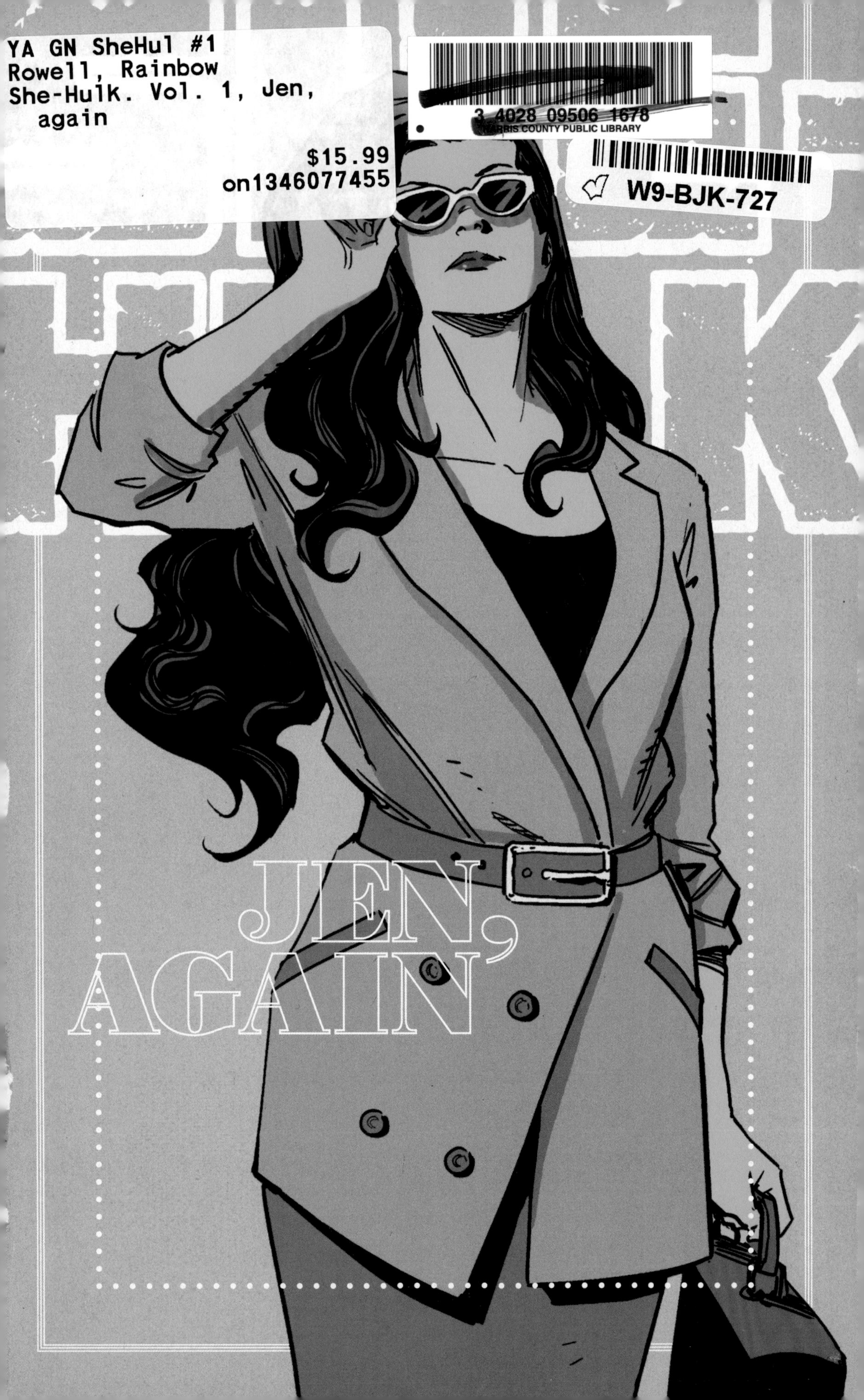
JEN,
AGAIN

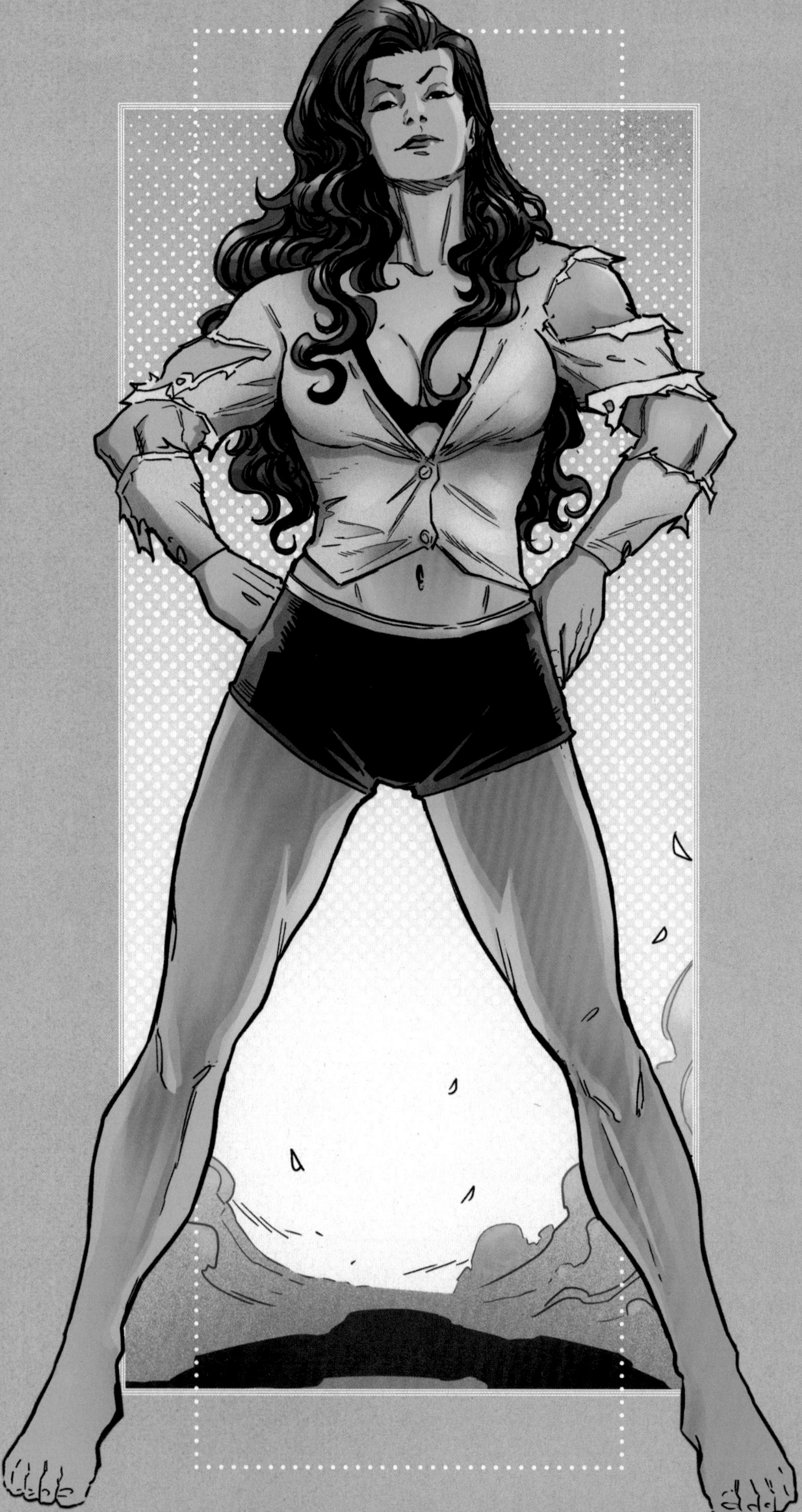

SHE-HULK

JEN, AGAIN

RAINBOW ROWELL
WRITER

ROGÊ ANTÔNIO (#1-3) &
LUCA MARESCA (#3-5)
ARTISTS

RICO RENZI
COLORIST

VC's JOE CARAMAGNA
LETTERER

JEN BARTEL
COVER ART

LINDSEY COHICK
ASSISTANT EDITOR

NICK LOWE
EDITOR

JENNIFER GRÜNWALD
COLLECTION EDITOR

DANIEL KIRCHHOFFER
ASSISTANT EDITOR

MAIA LOY
ASSISTANT MANAGING EDITOR

LISA MONTALBANO
ASSOCIATE MANAGER, TALENT RELATIONS

JEFF YOUNGQUIST
VP PRODUCTION & SPECIAL PROJECTS

ADAM DEL RE
BOOK DESIGNER

DAVID GABRIEL
SVP PRINT, SALES & MARKETING

C.B. CEBULSKI
EDITOR IN CHIEF

SHE-HULK BY RAINBOW ROWELL VOL. 1: JEN, AGAIN. Contains material originally published in magazine form as SHE-HULK (2022) #1-5. First printing 2022. ISBN 978-1-302-92907-7. Published by MARVEL WORLDWIDE, INC., a subsidiary of MARVEL ENTERTAINMENT, LLC. OFFICE OF PUBLICATION: 1290 Avenue of the Americas, New York, NY 10104. © 2022 MARVEL No similarity between any of the names, characters, persons, and/or institutions in this book with those of any living or dead person or institution is intended, and any such similarity which may exist is purely coincidental. **Printed in Canada.** KEVIN FEIGE, Chief Creative Officer; DAN BUCKLEY, President, Marvel Entertainment; DAVID BOGART, Associate Publisher & SVP of Talent Affairs; TOM BREVOORT, VP, Executive Editor; NICK LOWE, Executive Editor, VP of Content, Digital Publishing; DAVID GABRIEL, VP of Print & Digital Publishing; SVEN LARSEN, VP of Licensed Publishing; MARK ANNUNZIATO, VP of Planning & Forecasting; JEFF YOUNGQUIST, VP of Production & Special Projects; ALEX MORALES, Director of Publishing Operations; DAN EDINGTON, Director of Editorial Operations; RICKEY PURDIN, Director of Talent Relations; JENNIFER GRÜNWALD, Director of Production & Special Projects; SUSAN CRESPI, Production Manager; STAN LEE, Chairman Emeritus. For information regarding advertising in Marvel Comics or on Marvel.com, please contact Vit DeBellis, Custom Solutions & Integrated Advertising Manager, at vdebellis@marvel.com. For Marvel subscription inquiries, please call 888-511-5480. Manufactured between 7/22/2022 and 8/23/2022 by SOLISCO PRINTERS, SCOTT, QC, CANADA.

10 9 8 7 6 5 4 3 2 1

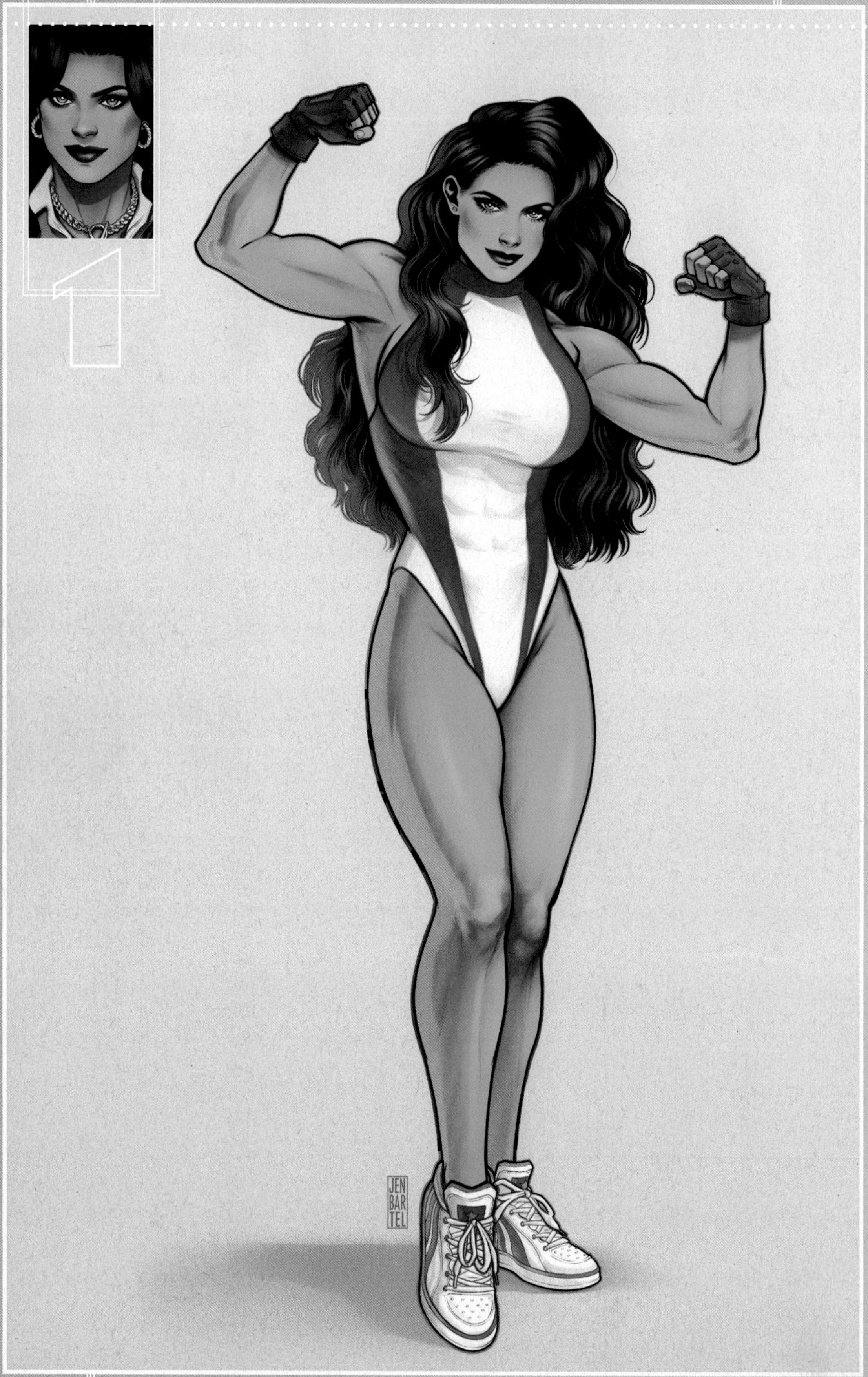
1
JEN BAR TEL

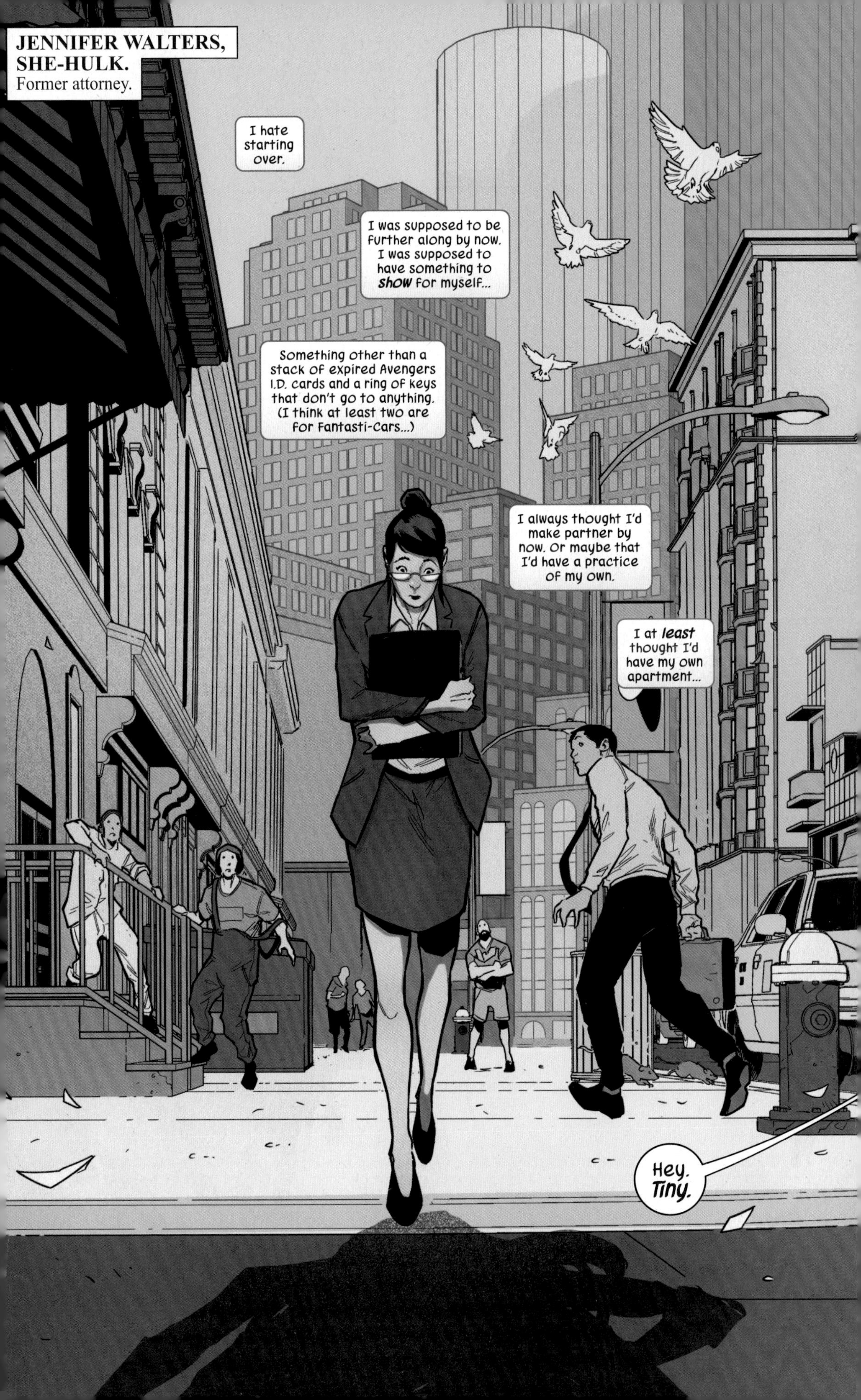
JENNIFER WALTERS, SHE-HULK.
Former attorney.
I hate starting over.
I was supposed to be further along by now. I was supposed to have something to *show* for myself...
Something other than a stack of expired Avengers I.D. cards and a ring of keys that don't go to anything. (I think at least two are for Fantasti-Cars...)
I always thought I'd make partner by now. Or maybe that I'd have a practice of my own.
I at *least* thought I'd have my own apartment...
Hey. *Tiny.*

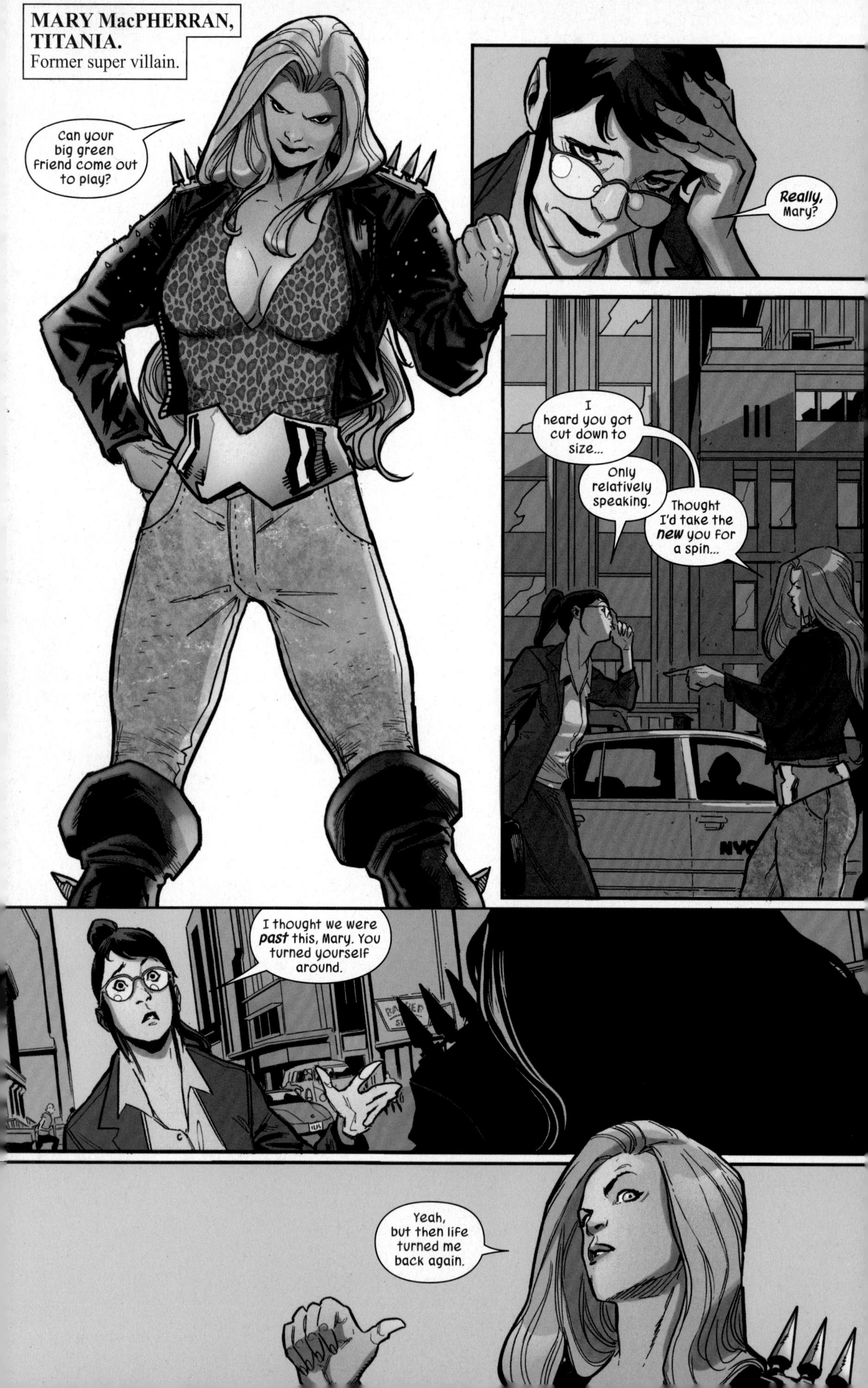
MARY MacPHERRAN, TITANIA.
Former super villain.
Can your big green friend come out to play?
Really, Mary?
I heard you got cut down to size...
Only relatively speaking.
Thought I'd take the new you for a spin...
NYC
I thought we were past this, Mary. You turned yourself around.
Yeah, but then life turned me back again.

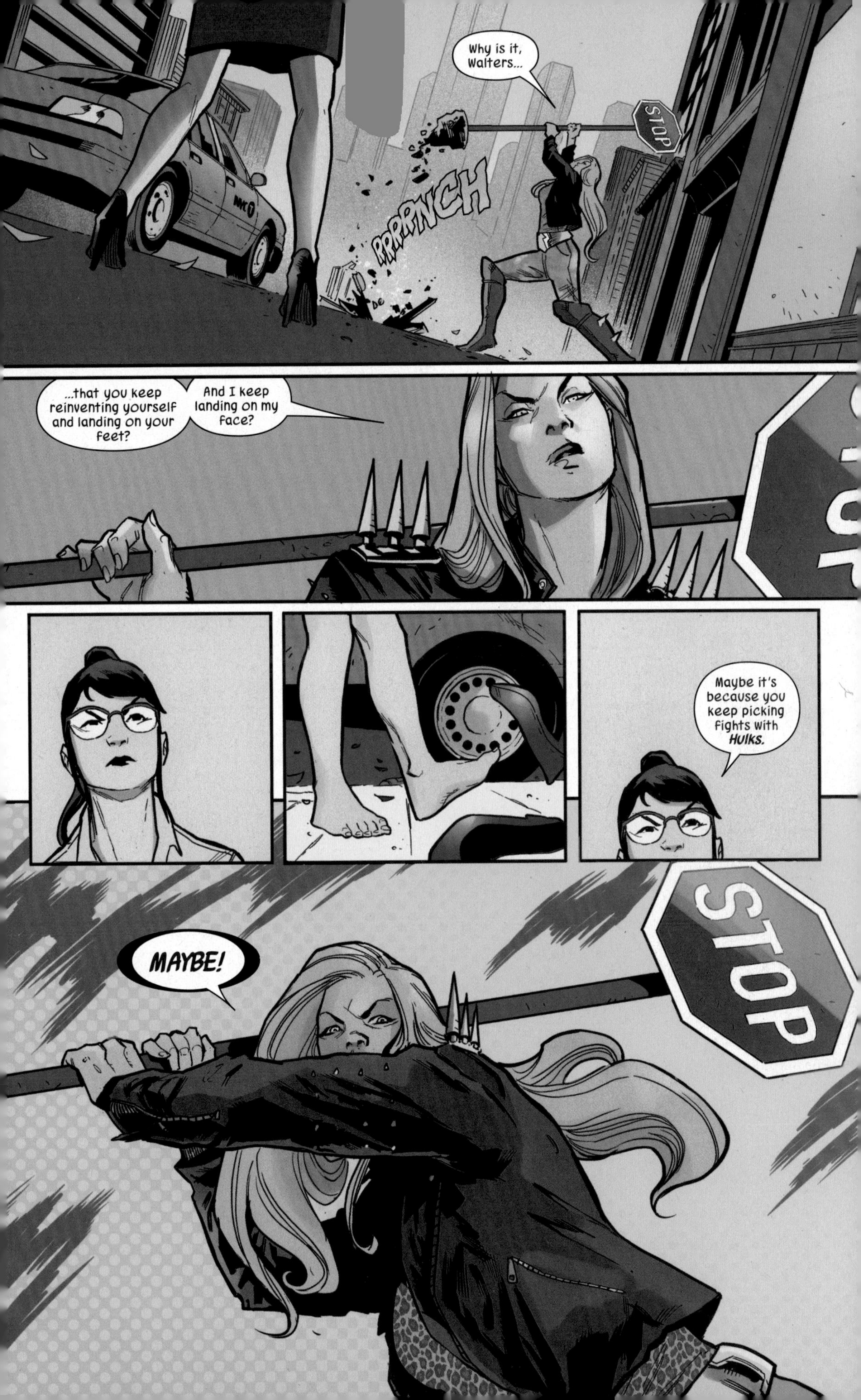

Why is it, Walters...
RRRRNCH
STOP
...that you keep reinventing yourself and landing on your feet?
And I keep landing on my face?
Maybe it's because you keep picking fights with HULKS.
STOP
MAYBE!

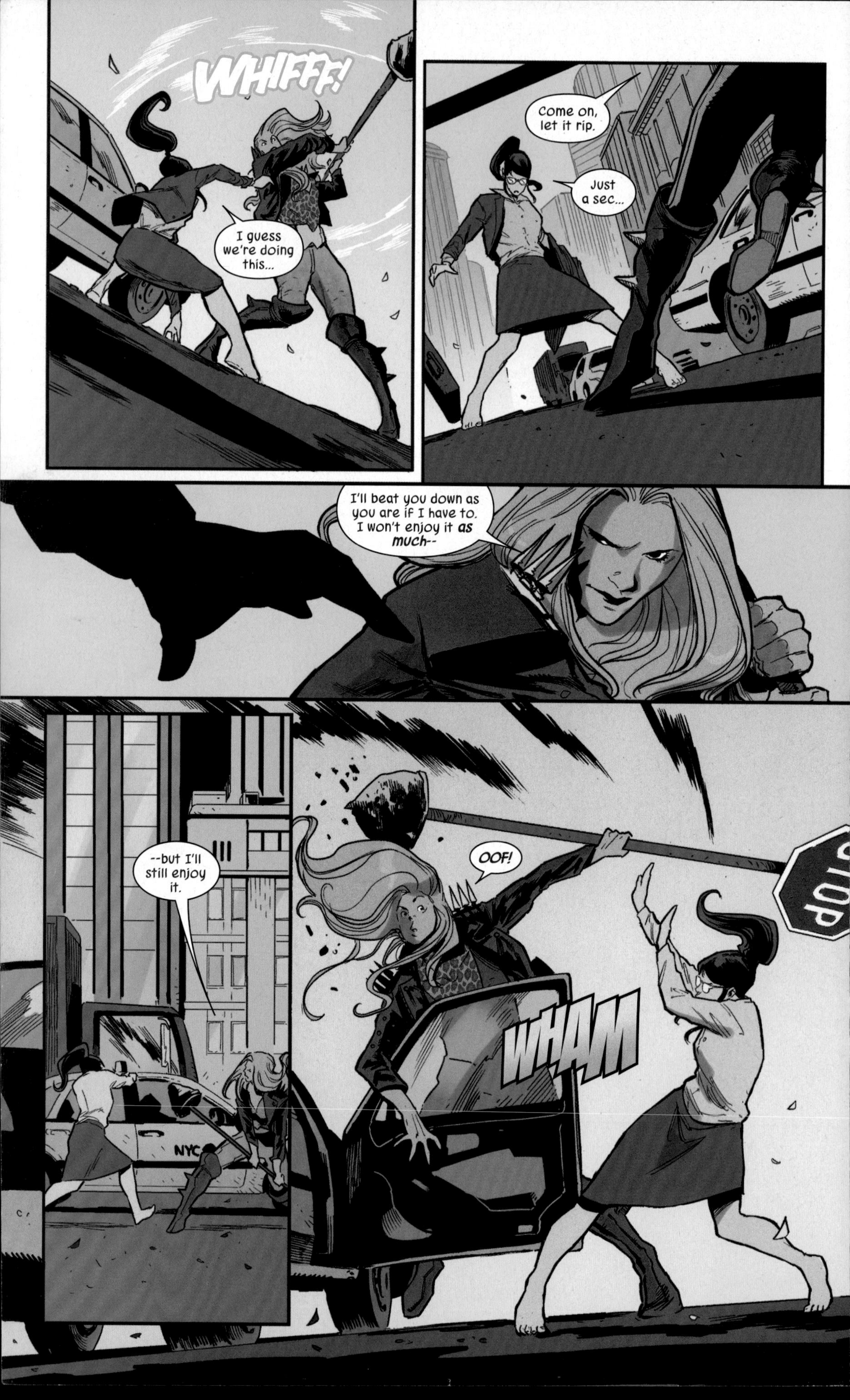
WHIFFF!
I guess we're doing this...
Come on, let it rip.
Just a sec...
I'll beat you down as you are if I have to. I won't enjoy it *as much*--
--but I'll still enjoy it.
OOF!
WHAM
STOP
NYC

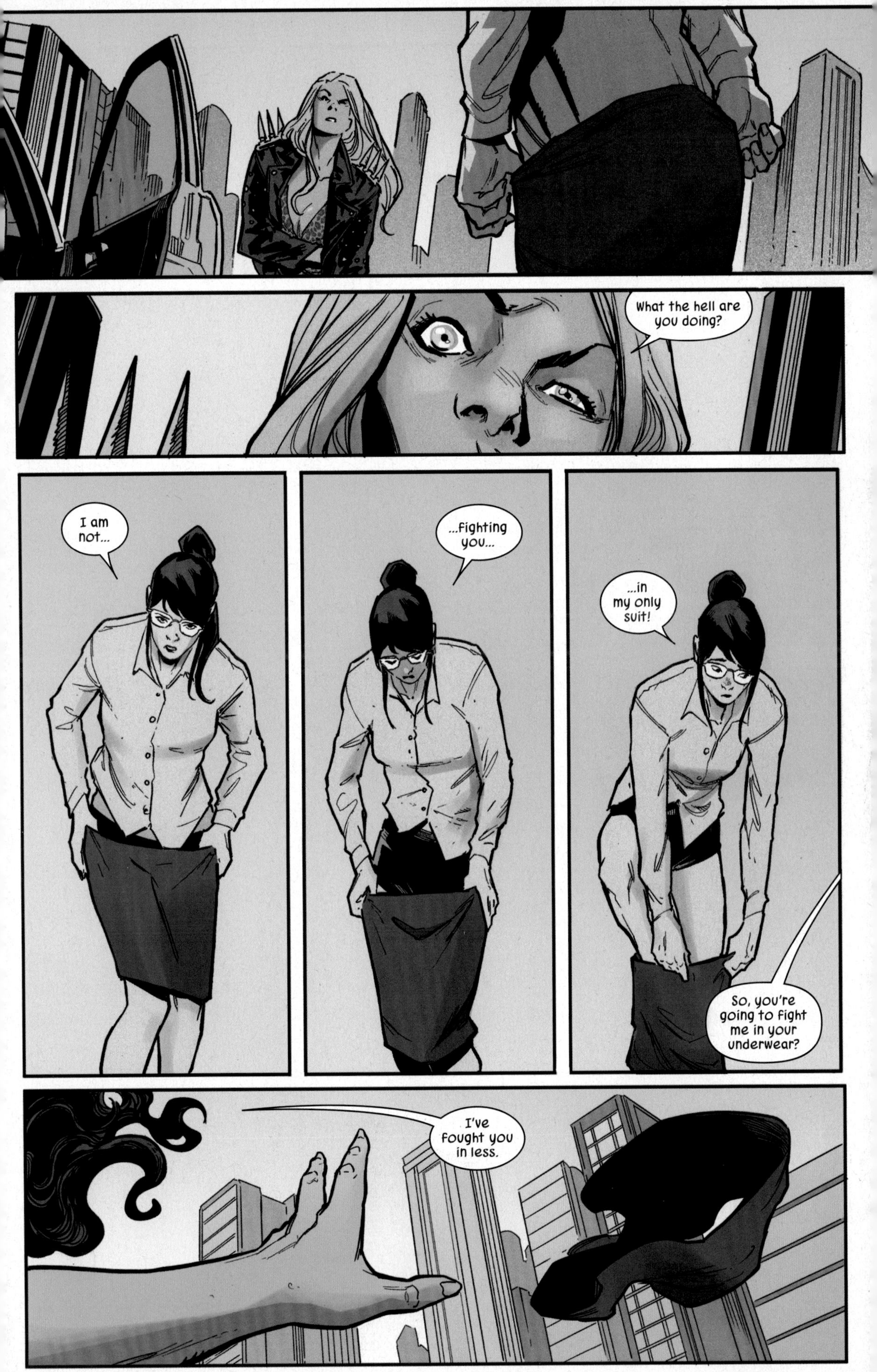
What the hell are you doing?
I am not...
...fighting you...
...in my only suit!
So, you're going to fight me in your underwear?
I've fought you in less.

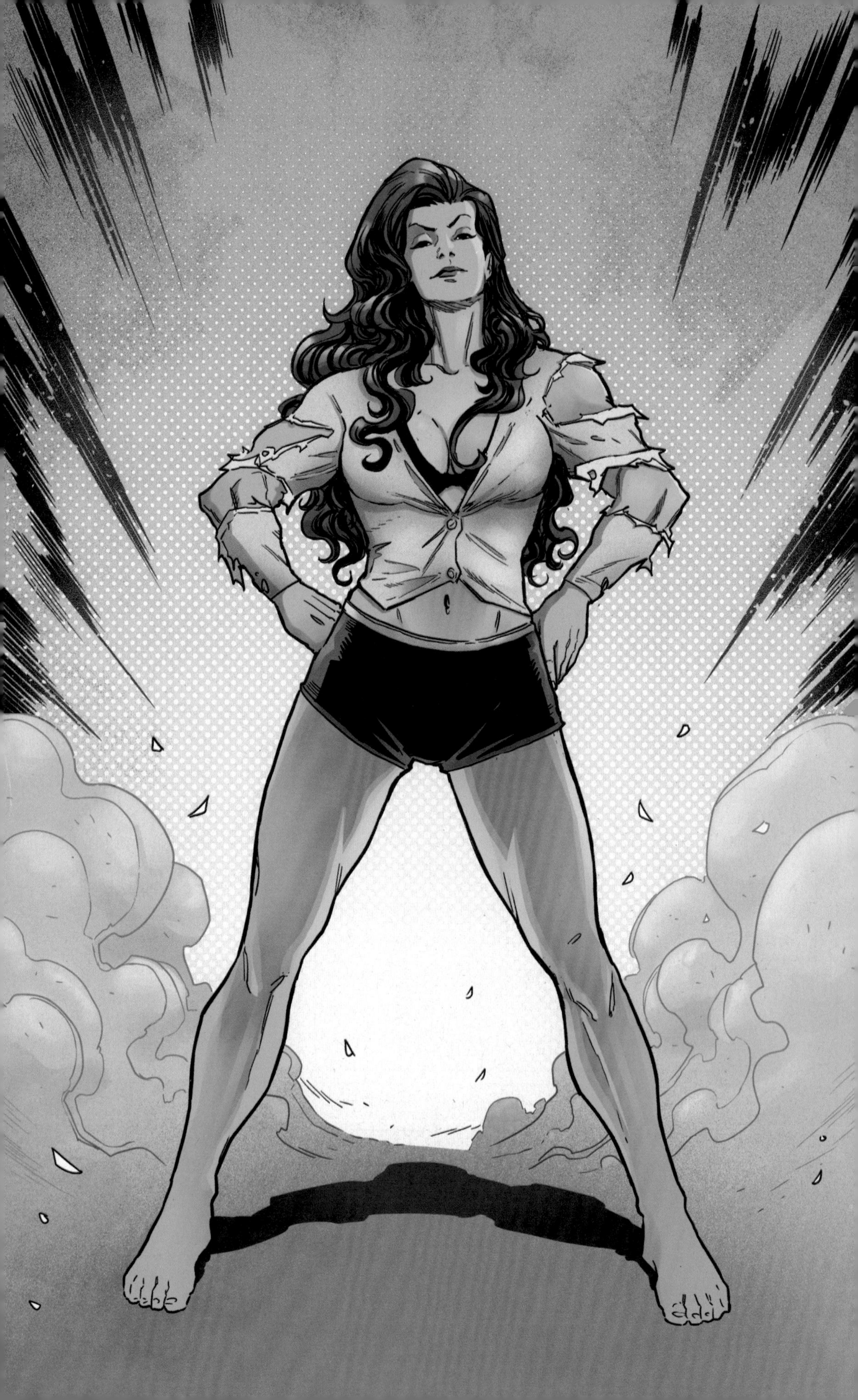

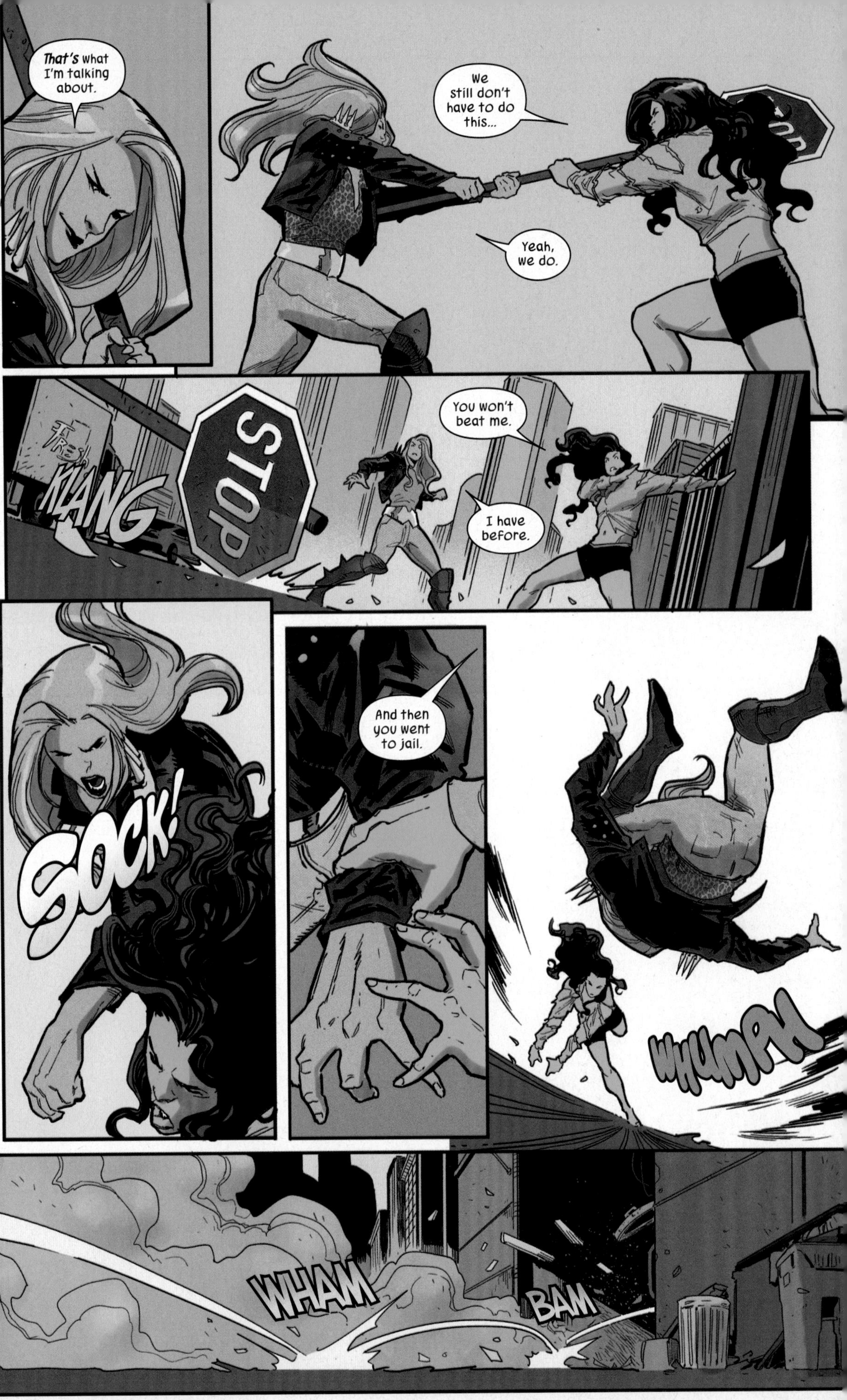
That's what I'm talking about.
We still don't have to do this...
Yeah, we do.
KLANG
You won't beat me.
I have before.
SOCK!
And then you went to jail.
WHUMPH
WHAM
BAM

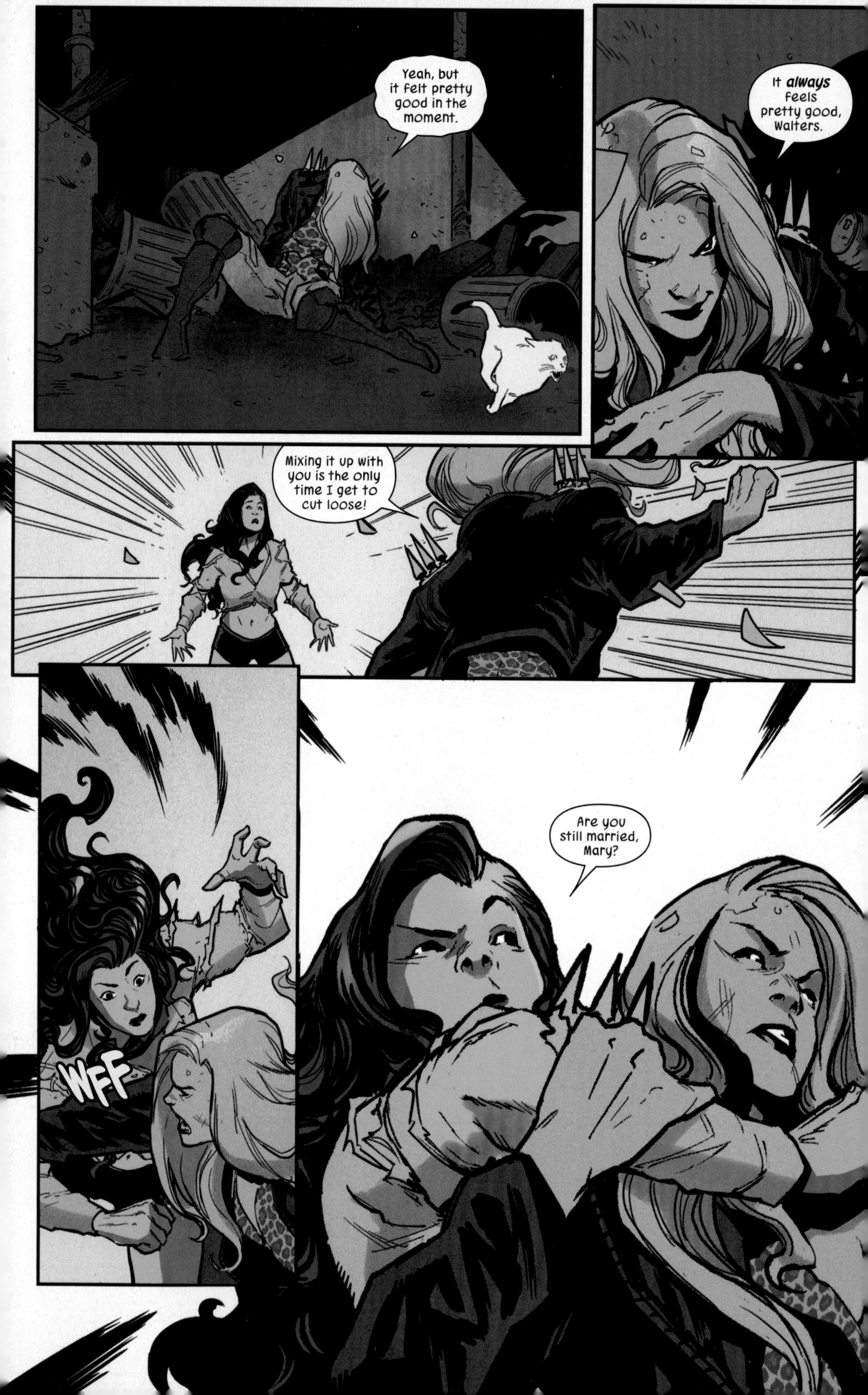
Yeah, but it felt pretty good in the moment.
It *always* feels pretty good, Walters.
Mixing it up with you is the only time I get to cut loose!
WFF
Are you still married, Mary?

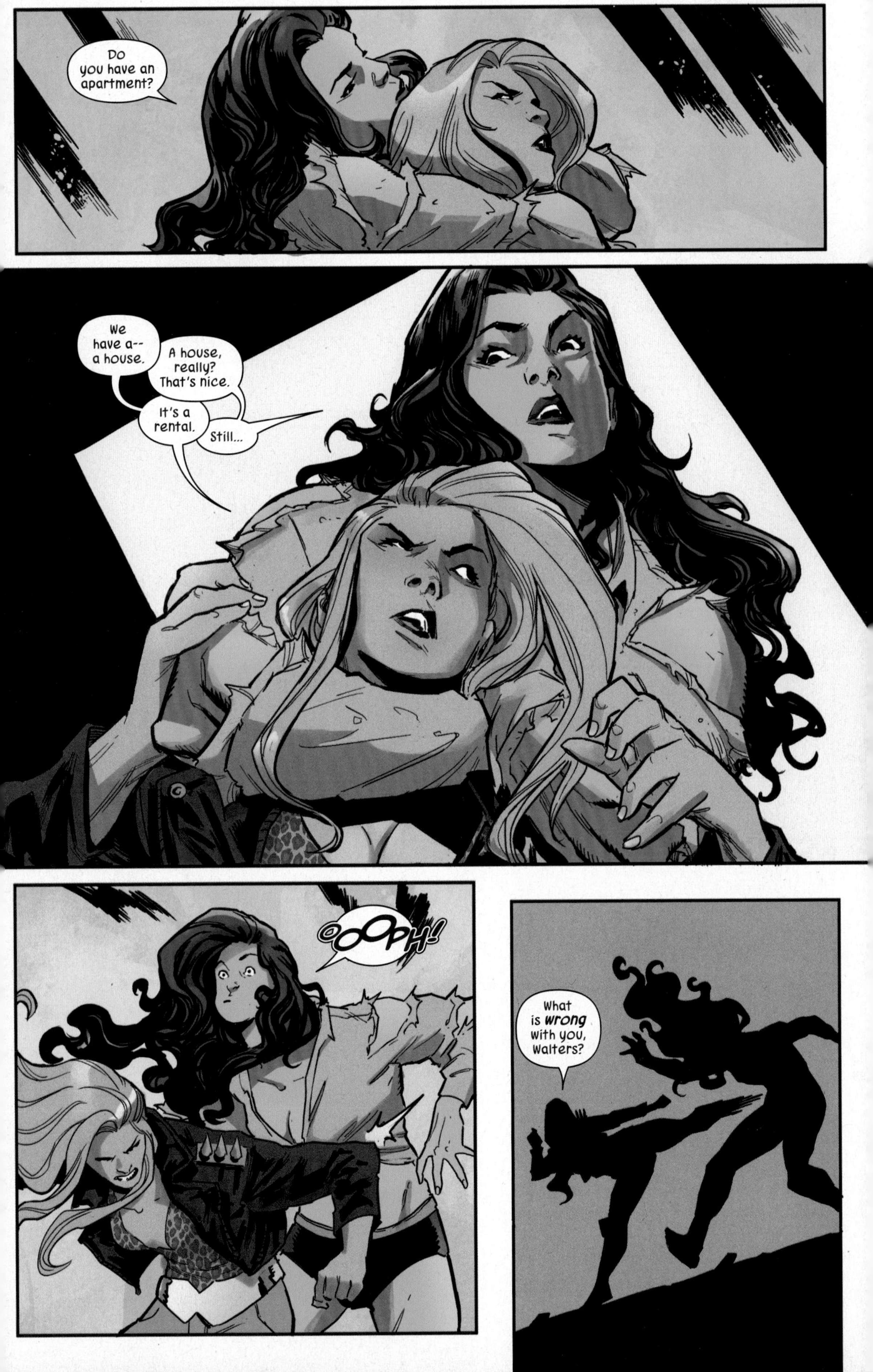
Do you have an apartment?
We have a-- a house.
A house, really? That's nice.
It's a rental.
Still...
OOOPH!
What is *wrong* with you, Walters?

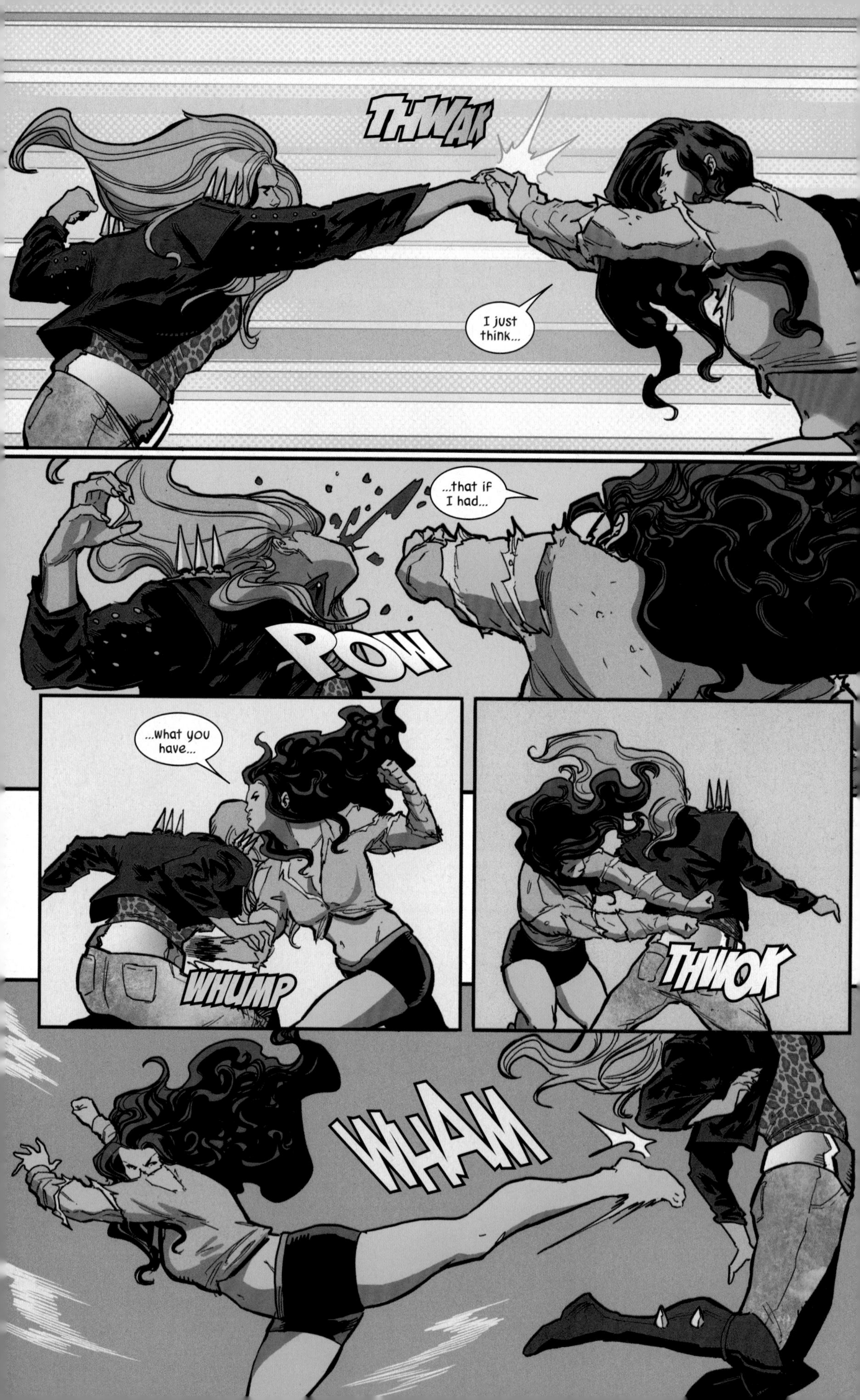
THWAK
I just think...
...that if I had...
POW
...what you have...
WHUMP
THWOK
WHAM

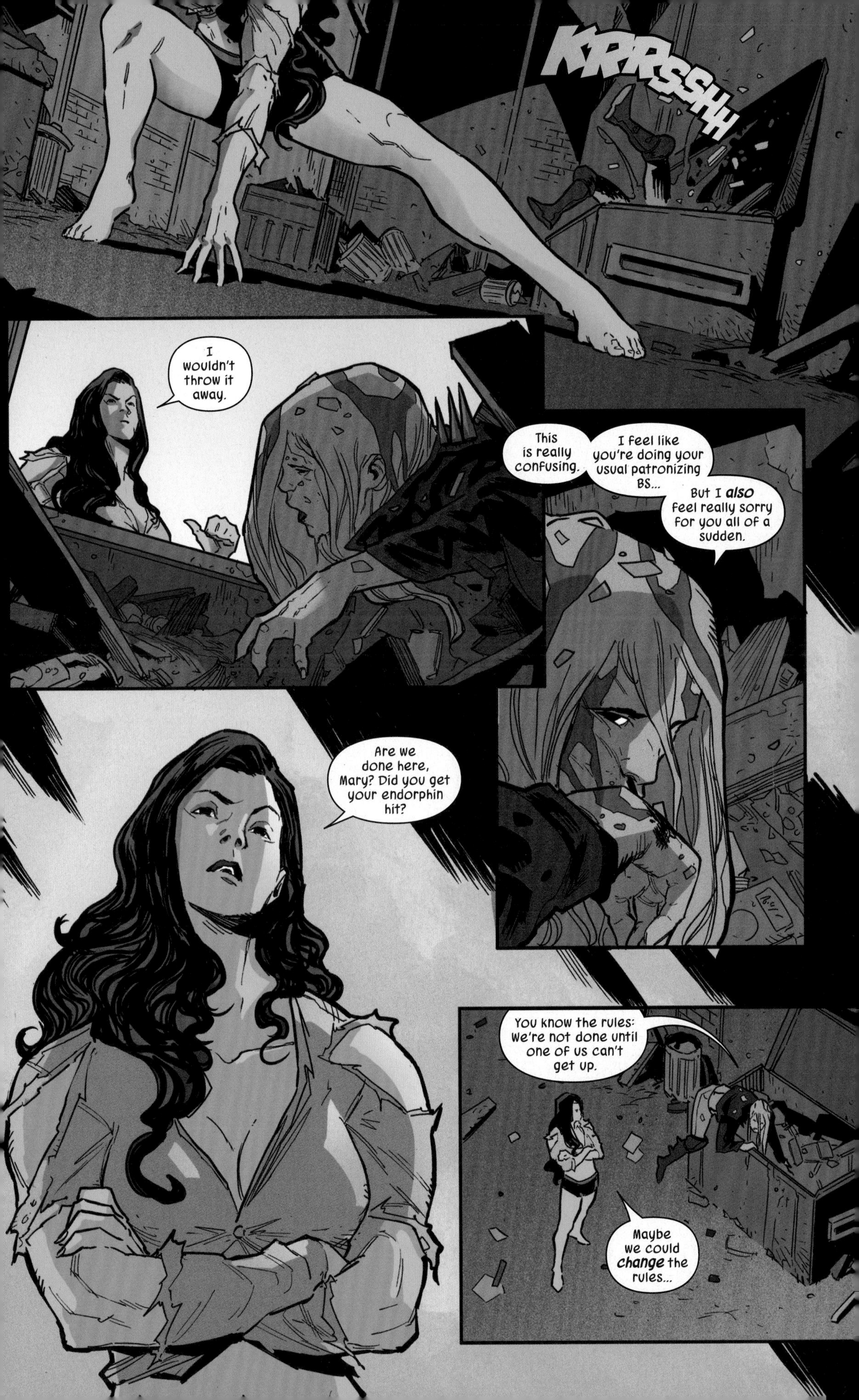
KRRSSHH
I wouldn't throw it away.
This is really confusing.
I feel like you're doing your usual patronizing BS...
But I *also* feel really sorry for you all of a sudden.
Are we done here, Mary? Did you get your endorphin hit?
You know the rules: We're not done until one of us can't get up.
Maybe we could *change* the rules...

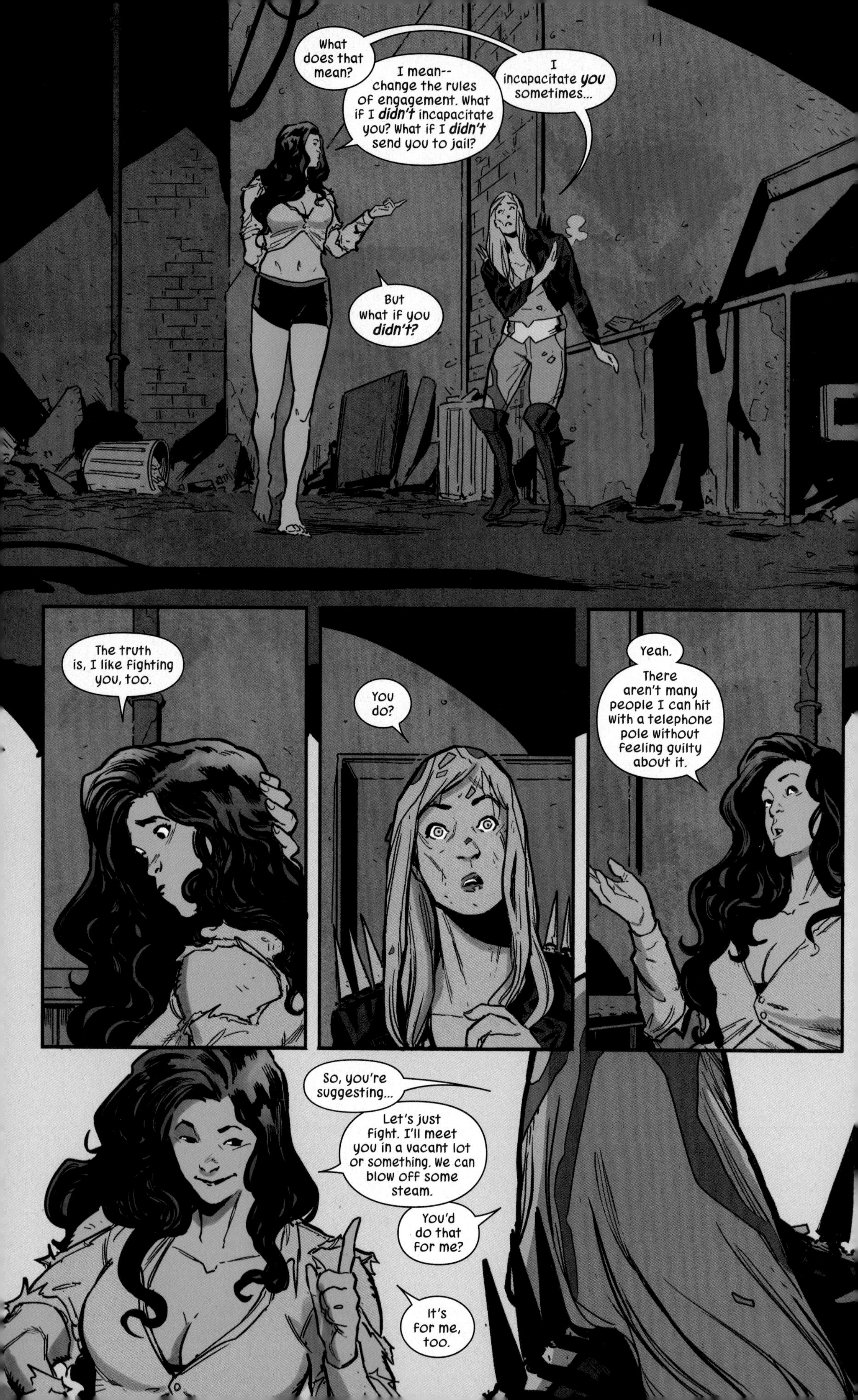

What does that mean?
I incapacitate *you* sometimes...
I mean-- change the rules of engagement. What if I *didn't* incapacitate you? What if I *didn't* send you to jail?
But what if you *didn't?*
The truth is, I like fighting you, too.
You do?
Yeah.
There aren't many people I can hit with a telephone pole without feeling guilty about it.
So, you're suggesting...
Let's just fight. I'll meet you in a vacant lot or something. We can blow off some steam.
You'd do that for me?
It's for me, too.

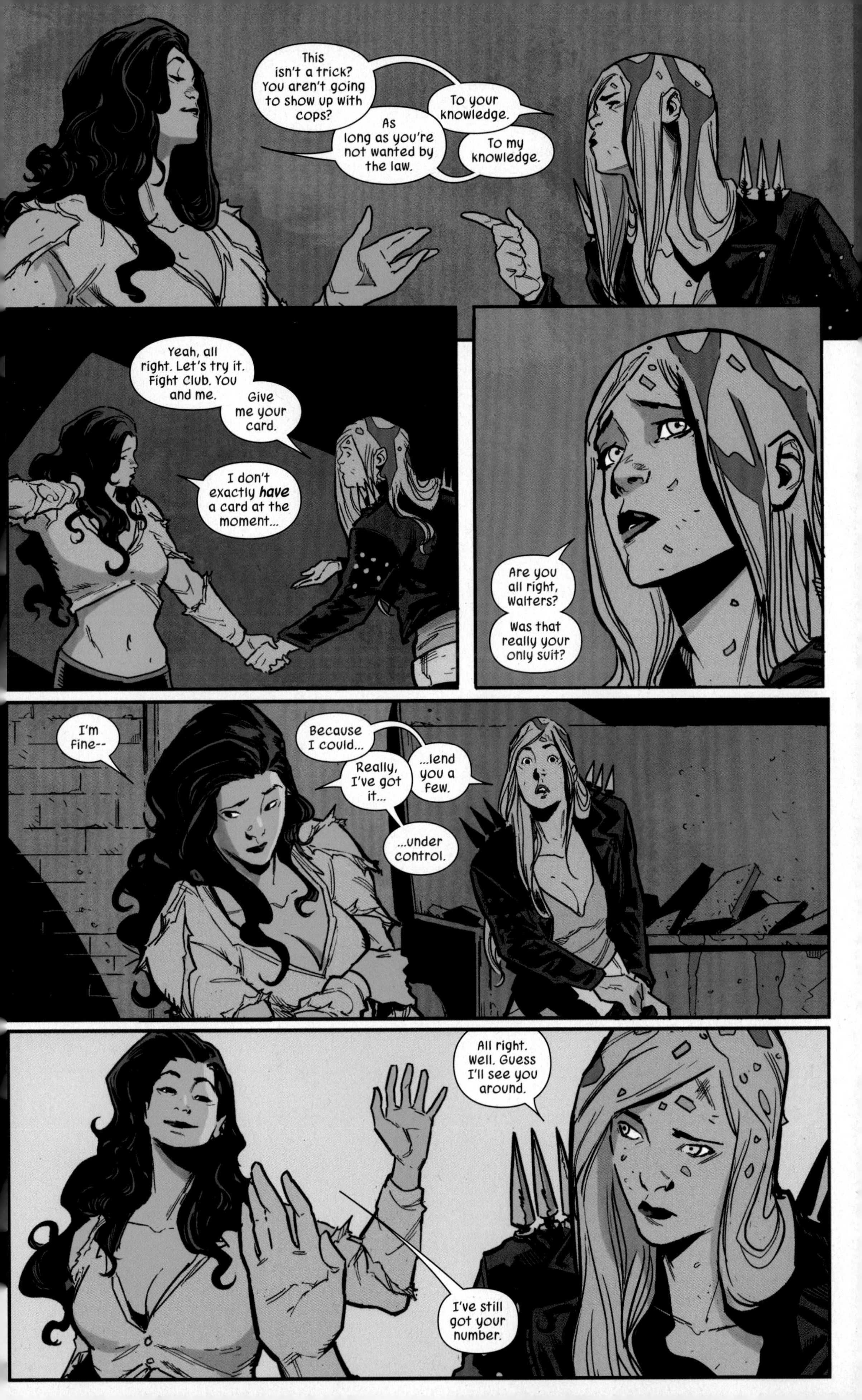
This isn't a trick? You aren't going to show up with cops?
To your knowledge.
As long as you're not wanted by the law.
To my knowledge.
Yeah, all right. Let's try it. Fight Club. You and me.
Give me your card.
I don't exactly *have* a card at the moment...
Are you all right, Walters?
Was that really your only suit?
I'm Fine--
Because I could...
Really, I've got it...
...lend you a few.
...under control.
All right. Well. Guess I'll see you around.
I've still got your number.

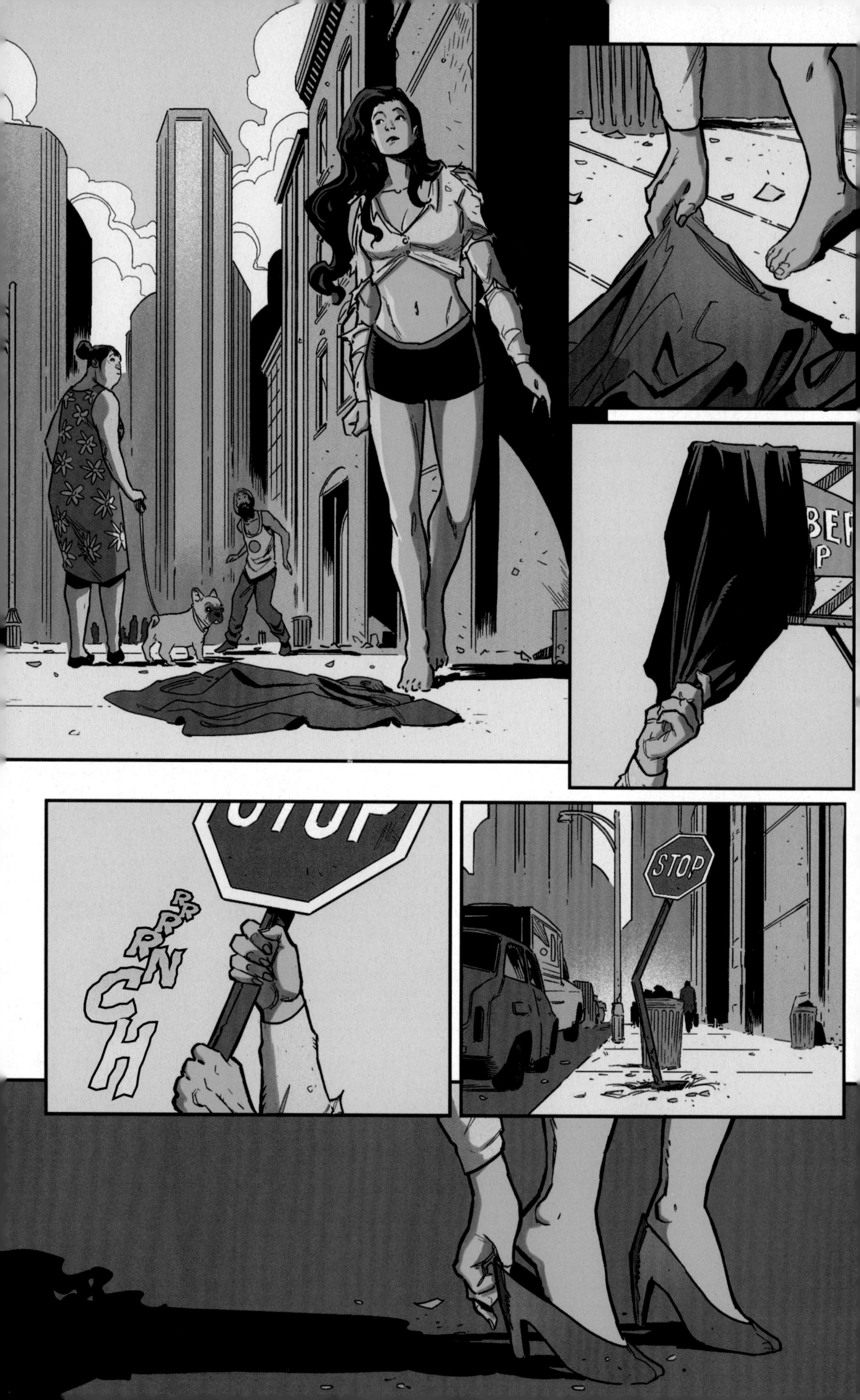

RRRNCH
STOP

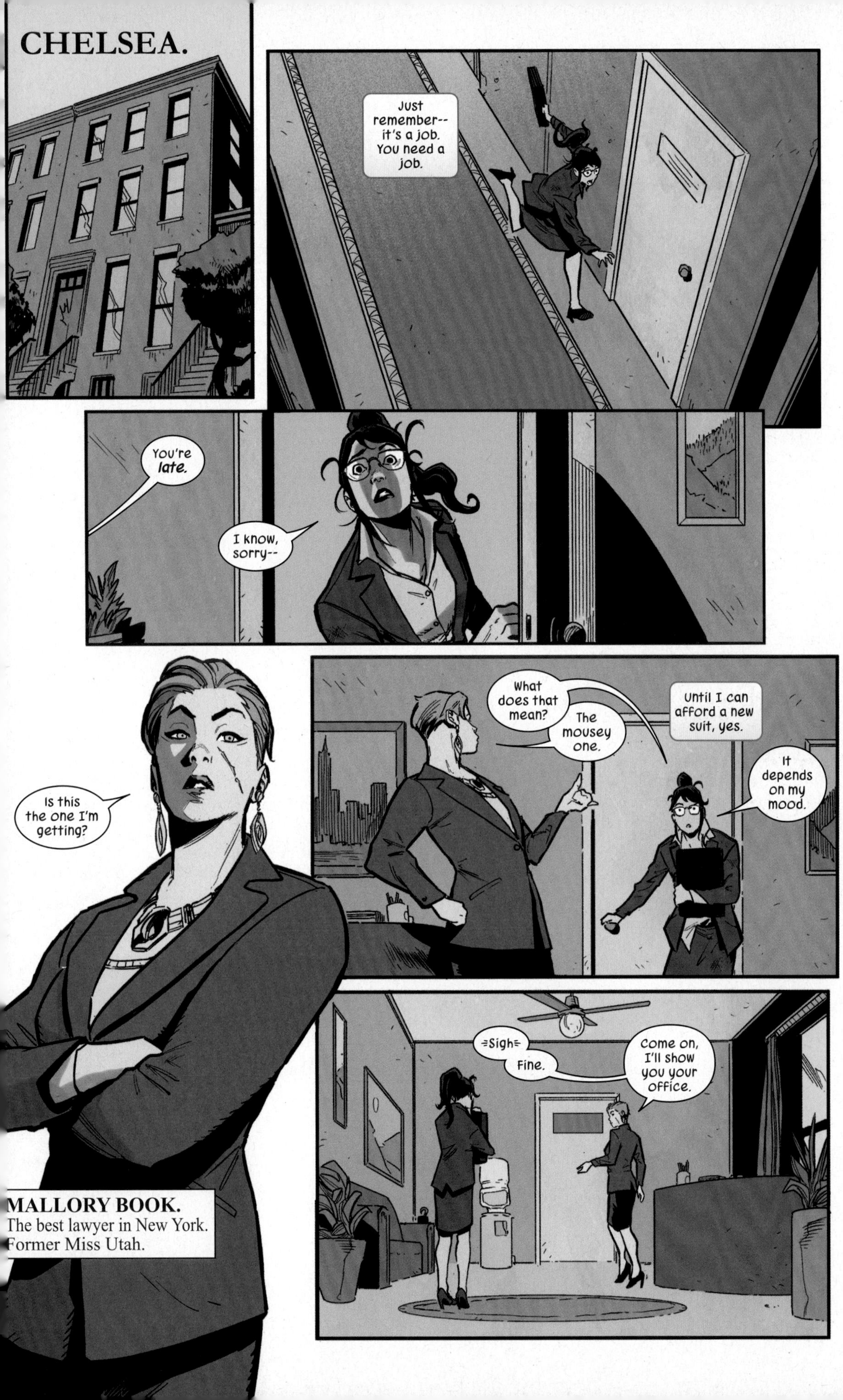
CHELSEA.
Just remember-- it's a job. You need a job.
You're late.
I know, sorry--
Is this the one I'm getting?
What does that mean?
The mousey one.
Until I can afford a new suit, yes.
It depends on my mood.
MALLORY BOOK.
The best lawyer in New York.
Former Miss Utah.
=Sigh=
Fine.
Come on, I'll show you your office.

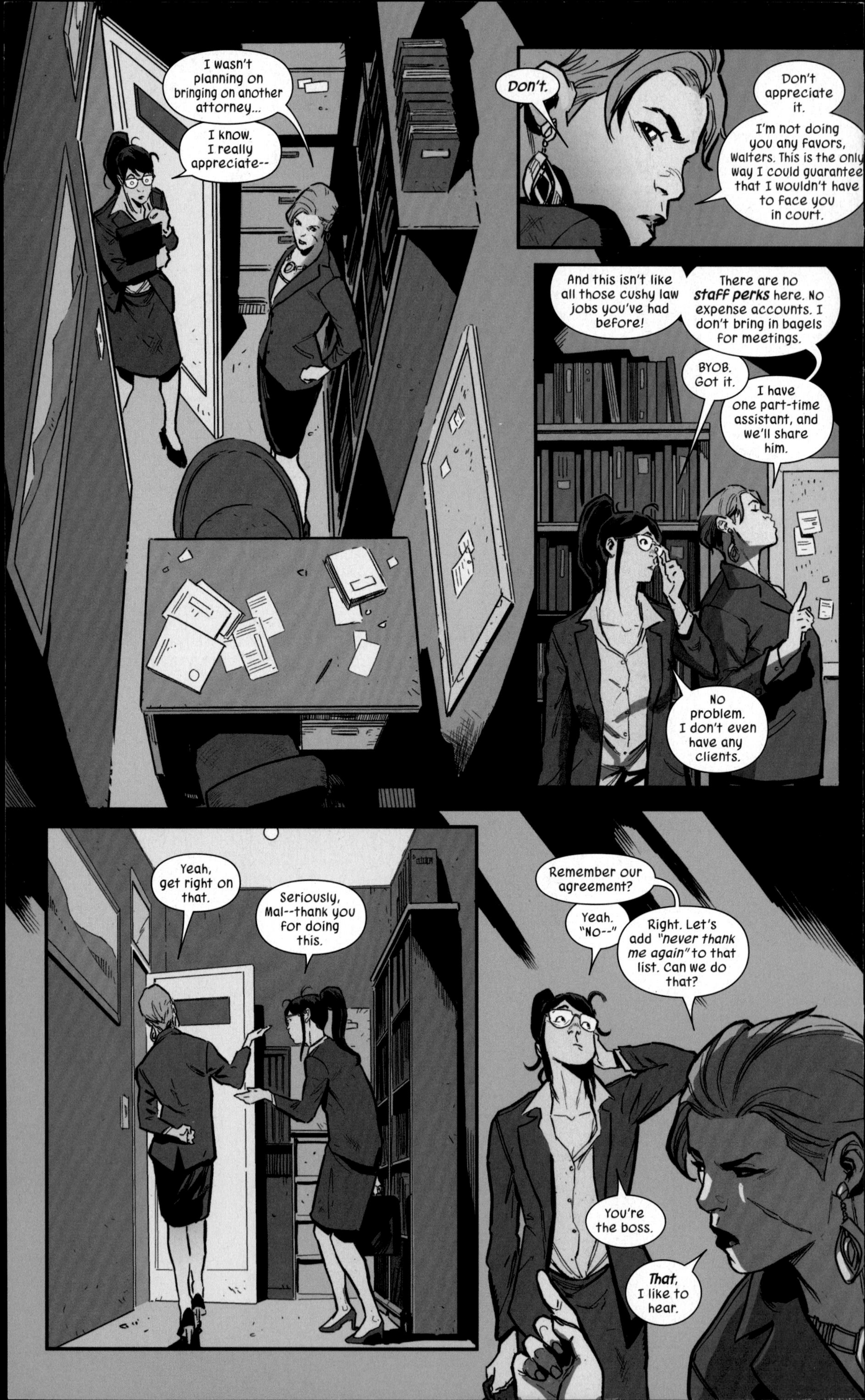
I wasn't planning on bringing on another attorney...
I know. I really appreciate--
Don't.
Don't appreciate it.
I'm not doing you any favors, Walters. This is the only way I could guarantee that I wouldn't have to face you in court.
And this isn't like all those cushy law jobs you've had before!
There are no staff perks here. No expense accounts. I don't bring in bagels for meetings.
BYOB. Got it.
I have one part-time assistant, and we'll share him.
No problem. I don't even have any clients.
Yeah, get right on that.
Seriously, Mal--thank you for doing this.
Remember our agreement?
Yeah. "No--"
Right. Let's add "never thank me again" to that list. Can we do that?
You're the boss.
That, I like to hear.

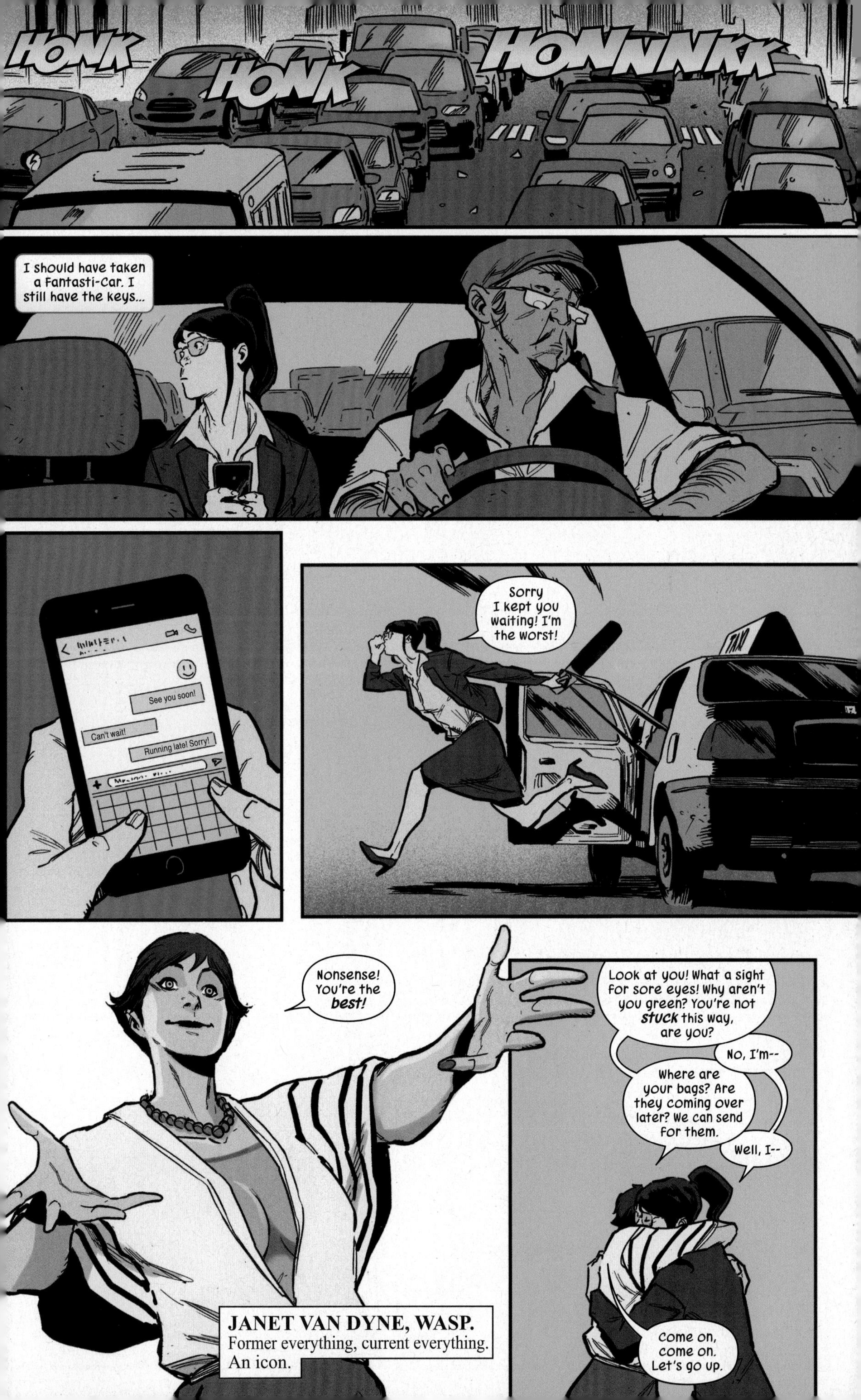
HONK
HONK
HONNNKK
I should have taken a Fantasti-Car. I still have the keys...
See you soon!
Can't wait!
Running late! Sorry!
Sorry I kept you waiting! I'm the worst!
TAXI
Nonsense! You're the best!
JANET VAN DYNE, WASP.
Former everything, current everything. An icon.
Look at you! What a sight for sore eyes! Why aren't you green? You're not stuck this way, are you?
No, I'm--
Where are your bags? Are they coming over later? We can send for them.
Well, I--
Come on, come on. Let's go up.

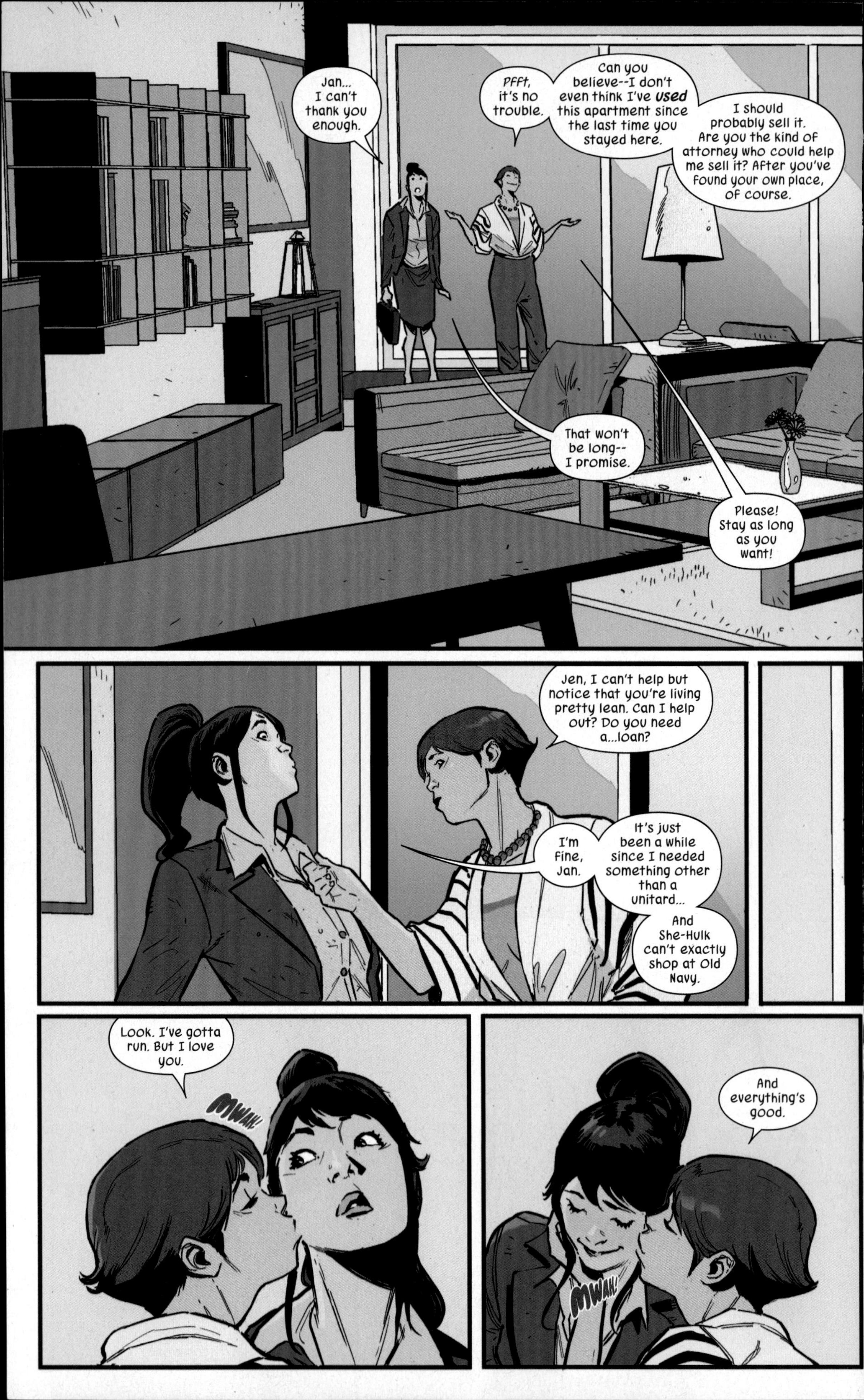
Jan... I can't thank you enough.
Pfft, it's no trouble.
Can you believe--I don't even think I've used this apartment since the last time you stayed here.
I should probably sell it. Are you the kind of attorney who could help me sell it? After you've found your own place, of course.
That won't be long-- I promise.
Please! Stay as long as you want!
Jen, I can't help but notice that you're living pretty lean. Can I help out? Do you need a...loan?
I'm fine, Jan.
It's just been a while since I needed something other than a unitard...
And She-Hulk can't exactly shop at Old Navy.
Look. I've gotta run. But I love you.
MWAH!
And everything's good.
MWAH!

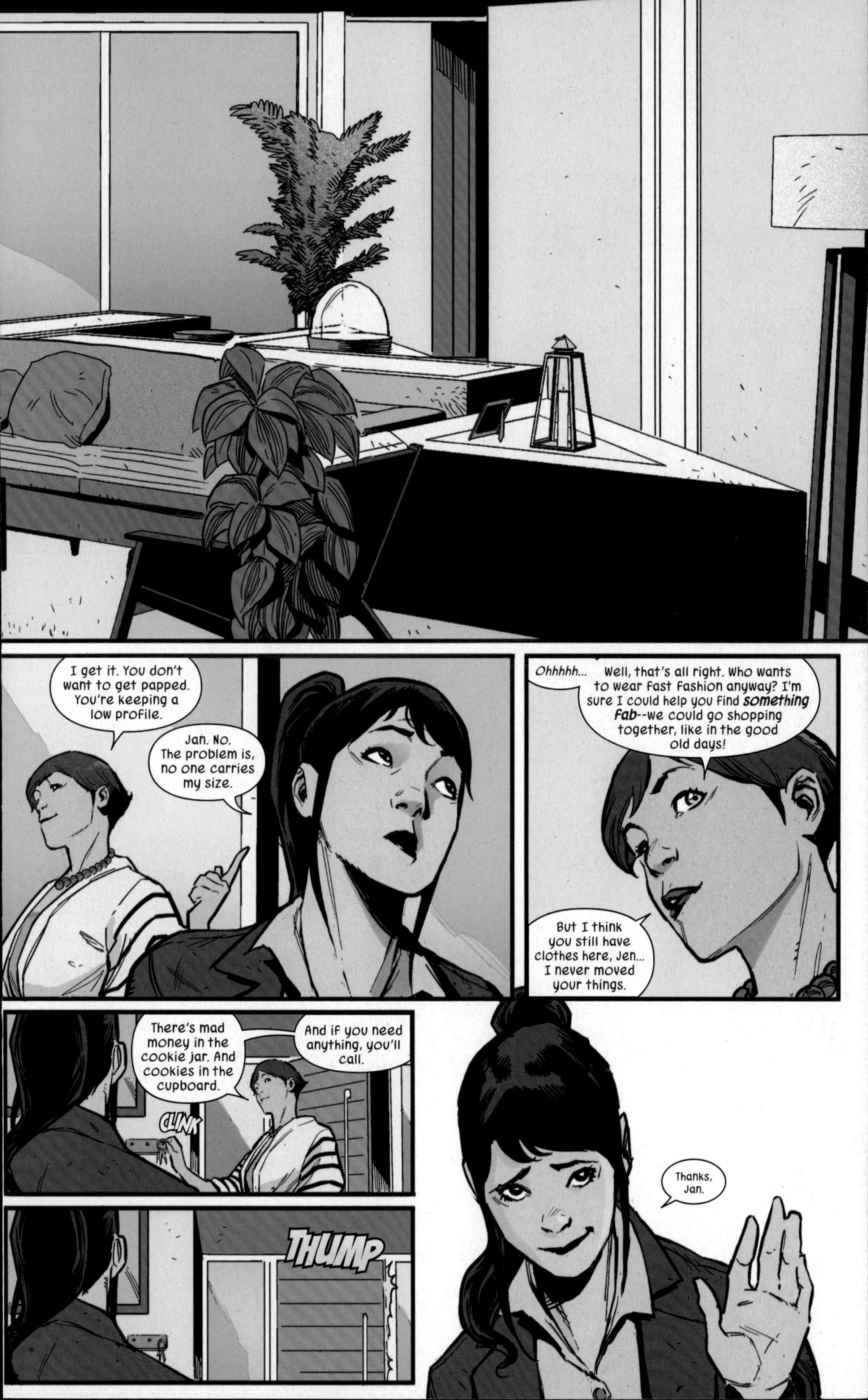

I get it. You don't want to get papped. You're keeping a low profile.
Jan. No. The problem is, no one carries my size.
Ohhhhh...
Well, that's all right. Who wants to wear fast fashion anyway? I'm sure I could help you find *something fab*--we could go shopping together, like in the good old days!
But I think you still have clothes here, Jen... I never moved your things.
There's mad money in the cookie jar. And cookies in the cupboard.
And if you need anything, you'll call.
CLINK
THUMP
Thanks, Jan.

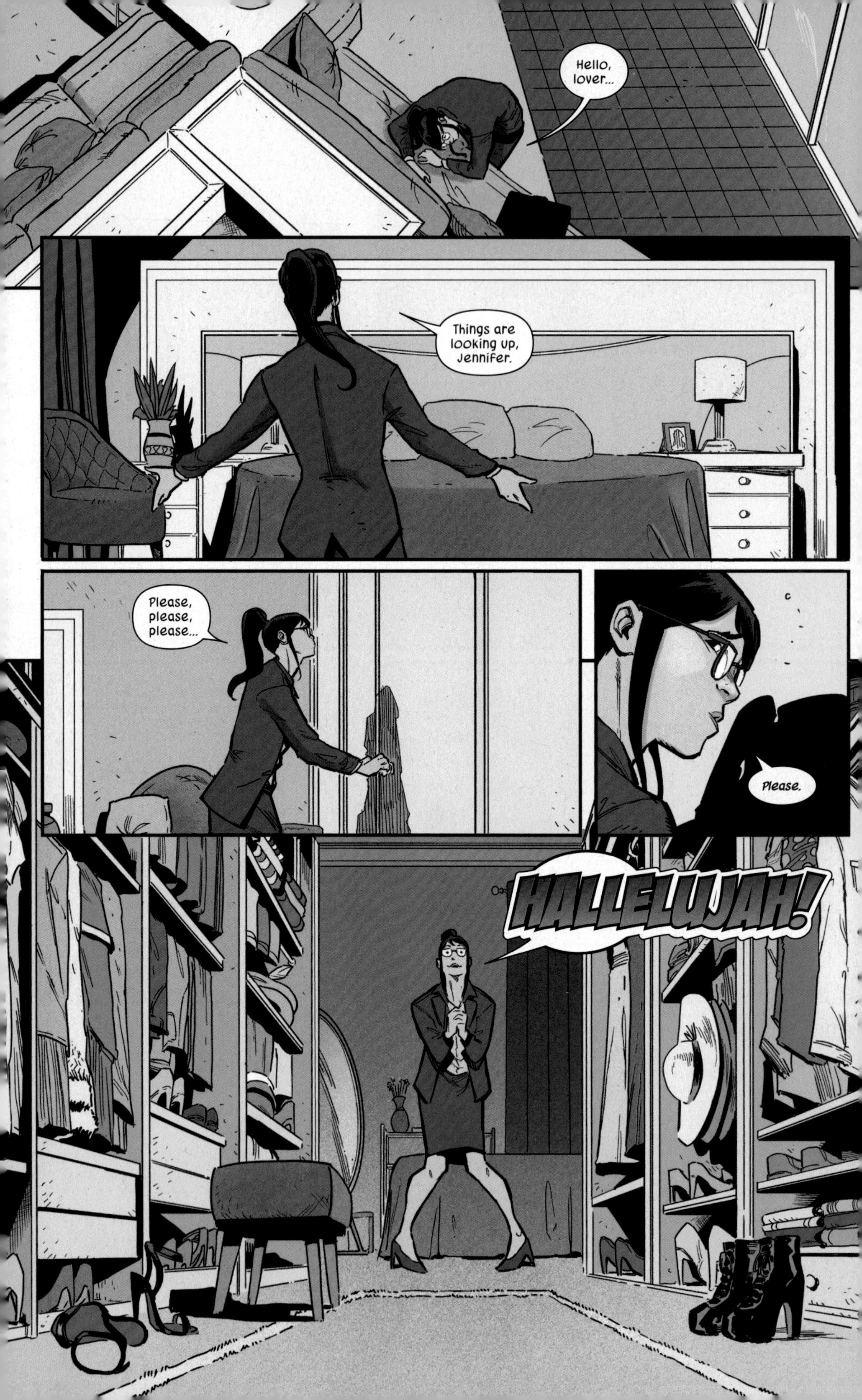

Hello, lover...
Things are looking up, Jennifer.
Please, please, please...
Please.
HALLELUJAH!

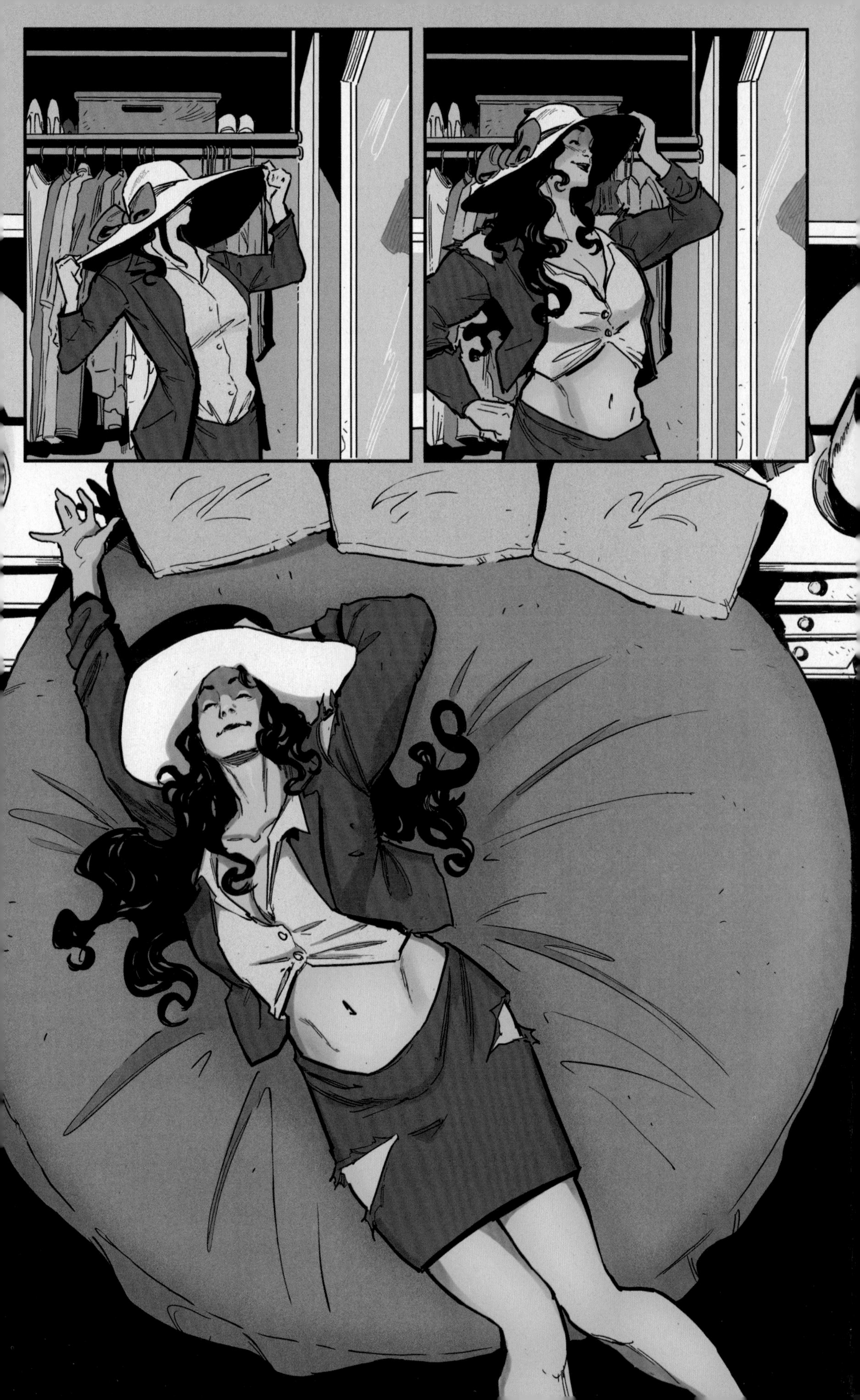

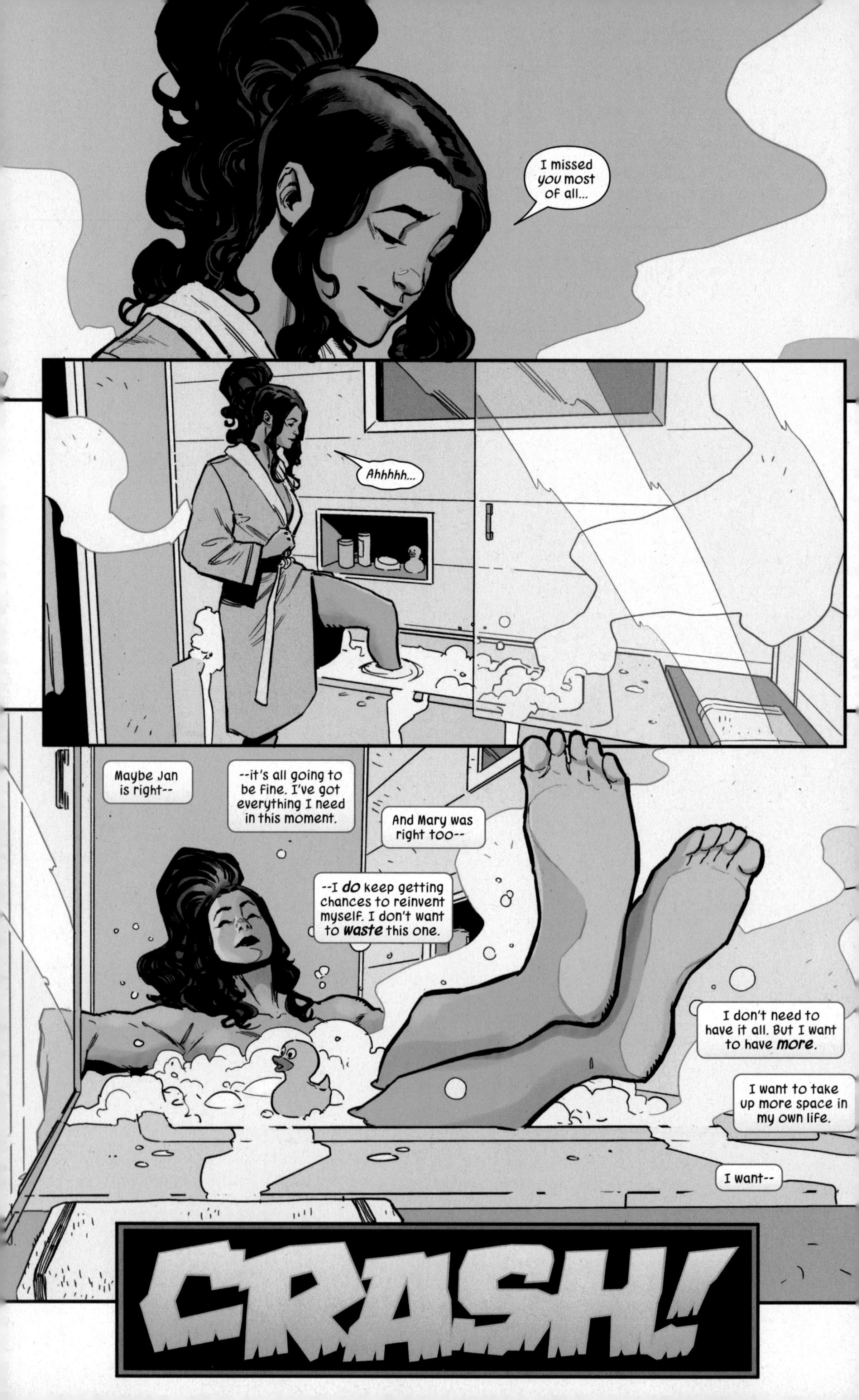
I missed you most of all...
Ahhhhh...
Maybe Jan is right--
--it's all going to be fine. I've got everything I need in this moment.
And Mary was right too--
--I do keep getting chances to reinvent myself. I don't want to waste this one.
I don't need to have it all. But I want to have more.
I want to take up more space in my own life.
I want--
CRASH!

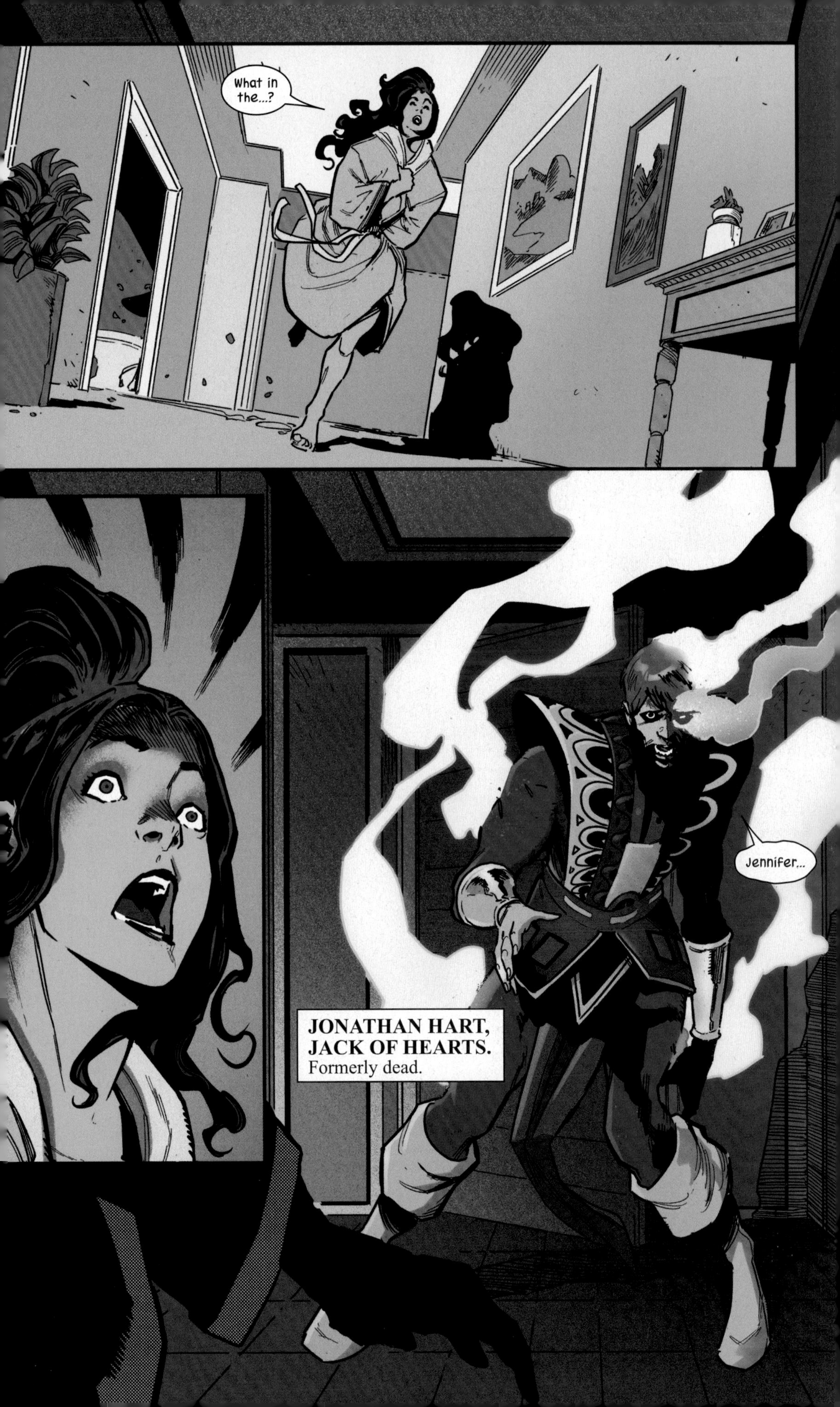

What in the...?
JONATHAN HART, JACK OF HEARTS.
Formerly dead.
Jennifer...

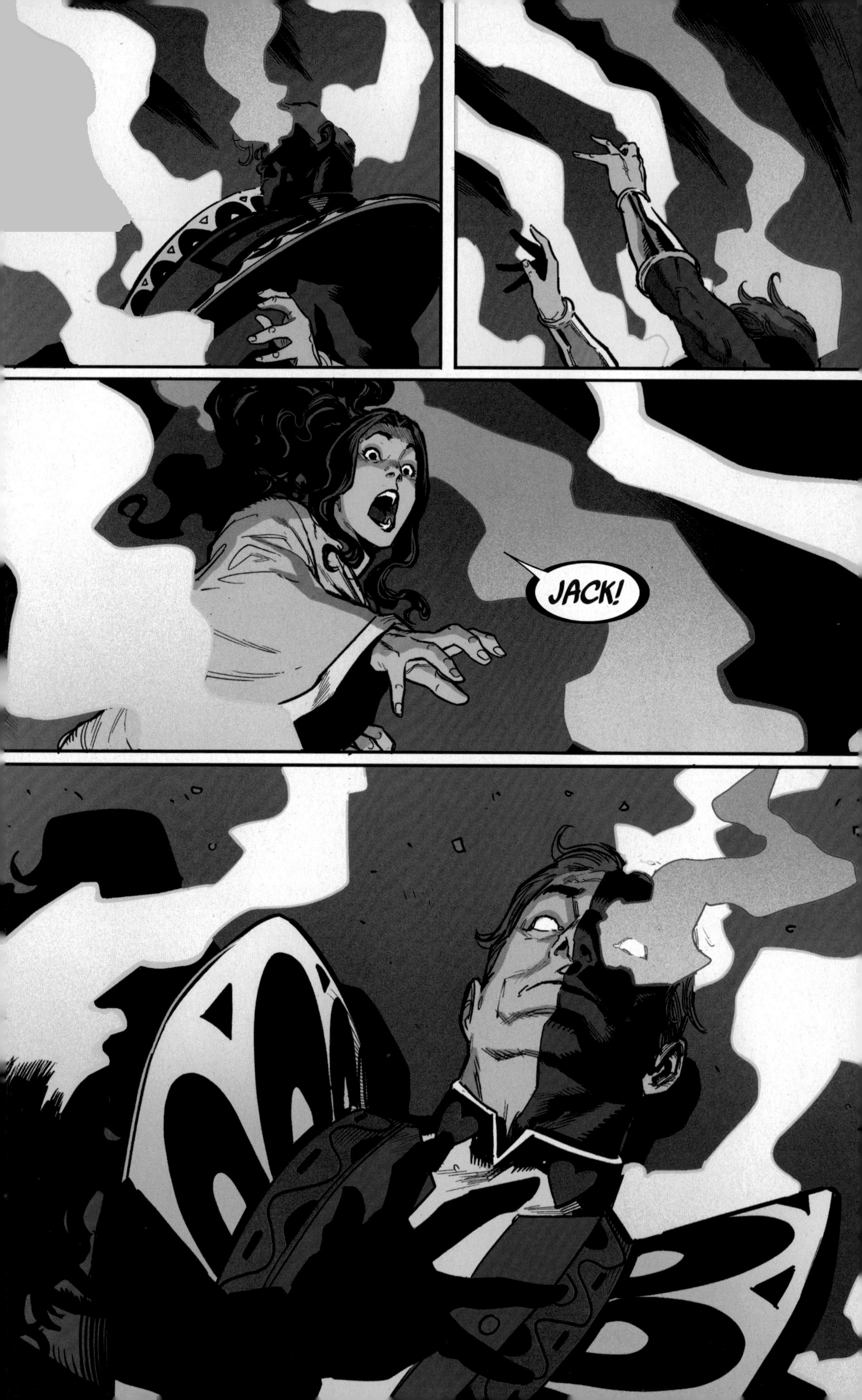
JACK!

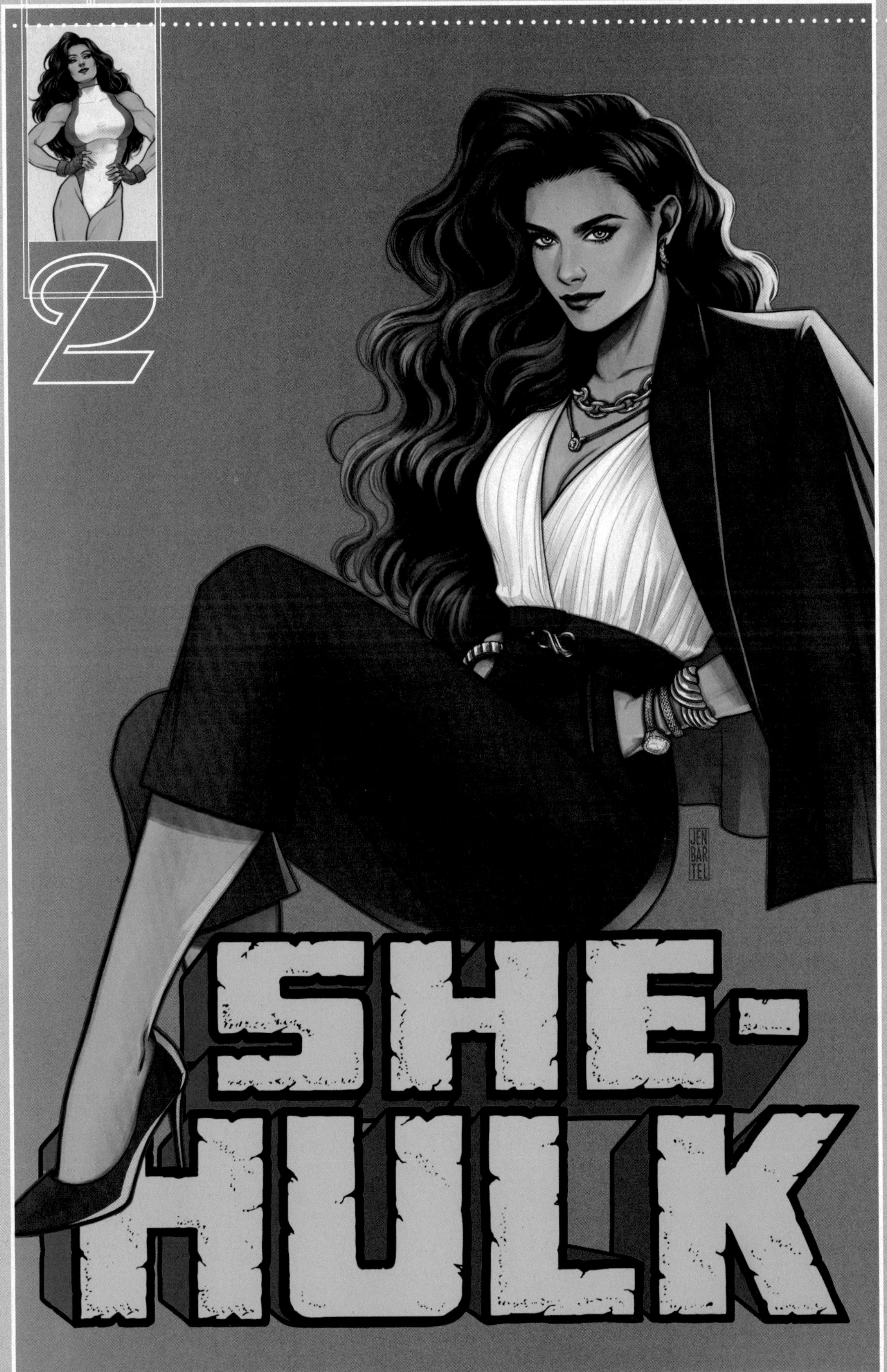
2
JEN BAR TEL
SHE-HULK

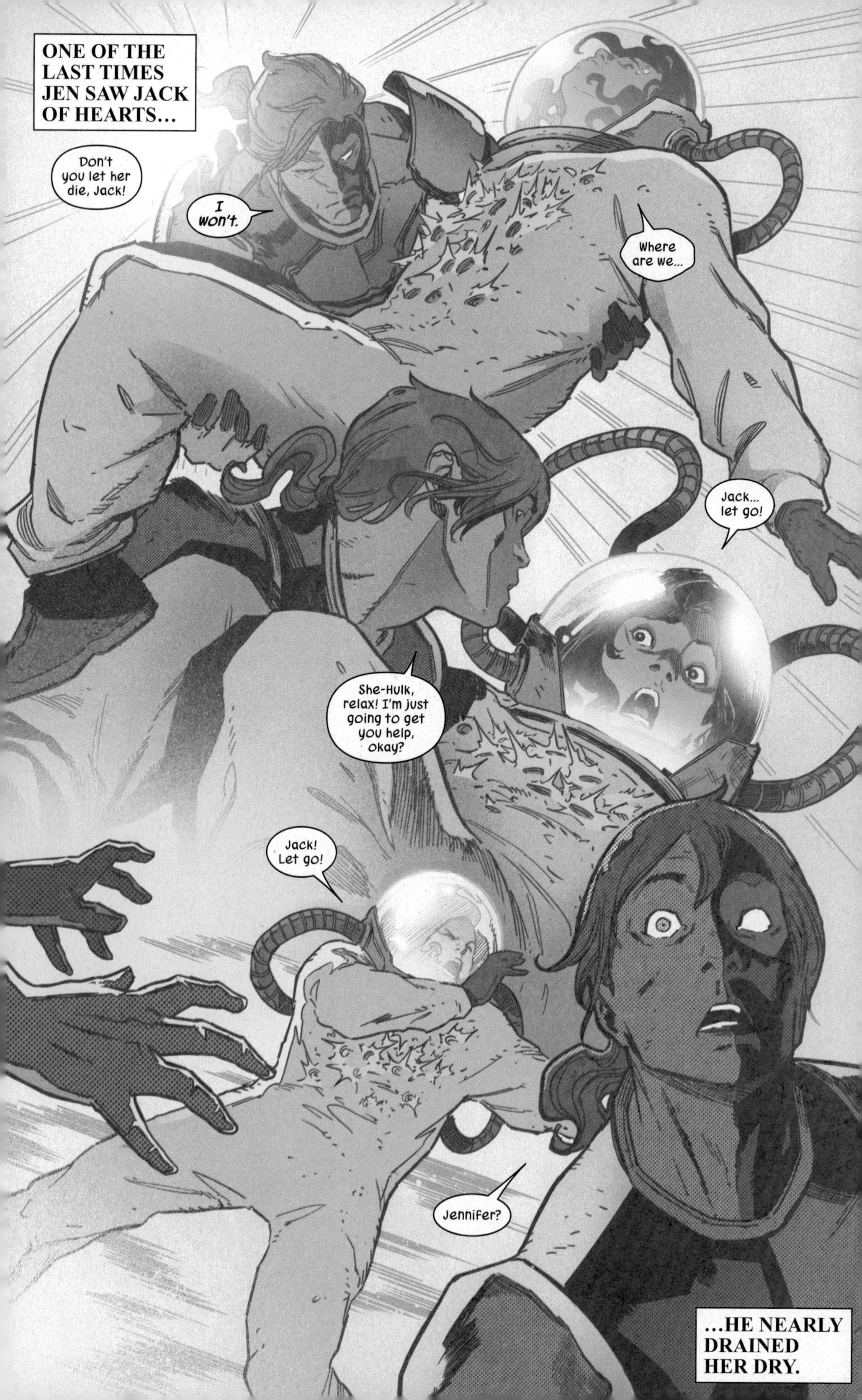
ONE OF THE LAST TIMES JEN SAW JACK OF HEARTS…
Don't you let her die, Jack!
I won't.
Where are we…
Jack… let go!
She-Hulk, relax! I'm just going to get you help, okay?
Jack! Let go!
Jennifer?
…HE NEARLY DRAINED HER DRY.

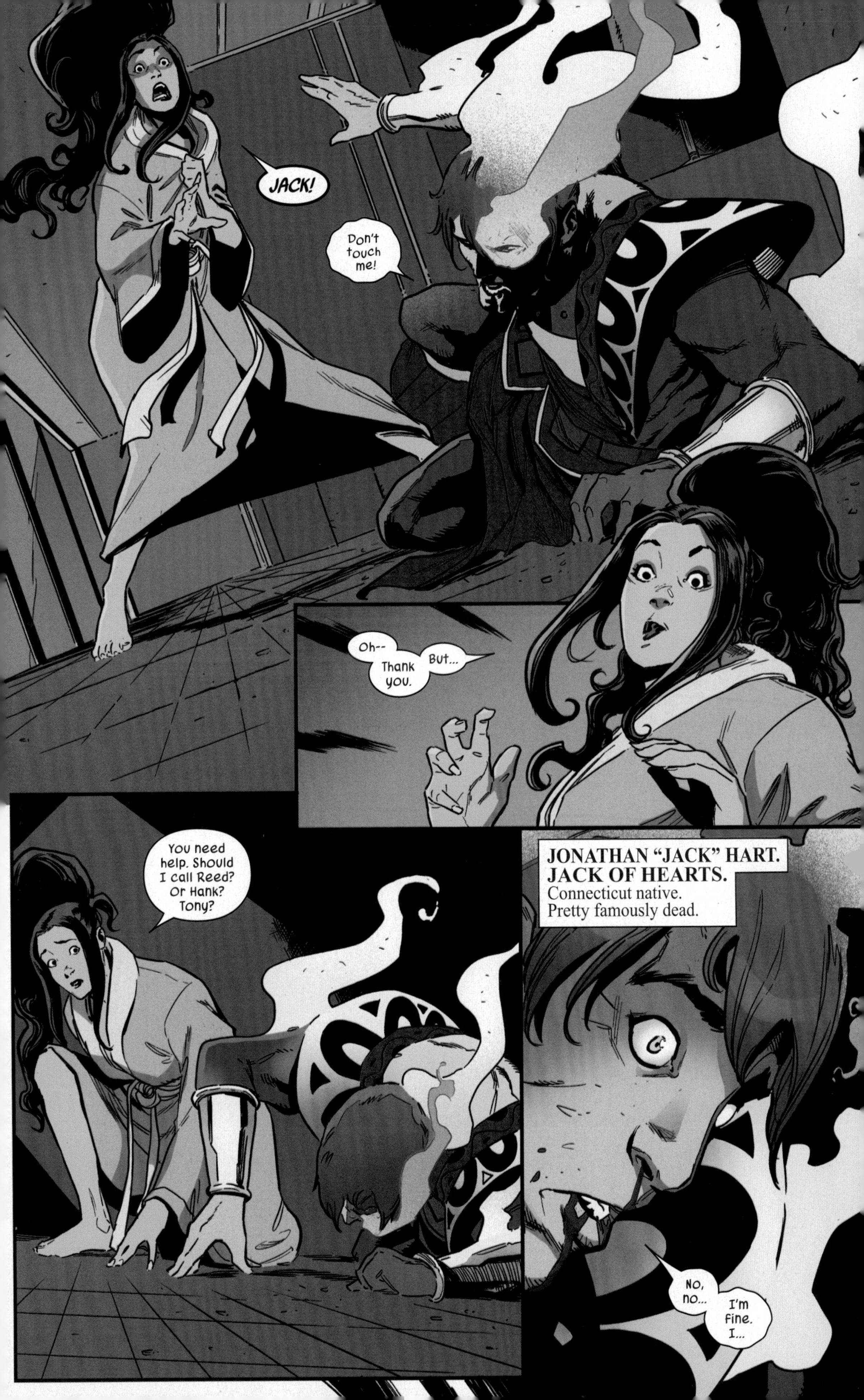
JACK!
Don't touch me!
Oh--
Thank you.
But...
You need help. Should I call Reed? Or Hank? Tony?
JONATHAN "JACK" HART. JACK OF HEARTS.
Connecticut native.
Pretty famously dead.
No, no...
I'm fine. I...

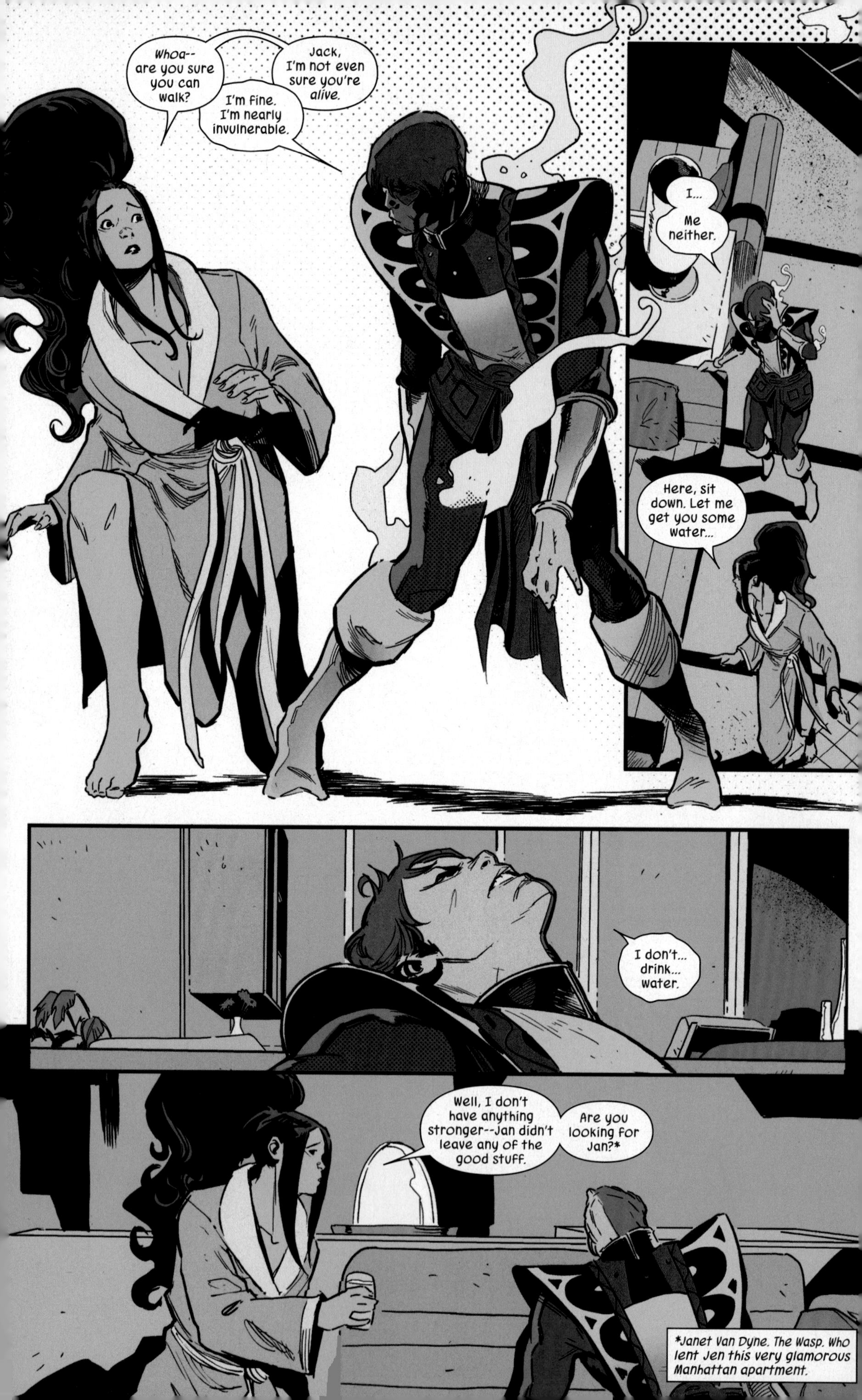
Whoa--
are you sure
you can
walk?
I'm fine.
I'm nearly
invulnerable.
Jack,
I'm not even
sure you're
alive.
I...
Me
neither.
Here, sit
down. Let me
get you some
water...
I don't...
drink...
water.
Well, I don't
have anything
stronger--Jan didn't
leave any of the
good stuff.
Are you
looking for
Jan?*
*Janet Van Dyne. The Wasp. Who
lent Jen this very glamorous
Manhattan apartment.

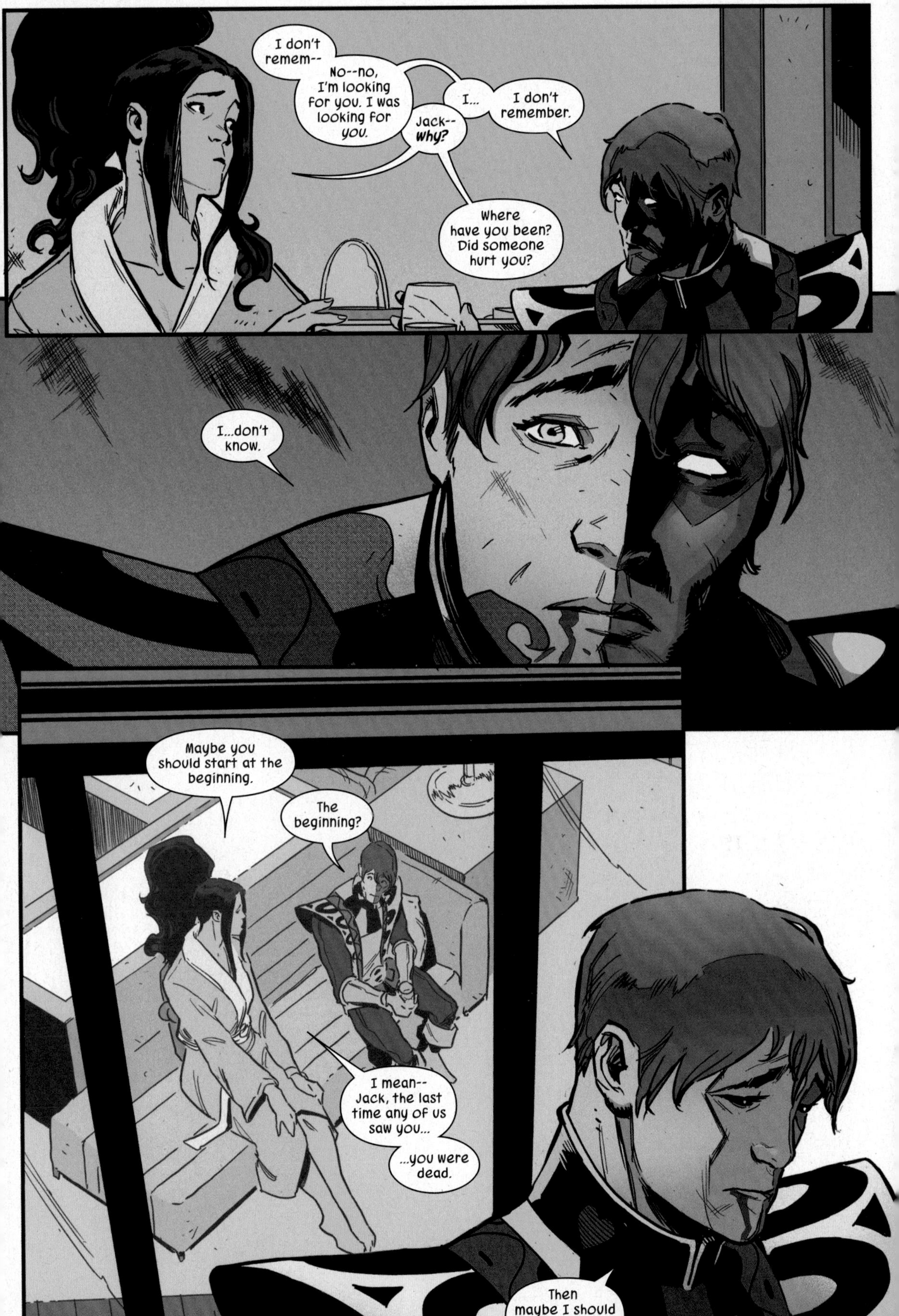

I don't remem--
No--no, I'm looking for you. I was looking for you.
I...
I don't remember.
Jack-- *Why?*
Where have you been? Did someone hurt you?
I...don't know.
Maybe you should start at the beginning.
The beginning?
I mean-- Jack, the last time any of us saw you...
...you were dead.
Then maybe I should start at the end.

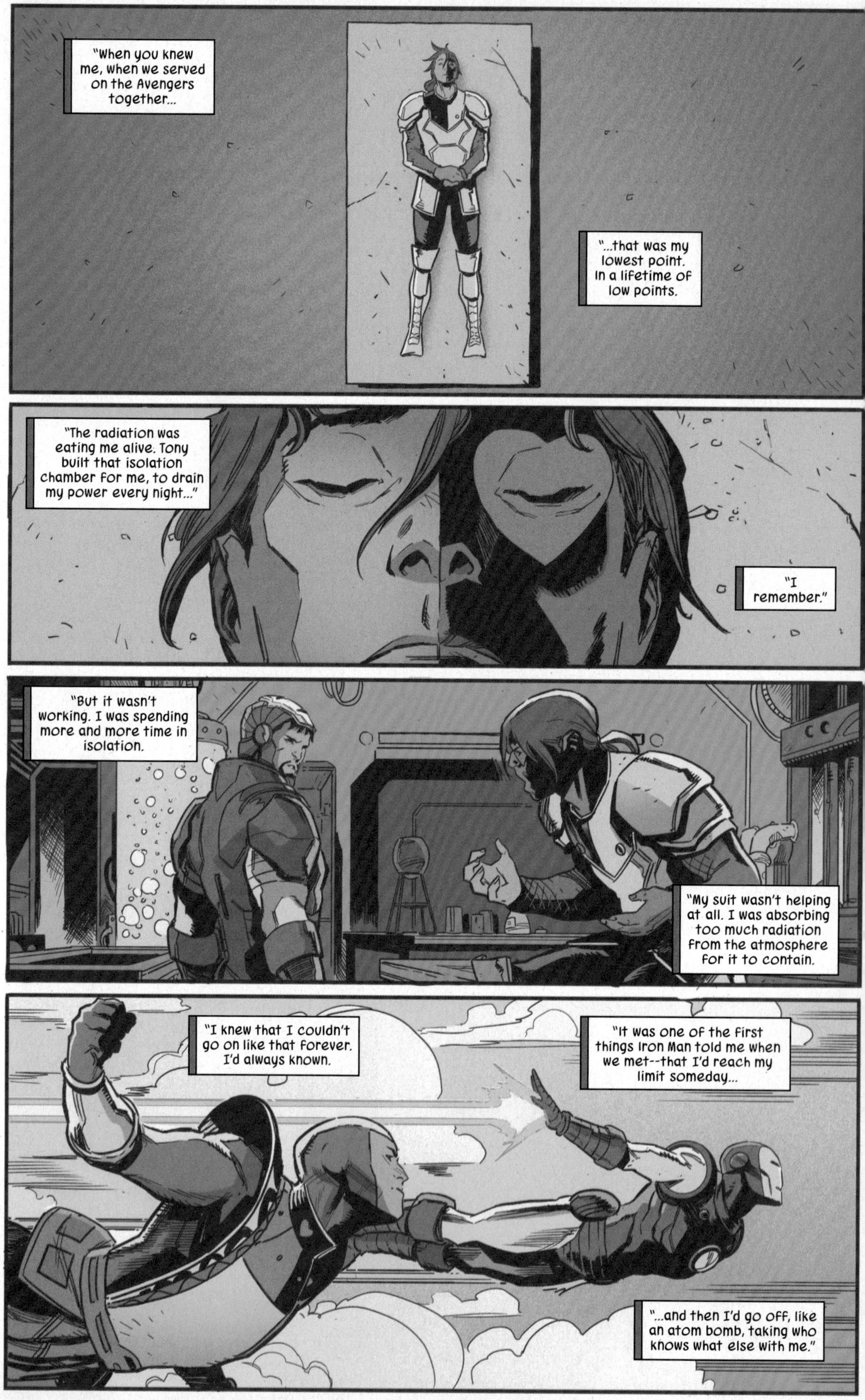
"When you knew me, when we served on the Avengers together...
"...that was my lowest point. In a lifetime of low points.
"The radiation was eating me alive. Tony built that isolation chamber for me, to drain my power every night..."
"I remember."
"But it wasn't working. I was spending more and more time in isolation.
"My suit wasn't helping at all. I was absorbing too much radiation from the atmosphere for it to contain.
"I knew that I couldn't go on like that forever. I'd always known.
"It was one of the first things Iron Man told me when we met--that I'd reach my limit someday...
"...and then I'd go off, like an atom bomb, taking who knows what else with me."

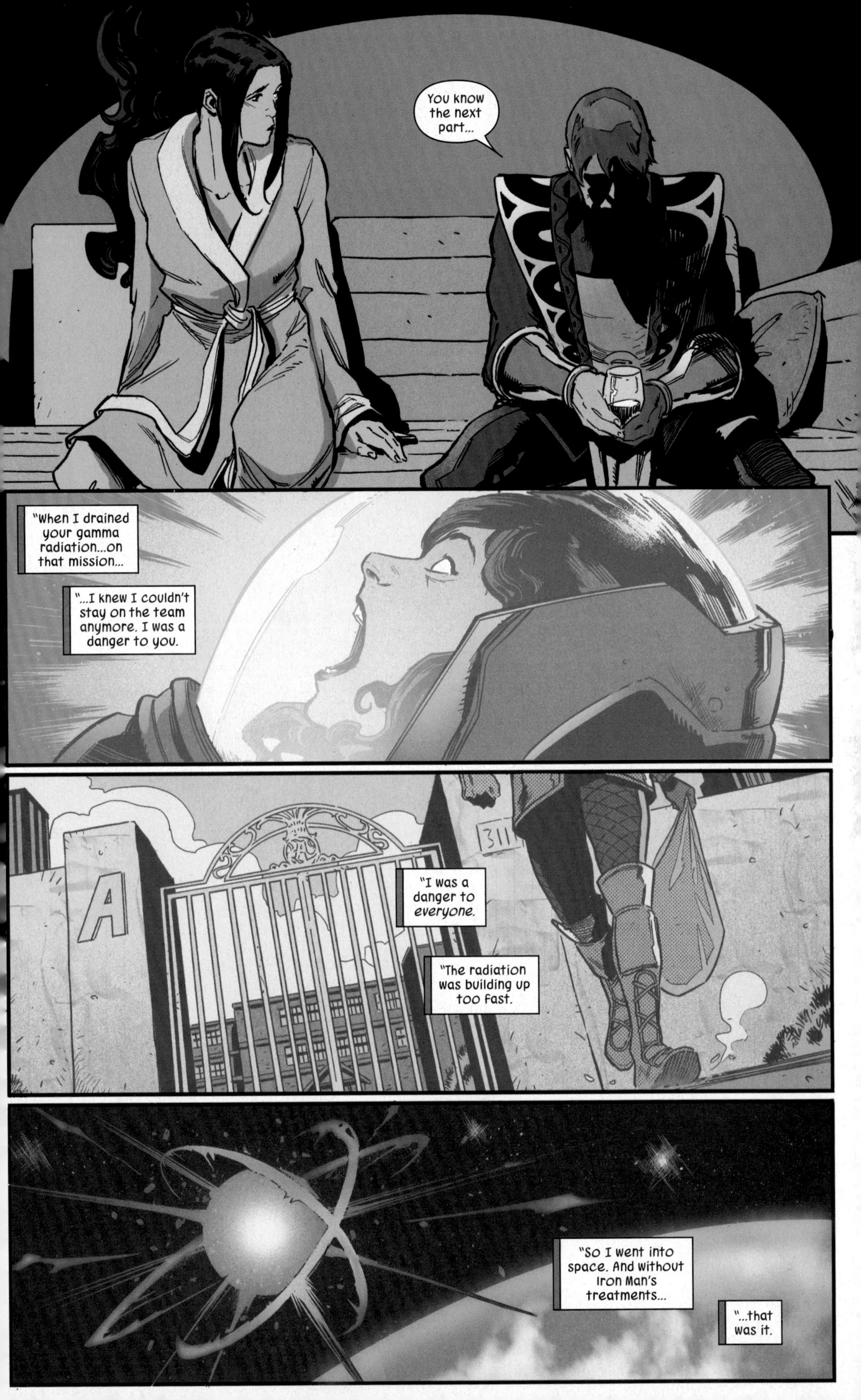
You know the next part...
"When I drained your gamma radiation...on that mission...
"...I knew I couldn't stay on the team anymore. I was a danger to you.
"I was a danger to everyone.
"The radiation was building up too fast.
"So I went into space. And without Iron Man's treatments...
"...that was it.

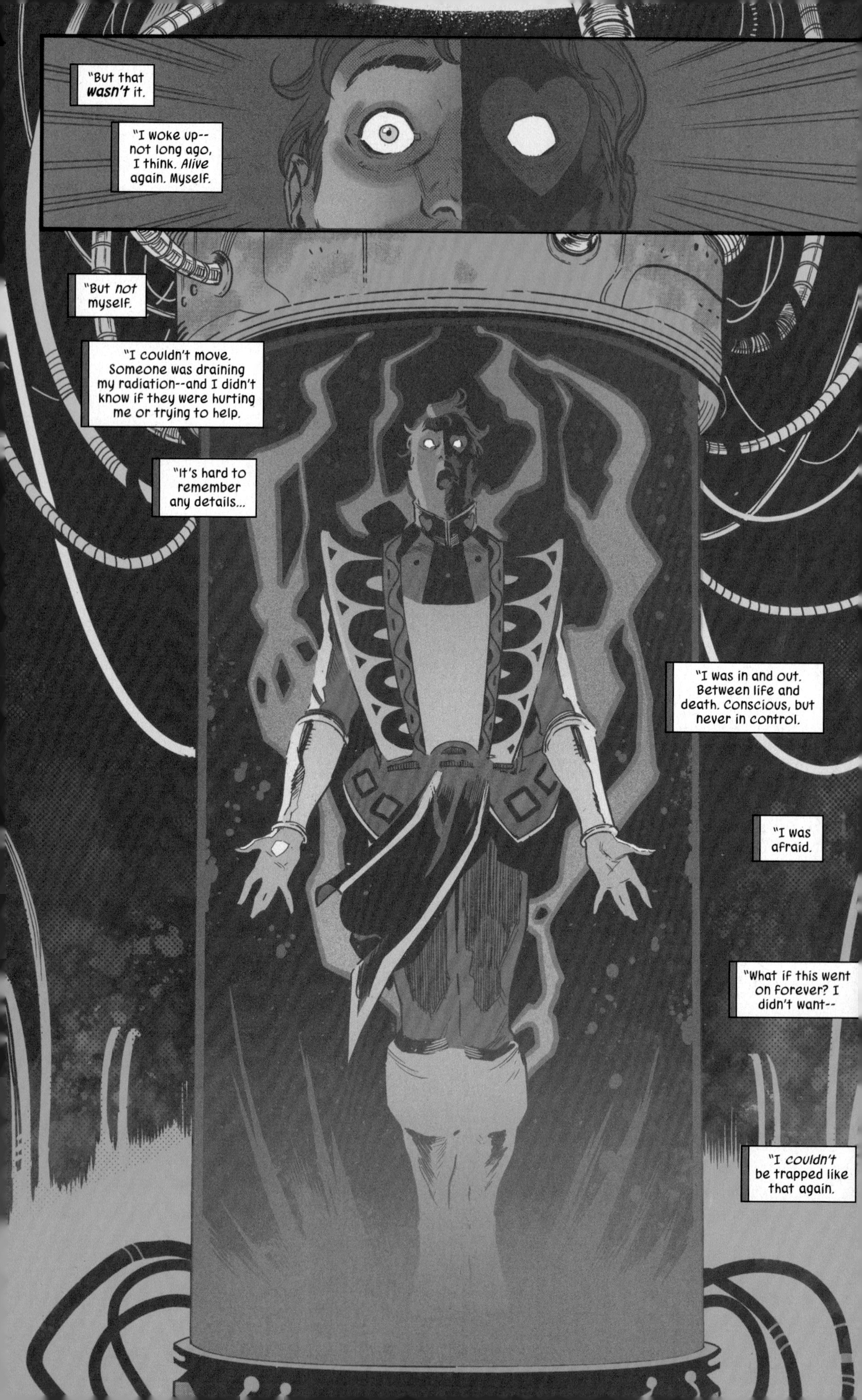
"But that *wasn't* it.
"I woke up--not long ago, I think. *Alive* again. Myself.
"But *not* myself.
"I couldn't move. Someone was draining my radiation--and I didn't know if they were hurting me or trying to help.
"It's hard to remember any details...
"I was in and out. Between life and death. Conscious, but never in control.
"I was afraid.
"What if this went on forever? I didn't want--
"I *couldn't* be trapped like that again.

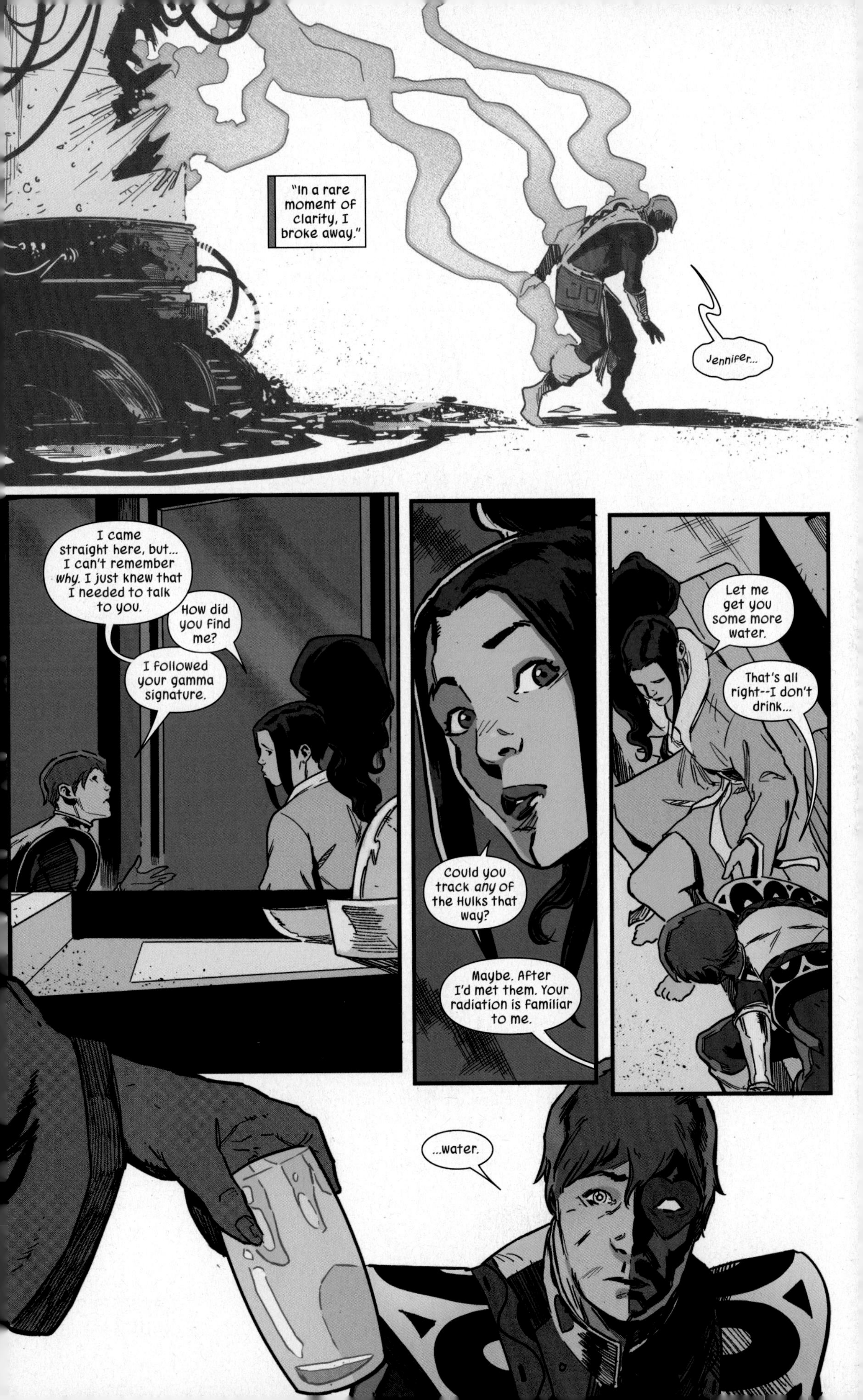
"In a rare moment of clarity, I broke away."
Jennifer...
I came straight here, but... I can't remember why. I just knew that I needed to talk to you.
How did you find me?
I followed your gamma signature.
Could you track any of the Hulks that way?
Maybe. After I'd met them. Your radiation is familiar to me.
Let me get you some more water.
That's all right--I don't drink...
...water.

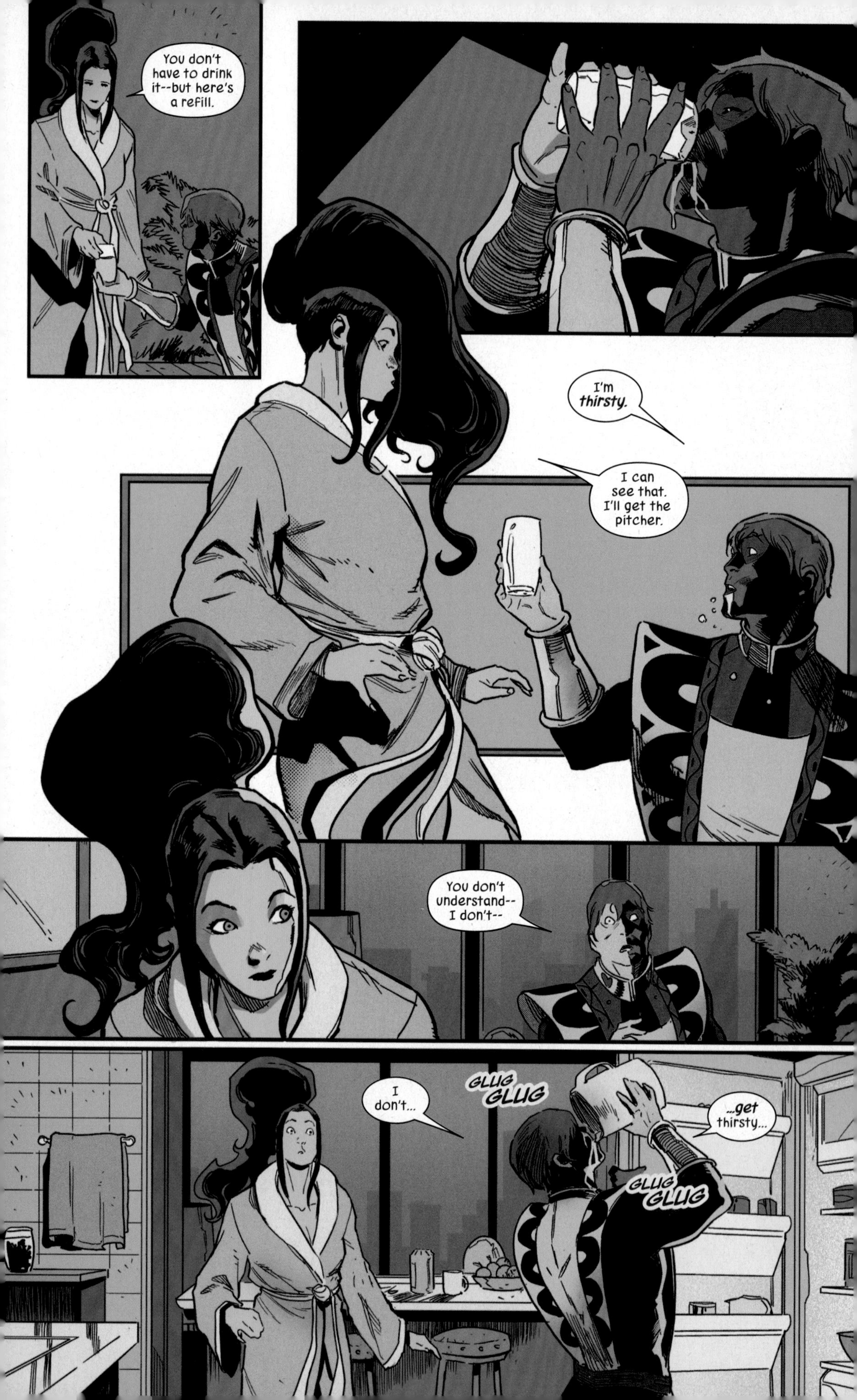

You don't have to drink it--but here's a refill.
I'm *thirsty.*
I can see that. I'll get the pitcher.
You don't understand-- I don't--
I don't...
GLUG GLUG
...get thirsty...
GLUG GLUG

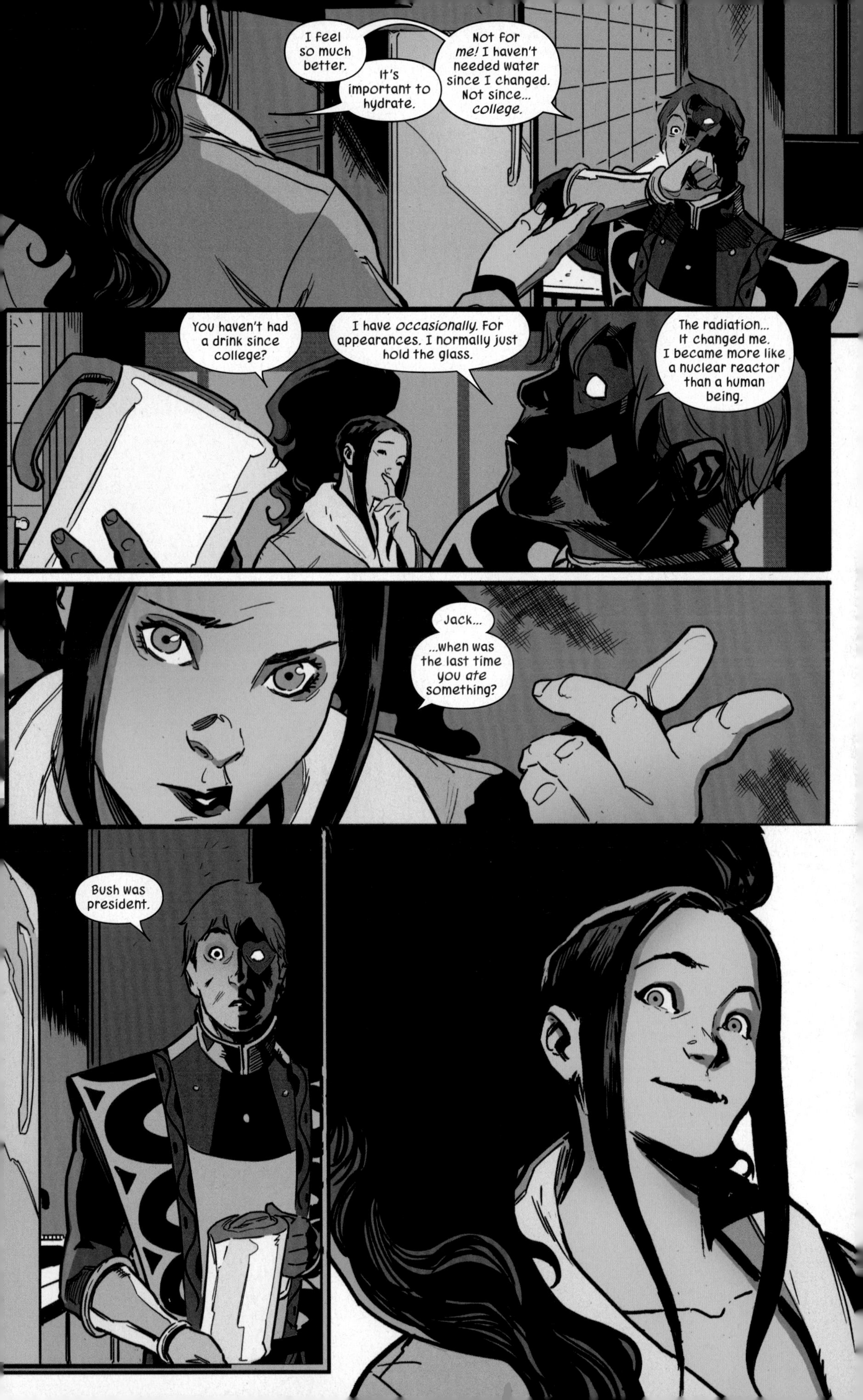
I feel so much better.
It's important to hydrate.
Not for *me!* I haven't needed water since I changed. Not since... *college.*
You haven't had a drink since college?
I have *occasionally.* For appearances. I normally just hold the glass.
The radiation... It changed me. I became more like a nuclear reactor than a human being.
Jack...
...when was the last time you *ate* something?
Bush was president.

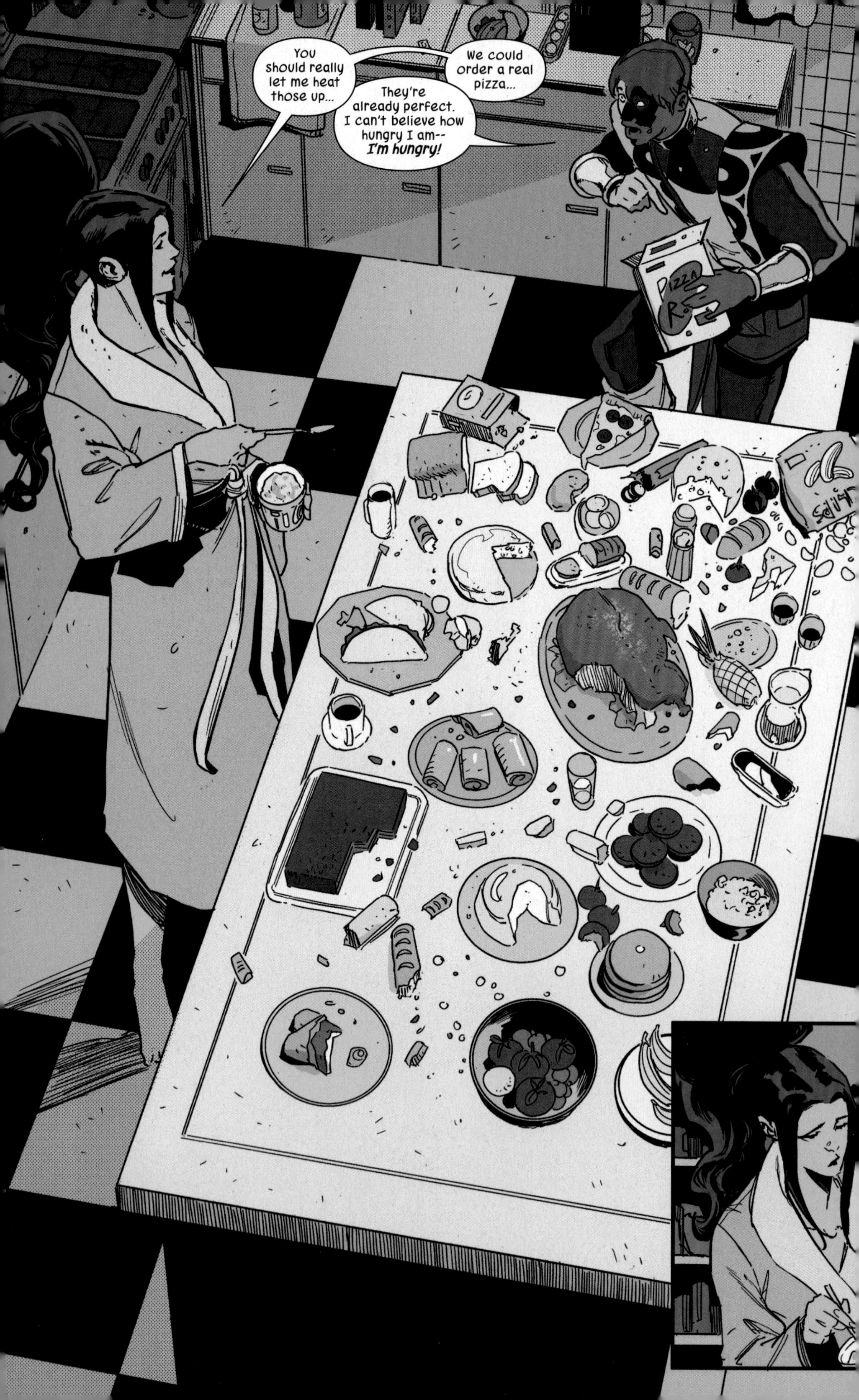
You should really let me heat those up...
We could order a real pizza...
They're already perfect. I can't believe how hungry I am-- *I'm hungry!*

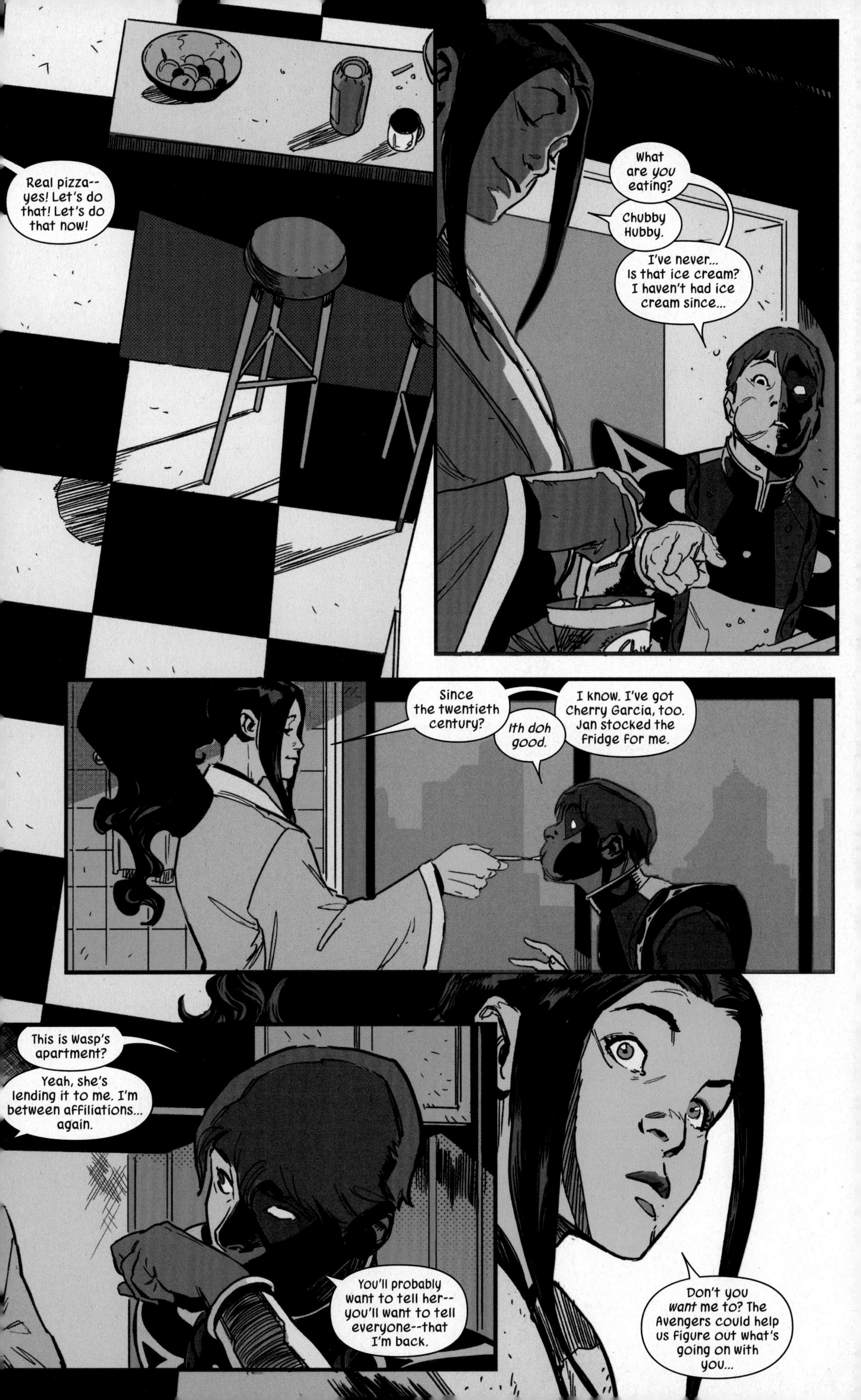
Real pizza--
yes! Let's do
that! Let's do
that now!
What
are *you*
eating?
Chubby
Hubby.
I've never...
Is that ice cream?
I haven't had ice
cream since...
Since
the twentieth
century?
I know. I've got
Cherry Garcia, too.
Jan stocked the
fridge for me.
*Ith doh
good.*
This is Wasp's
apartment?
Yeah, she's
lending it to me. I'm
between affiliations...
again.
You'll probably
want to tell her--
you'll want to tell
everyone--that
I'm back.
Don't you
want me to? The
Avengers could help
us figure out what's
going on with
you...

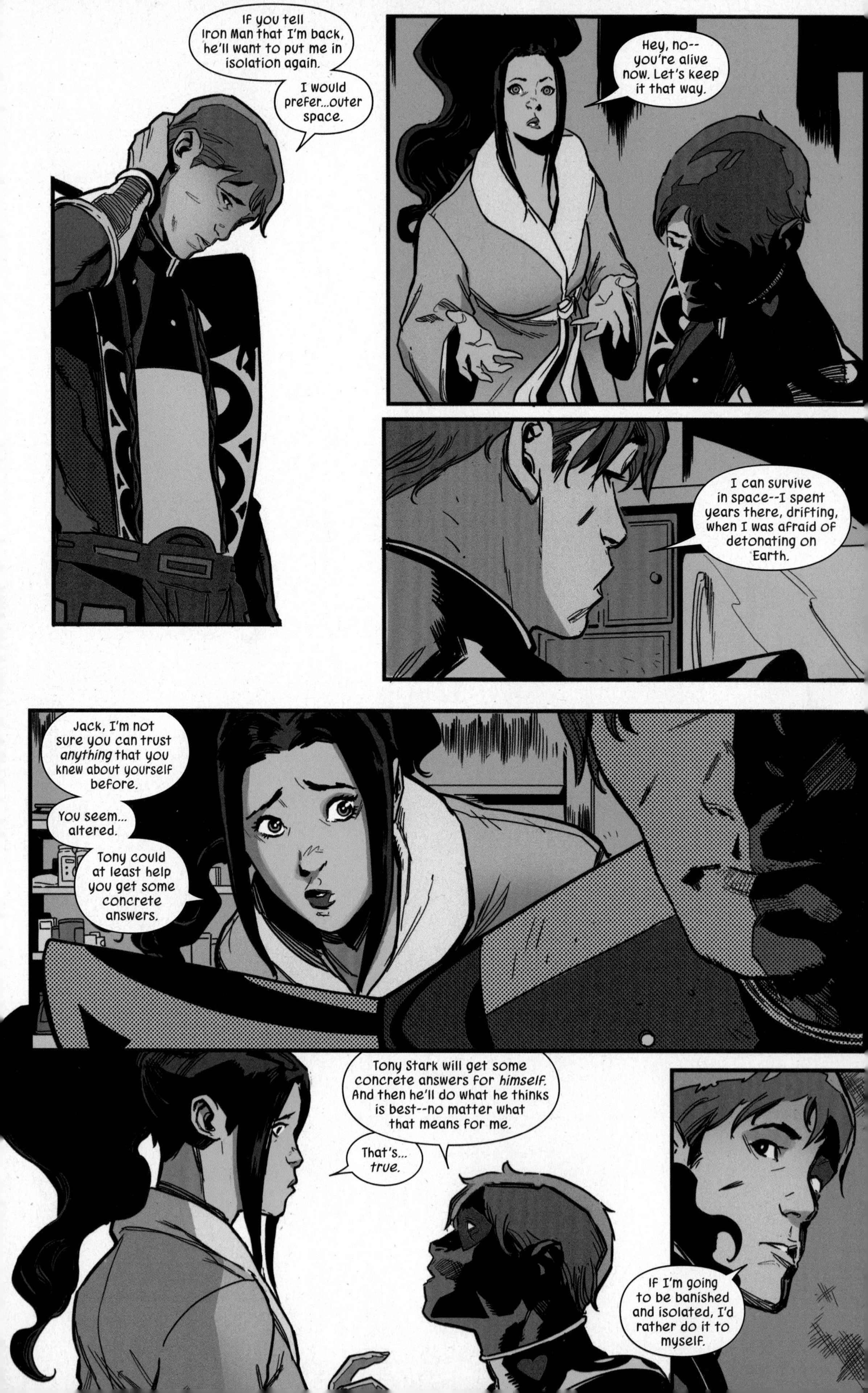
If you tell Iron Man that I'm back, he'll want to put me in isolation again.
I would prefer...outer space.
Hey, no-- you're alive now. Let's keep it that way.
I can survive in space--I spent years there, drifting, when I was afraid of detonating on Earth.
Jack, I'm not sure you can trust *anything* that you knew about yourself before.
You seem... altered.
Tony could at least help you get some concrete answers.
Tony Stark will get some concrete answers for *himself*. And then he'll do what he thinks is best--no matter what that means for me.
That's... *true*.
If I'm going to be banished and isolated, I'd rather do it to myself.

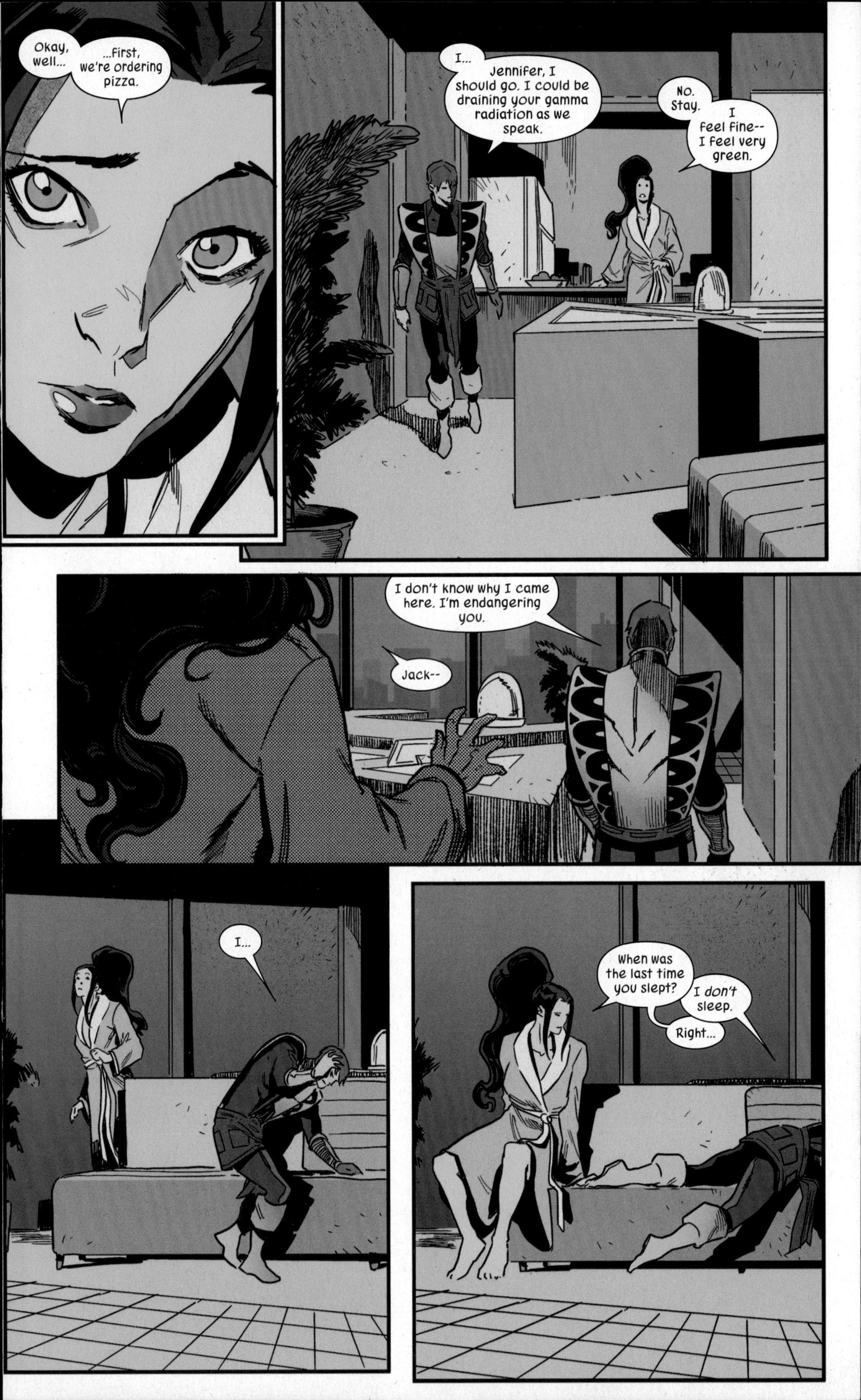
Okay, well...
...first, we're ordering pizza.
I...
Jennifer, I should go. I could be draining your gamma radiation as we speak.
No. Stay.
I feel fine-- I feel very green.
I don't know why I came here. I'm endangering you.
Jack--
I...
When was the last time you slept?
I don't sleep.
Right...

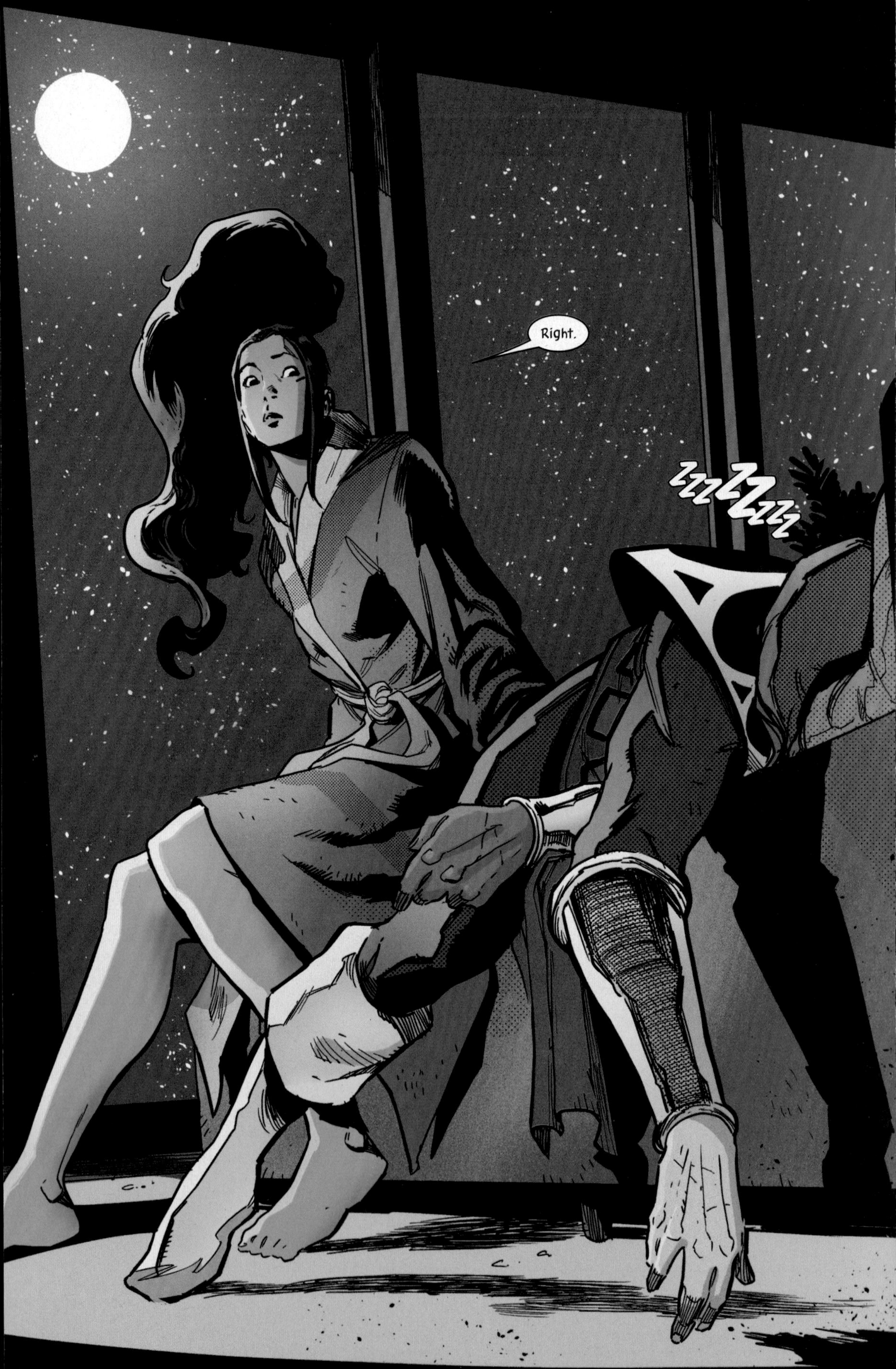
Right.
ZZZZZZZZZ

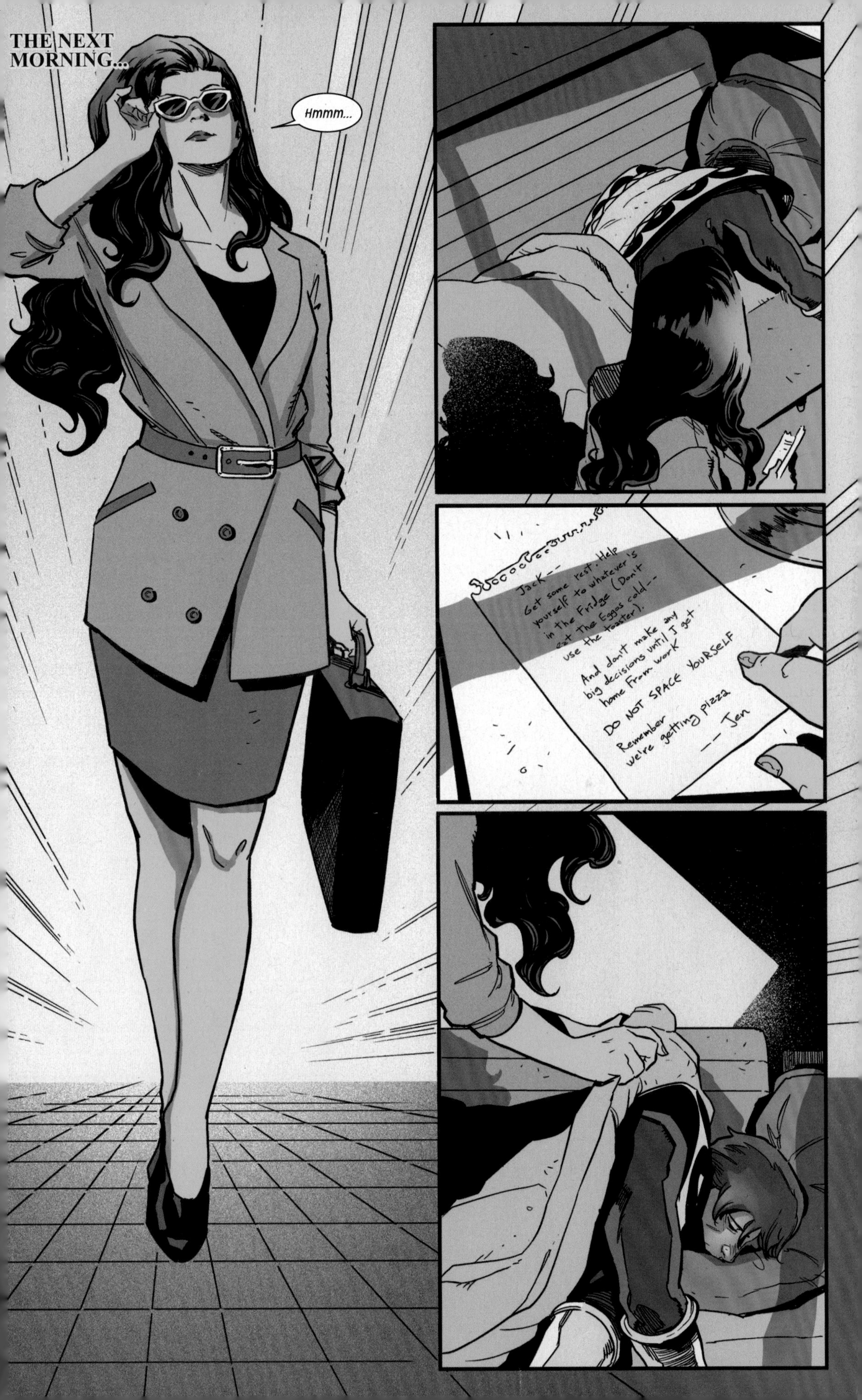
THE NEXT MORNING...
Hmmm...
Jack--
Get some rest. Help yourself to whatever's in the fridge (Don't eat the Eggos cold--use the toaster).
And don't make any big decisions until I get home from work
DO NOT SPACE YOURSELF
Remember we're getting pizza
-- Jen

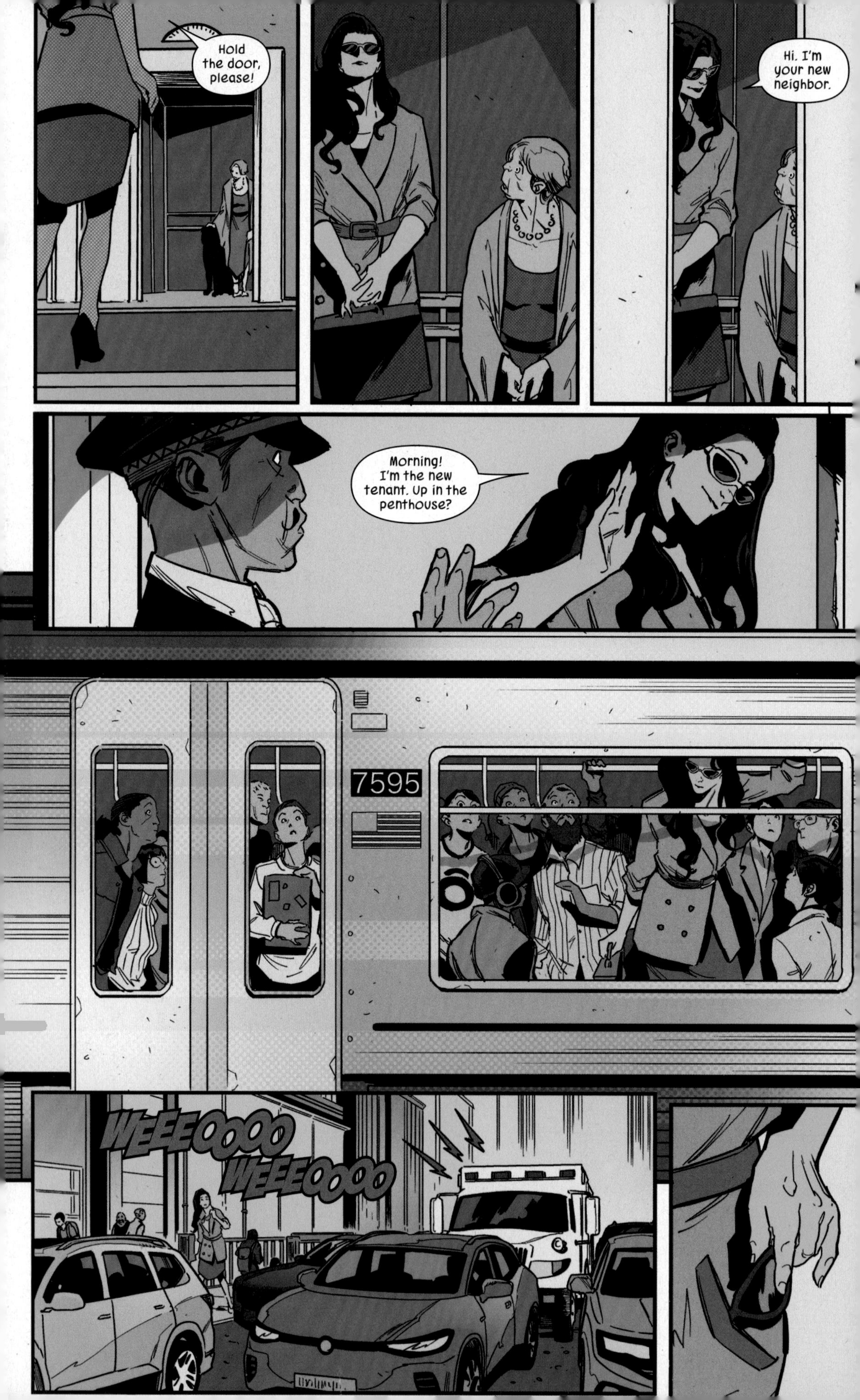
Hold the door, please!
Hi. I'm your new neighbor.
Morning! I'm the new tenant. Up in the penthouse?
7595
WEEEOOOO
WEEEOOOO

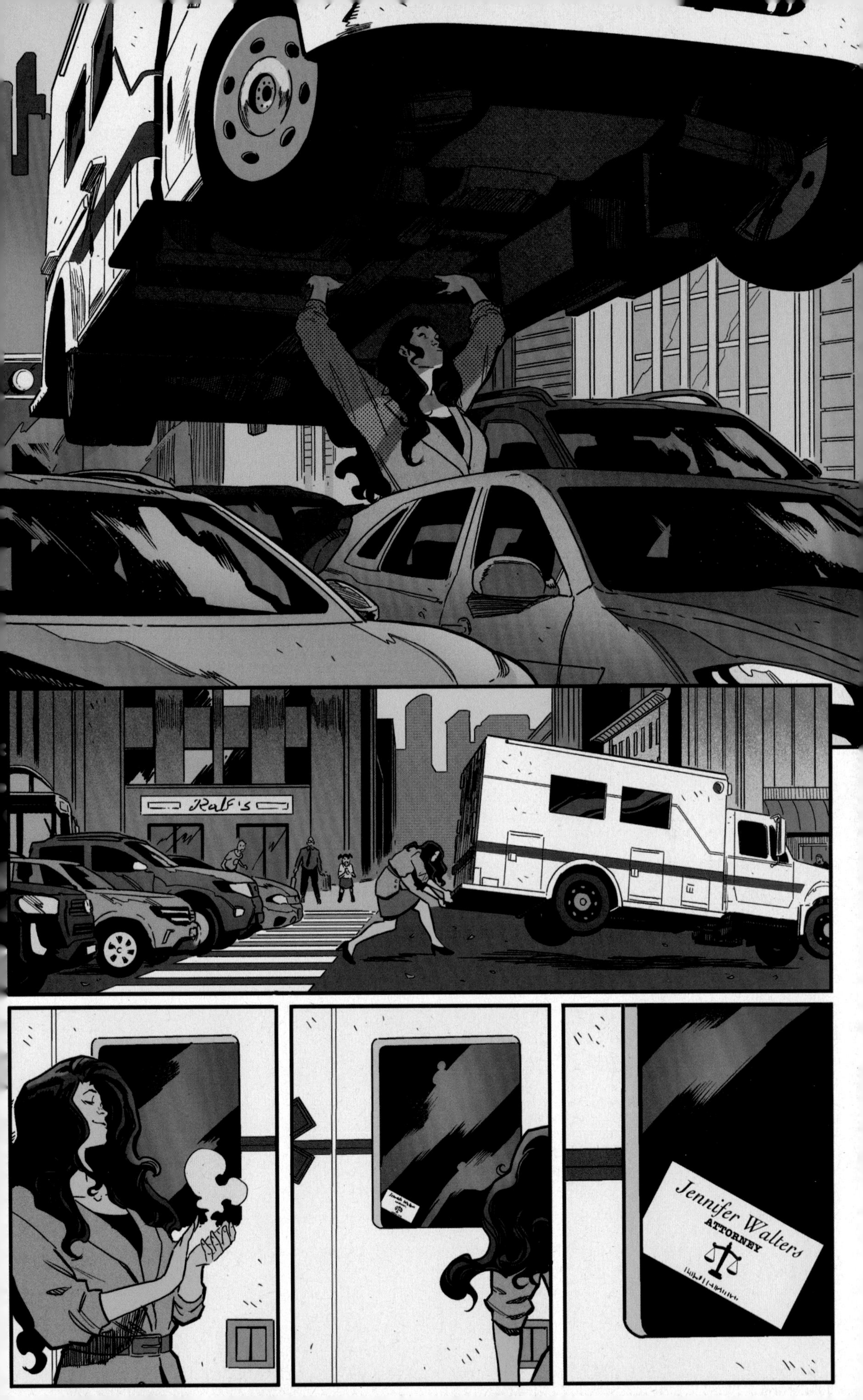
Ralf's
Jennifer Walters
ATTORNEY

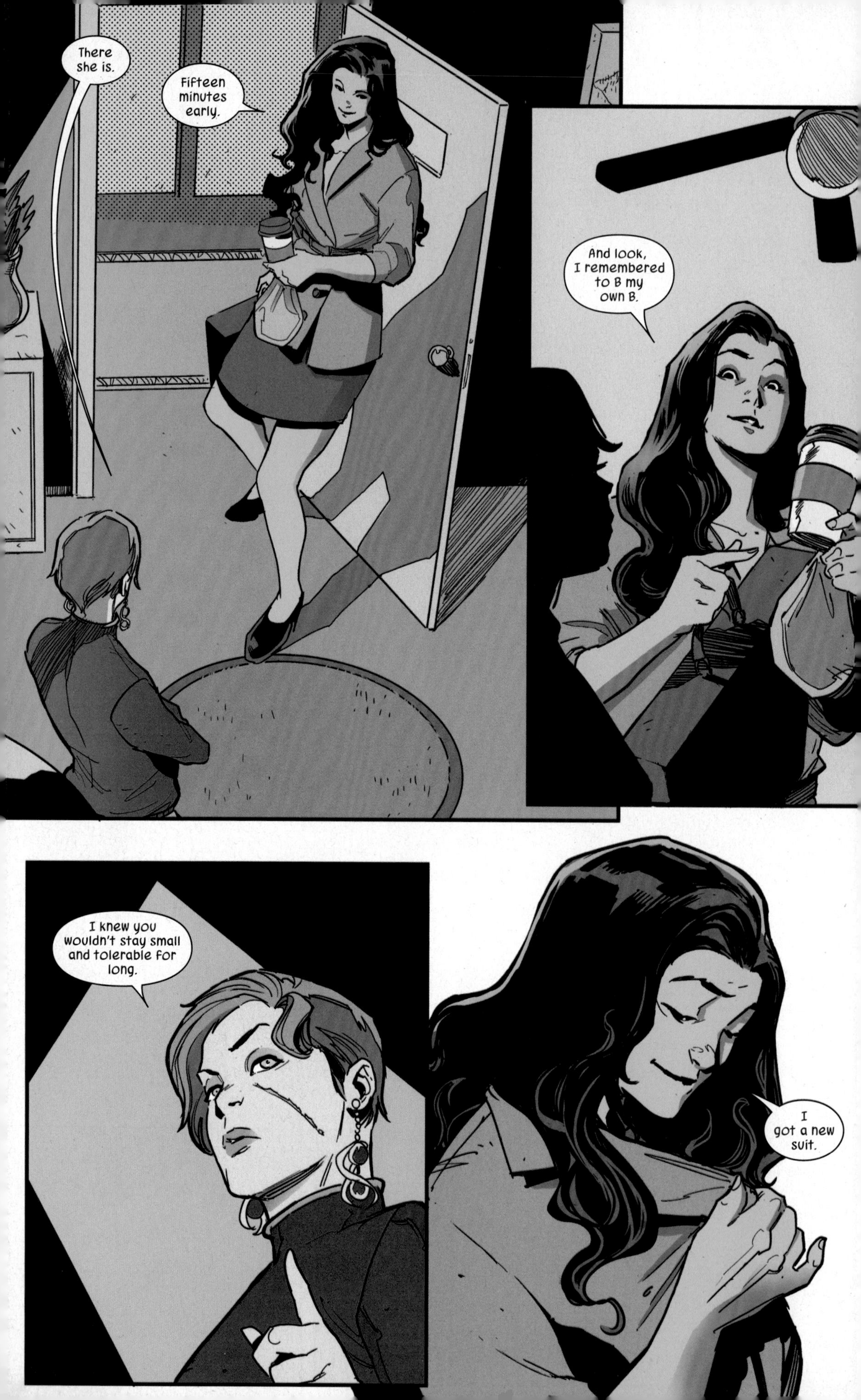
There she is.
Fifteen minutes early.
And look, I remembered to B my own B.
I knew you wouldn't stay small and tolerable for long.
I got a new suit.

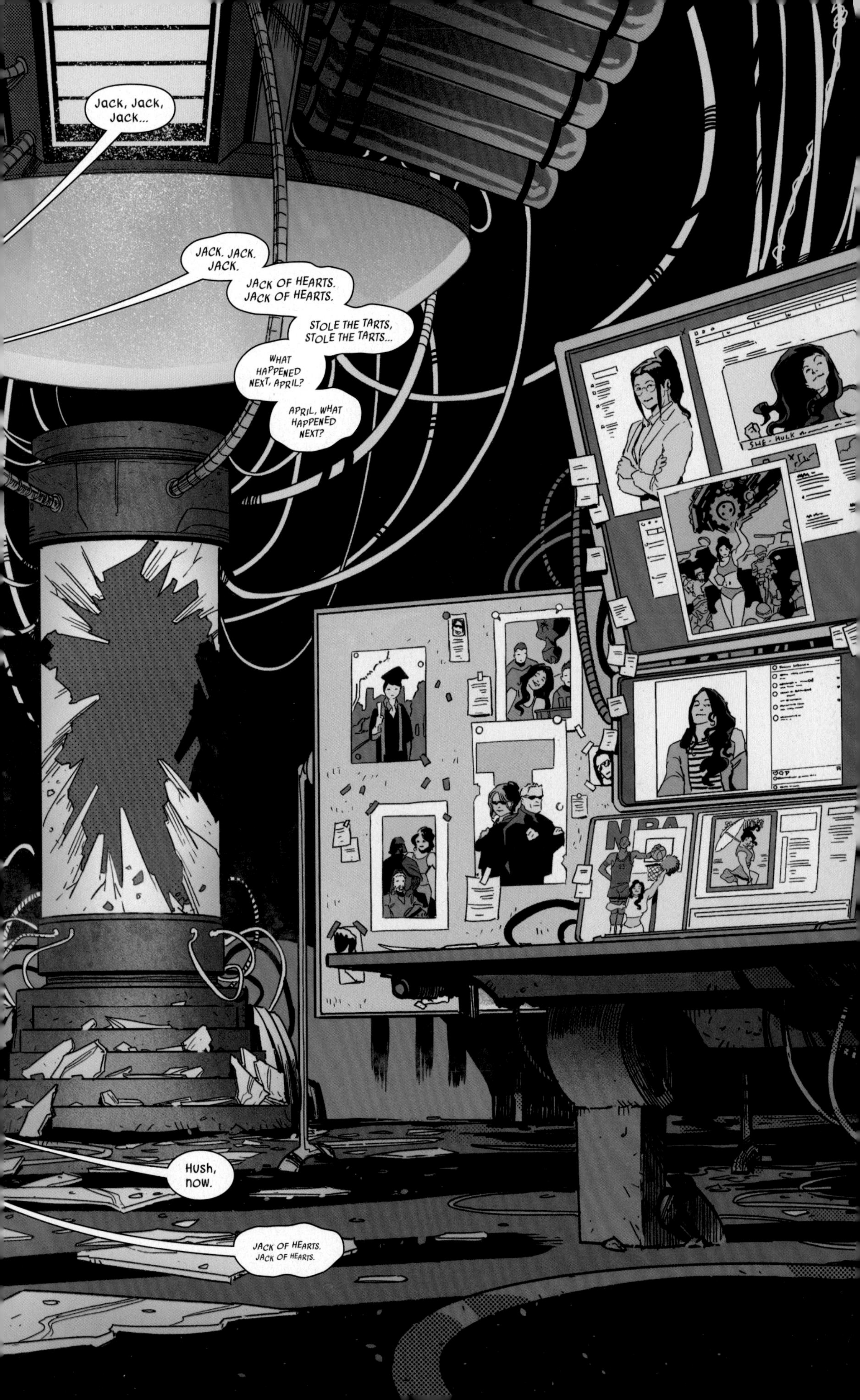
Jack, Jack, Jack...
JACK. JACK. JACK.
JACK OF HEARTS. JACK OF HEARTS.
STOLE THE TARTS, STOLE THE TARTS...
WHAT HAPPENED NEXT, APRIL?
APRIL, WHAT HAPPENED NEXT?
NBA
Hush, now.
JACK OF HEARTS. JACK OF HEARTS.

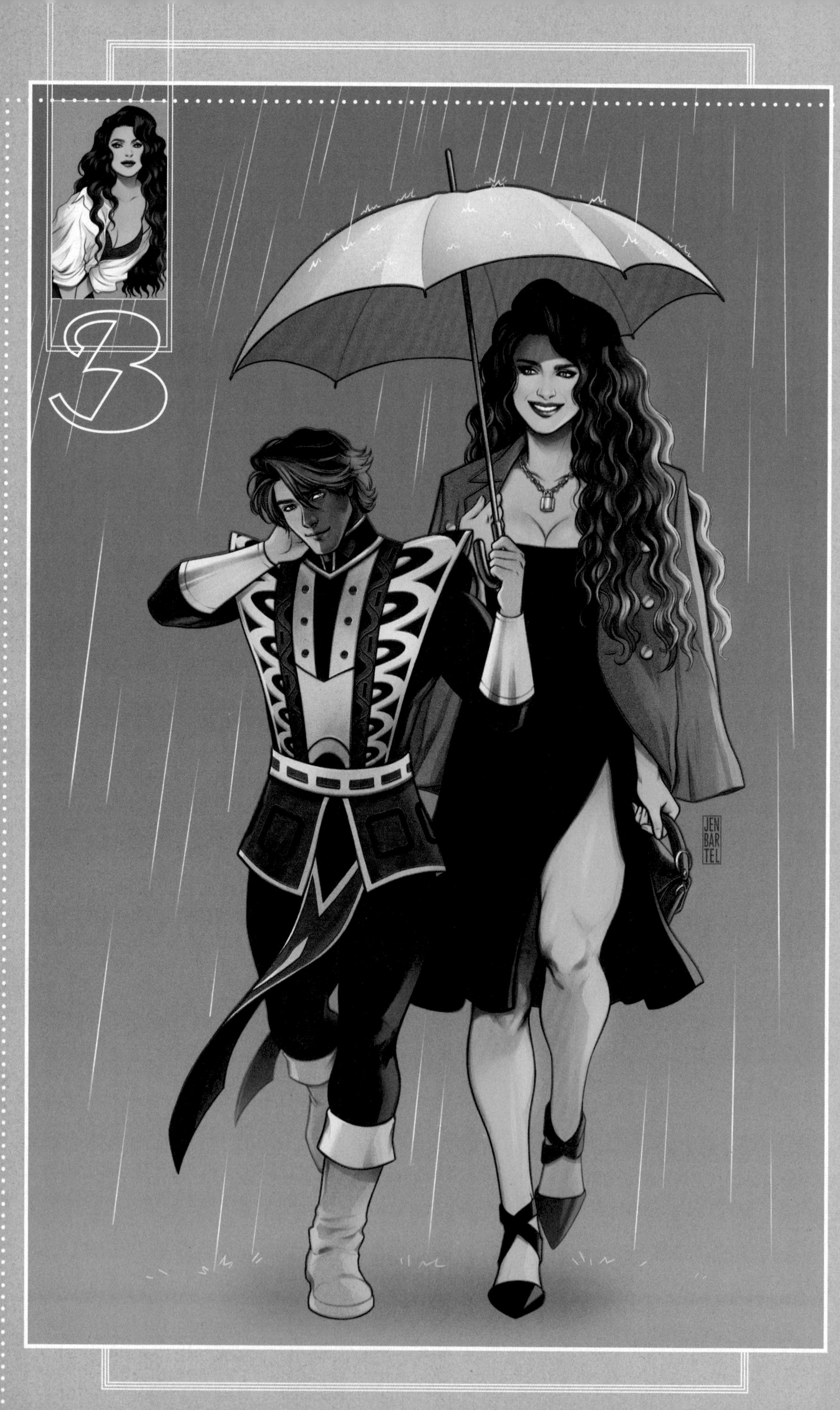
3
JEN
BAR
TEL

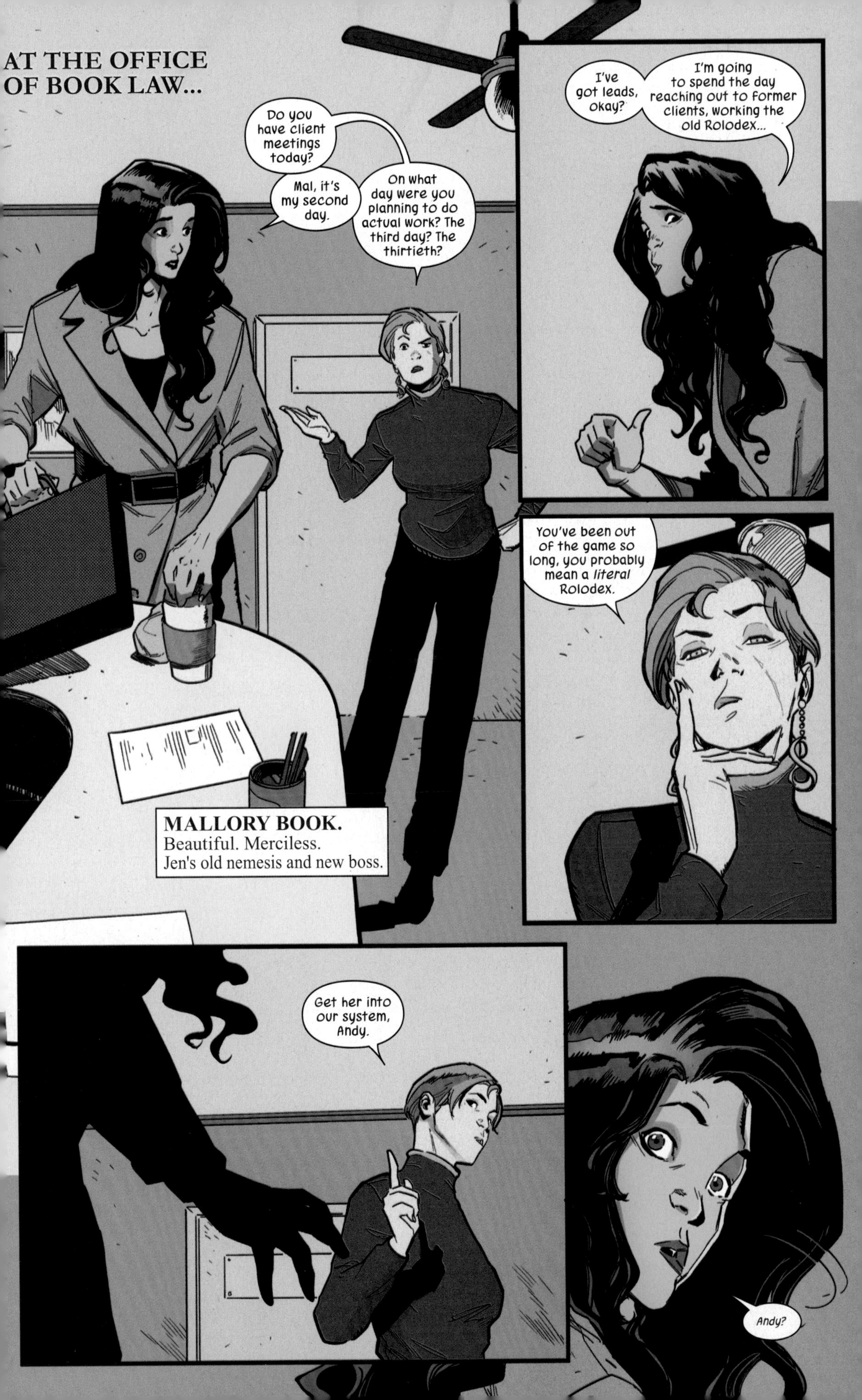
AT THE OFFICE OF BOOK LAW...
Do you have client meetings today?
Mal, it's my second day.
On what day were you planning to do actual work? The third day? The thirtieth?
I've got leads, okay?
I'm going to spend the day reaching out to former clients, working the old Rolodex...
You've been out of the game so long, you probably mean a *literal* Rolodex.
MALLORY BOOK.
Beautiful. Merciless.
Jen's old nemesis and new boss.
Get her into our system, Andy.
Andy?

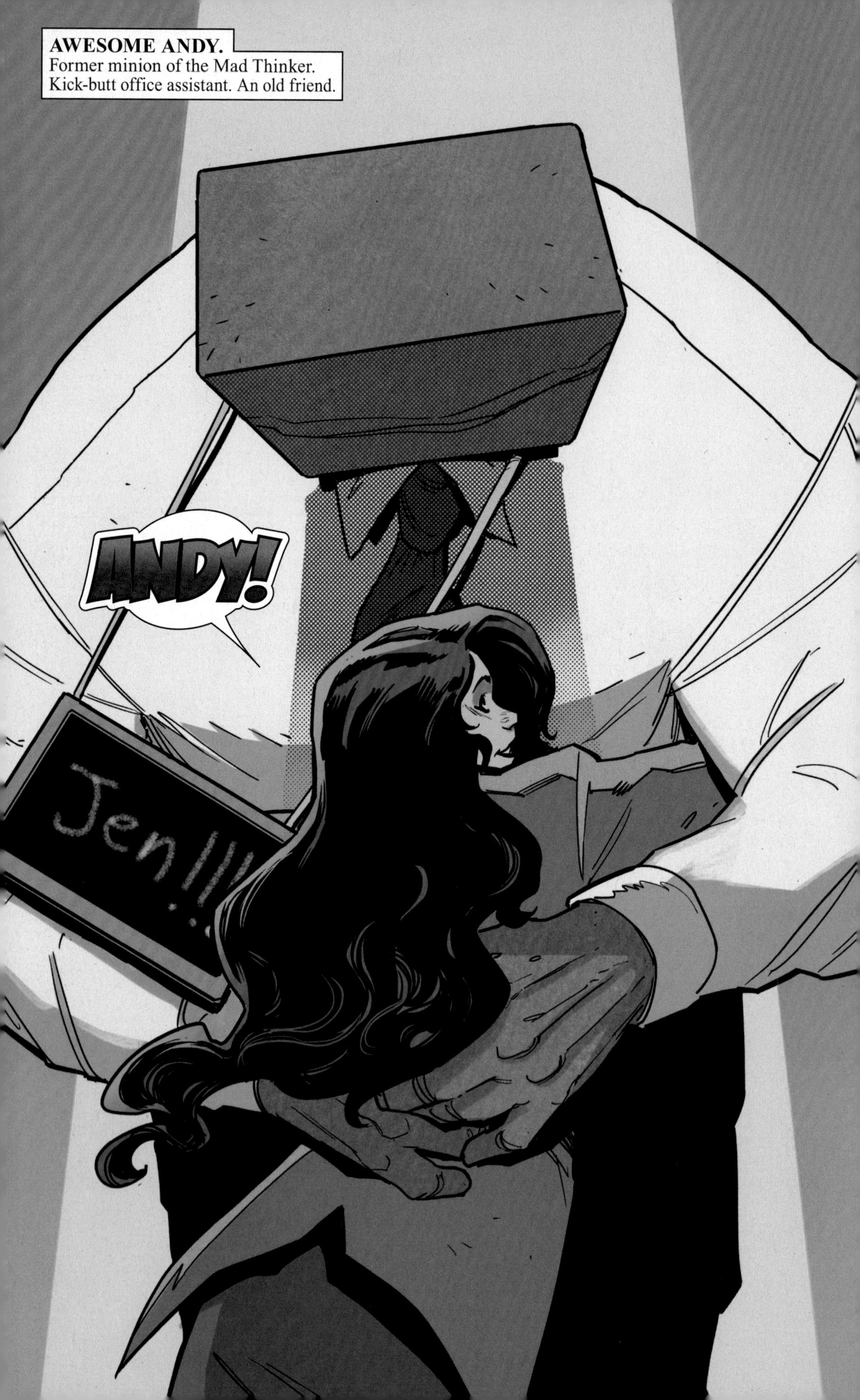
AWESOME ANDY.
Former minion of the Mad Thinker.
Kick-butt office assistant. An old friend.
ANDY!
Jen!!!!

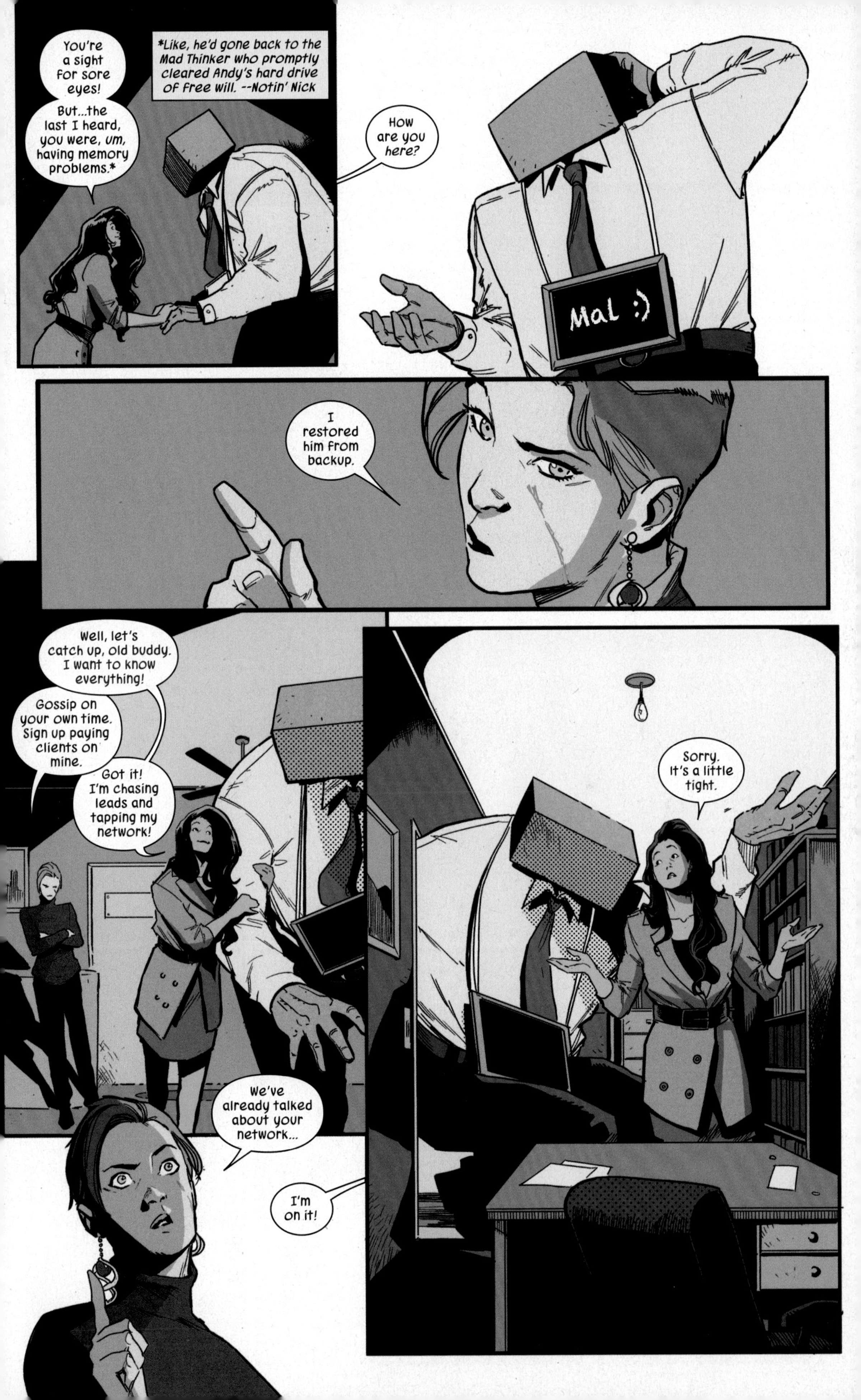
You're a sight for sore eyes!
*Like, he'd gone back to the Mad Thinker who promptly cleared Andy's hard drive of free will. --Notin' Nick
But...the last I heard, you were, um, having memory problems.*
How are you here?
Mal :)
I restored him from backup.
Well, let's catch up, old buddy. I want to know everything!
Gossip on your own time. Sign up paying clients on mine.
Got it! I'm chasing leads and tapping my network!
We've already talked about your network...
Sorry. It's a little tight.
I'm on it!

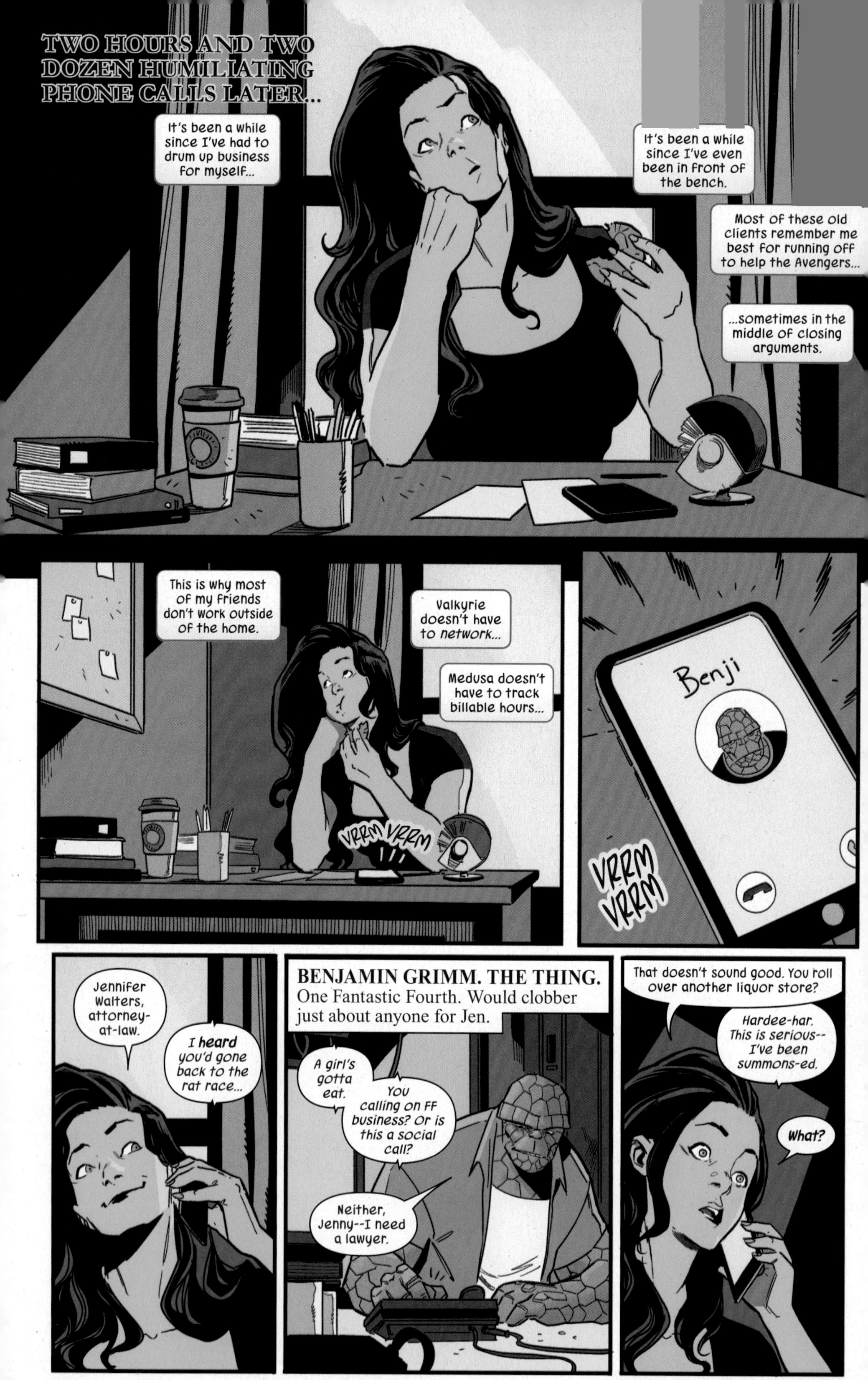
TWO HOURS AND TWO DOZEN HUMILIATING PHONE CALLS LATER...
It's been a while since I've had to drum up business for myself...
It's been a while since I've even been in front of the bench.
Most of these old clients remember me best for running off to help the Avengers...
...sometimes in the middle of closing arguments.
This is why most of my friends don't work outside of the home.
Valkyrie doesn't have to *network*...
Medusa doesn't have to track billable hours...
VRRM VRRM
Benji
VRRM VRRM
Jennifer Walters, attorney-at-law.
I *heard* you'd gone back to the rat race...
BENJAMIN GRIMM. THE THING.
One Fantastic Fourth. Would clobber just about anyone for Jen.
A girl's gotta eat.
You calling on FF business? Or is this a social call?
Neither, Jenny--I need a lawyer.
That doesn't sound good. You roll over another liquor store?
Hardee-har. This is serious--I've been summons-ed.
What?

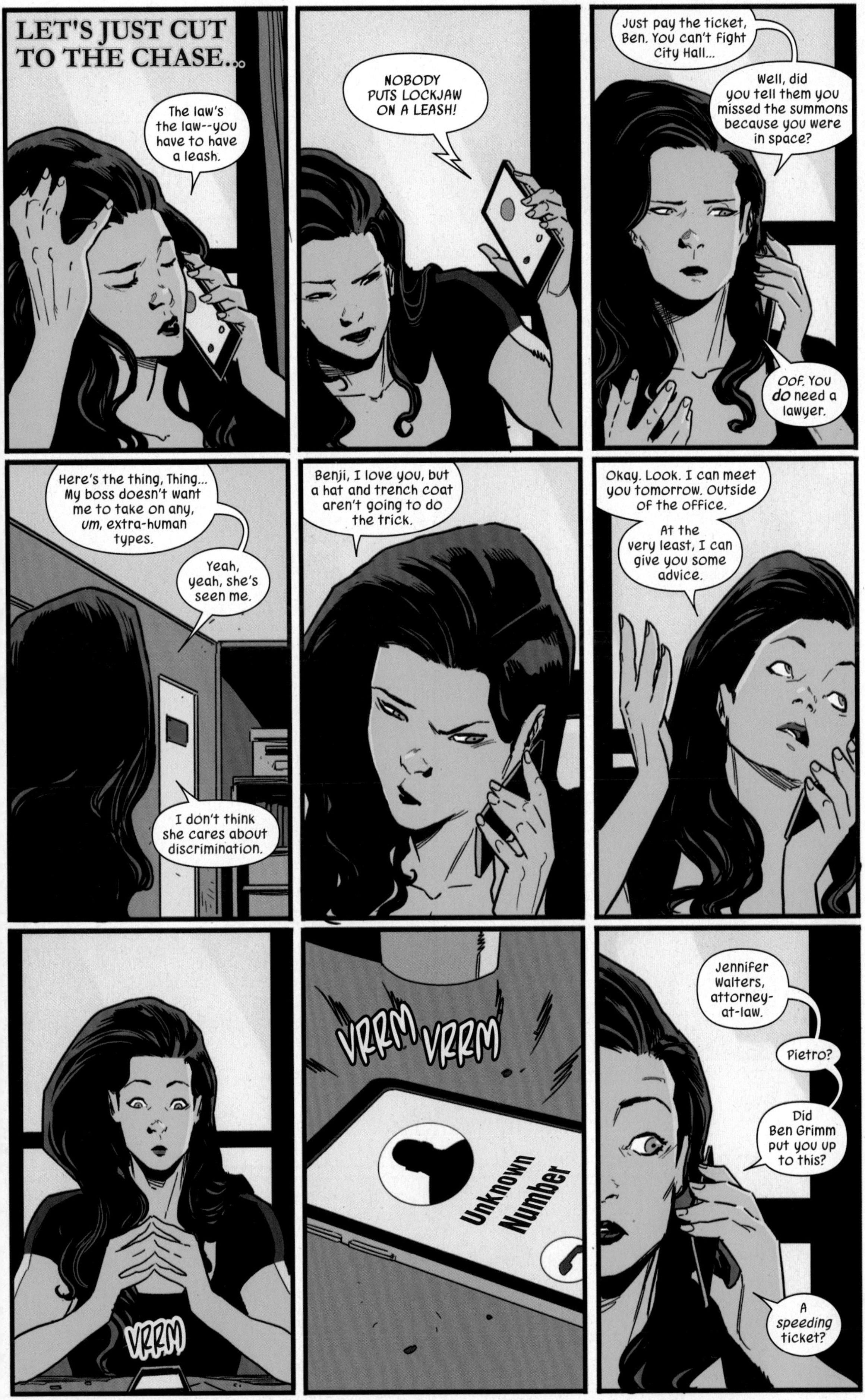
LET'S JUST CUT TO THE CHASE...
The law's the law--you have to have a leash.
NOBODY PUTS LOCKJAW ON A LEASH!
Just pay the ticket, Ben. You can't fight City Hall...
Well, did you tell them you missed the summons because you were in space?
OOF. You do need a lawyer.
Here's the thing, Thing... My boss doesn't want me to take on any, um, extra-human types.
Yeah, yeah, she's seen me.
I don't think she cares about discrimination.
Benji, I love you, but a hat and trench coat aren't going to do the trick.
Okay. Look. I can meet you tomorrow. Outside of the office.
At the very least, I can give you some advice.
VRRM
VRRM VRRM
Unknown Number
Jennifer Walters, attorney-at-law.
Pietro?
Did Ben Grimm put you up to this?
A speeding ticket?

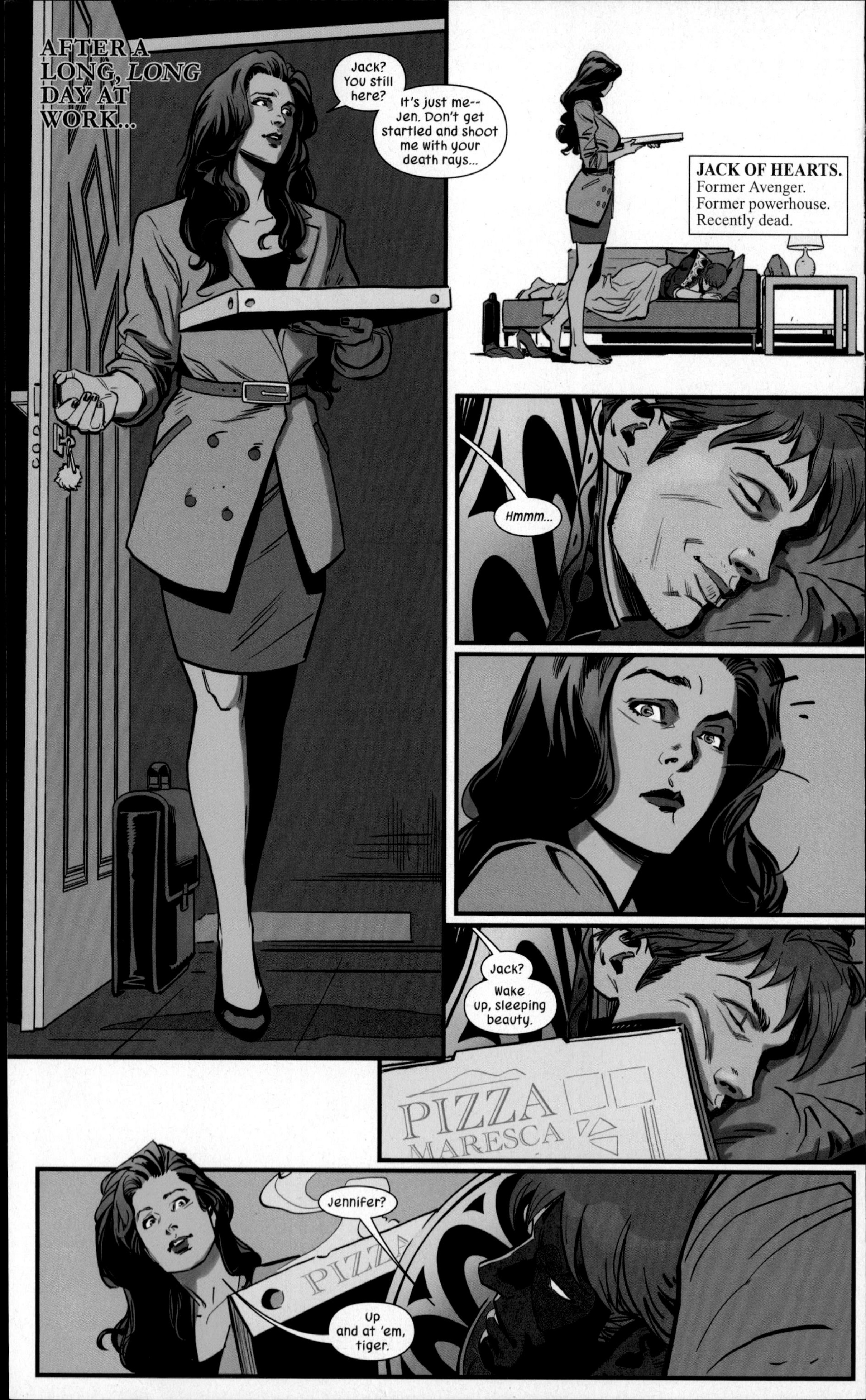
AFTER A LONG, *LONG* DAY AT WORK...
Jack? You still here?
It's just me-- Jen. Don't get startled and shoot me with your death rays...
JACK OF HEARTS.
Former Avenger.
Former powerhouse.
Recently dead.
Hmmm...
Jack?
Wake up, sleeping beauty.
PIZZA MARESCA
Jennifer?
PIZZA
Up and at 'em, tiger.

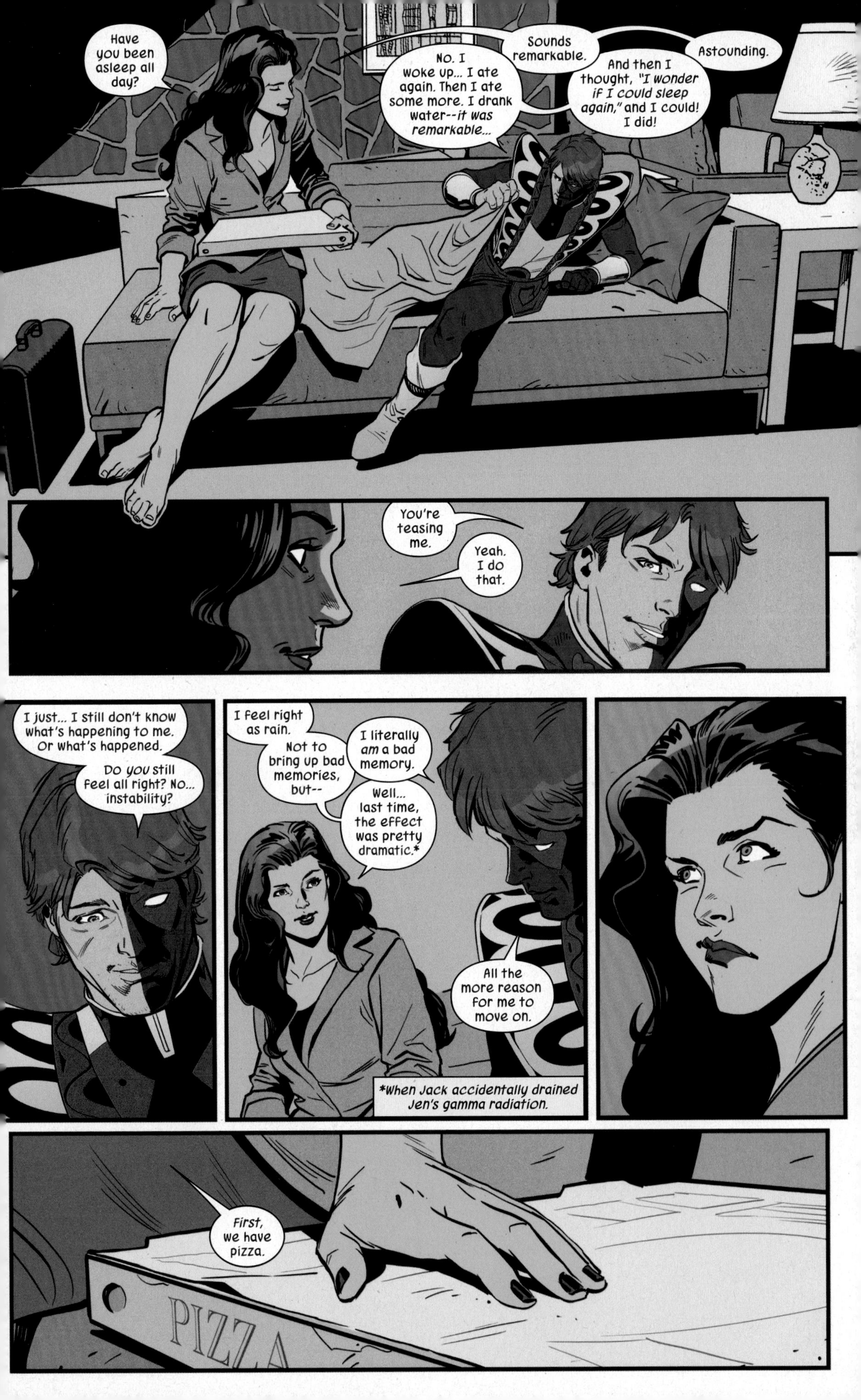
Have you been asleep all day?
No. I woke up... I ate again. Then I ate some more. I drank water--it was remarkable...
Sounds remarkable.
And then I thought, "I wonder if I could sleep again," and I could! I did!
Astounding.
You're teasing me.
Yeah. I do that.
I just... I still don't know what's happening to me. Or what's happened.
Do you still feel all right? No... instability?
I feel right as rain.
Not to bring up bad memories, but--
I literally am a bad memory.
Well... last time, the effect was pretty dramatic.*
All the more reason for me to move on.
*When Jack accidentally drained Jen's gamma radiation.
First, we have pizza.
PIZZA

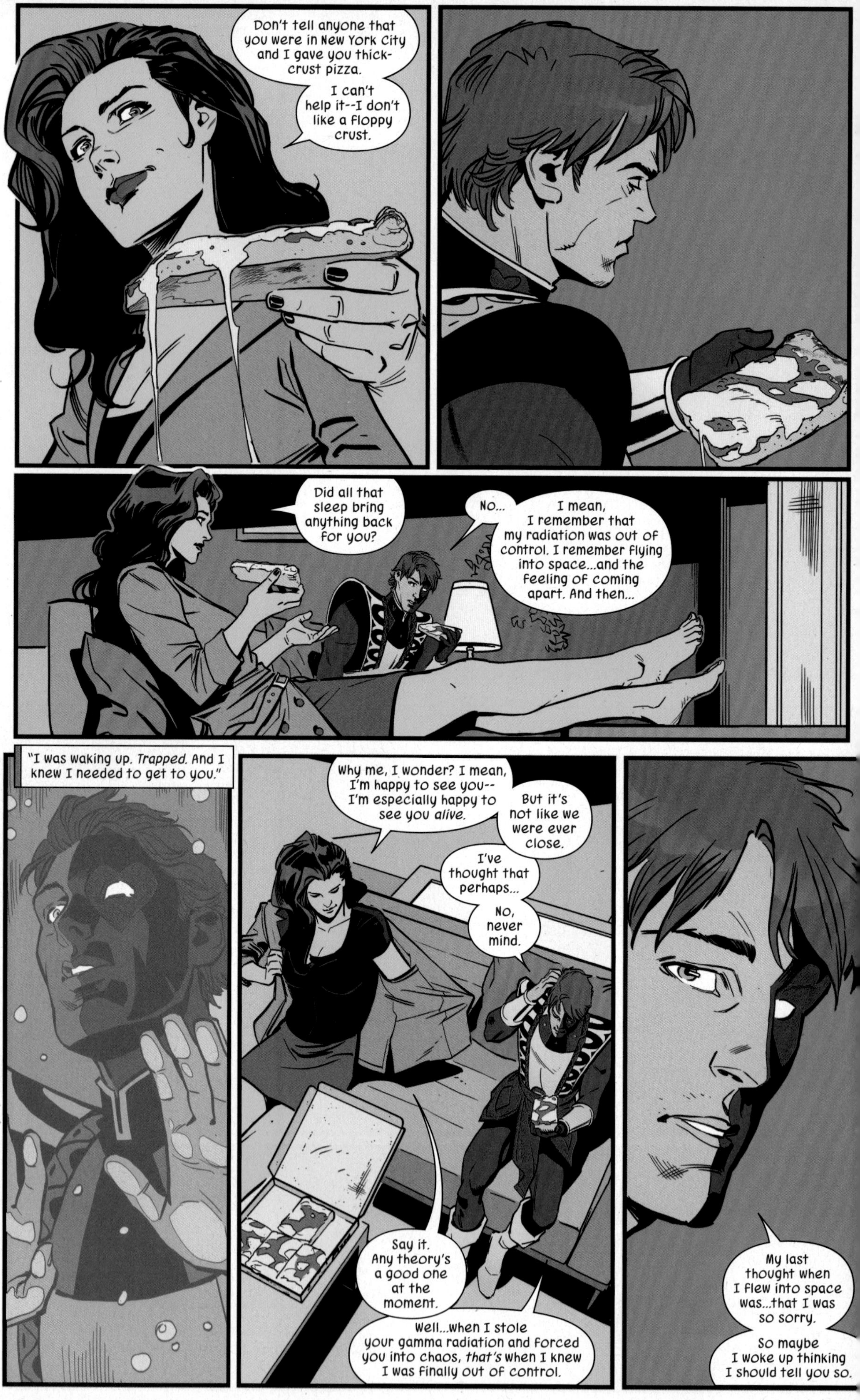
Don't tell anyone that you were in New York City and I gave you thick-crust pizza.
I can't help it--I don't like a floppy crust.
Did all that sleep bring anything back for you?
No...
I mean, I remember that my radiation was out of control. I remember flying into space...and the feeling of coming apart. And then...
"I was waking up. *Trapped.* And I knew I needed to get to you."
Why me, I wonder? I mean, I'm happy to see you-- I'm especially happy to see you *alive.*
But it's not like we were ever close.
I've thought that perhaps...
No, never mind.
Say it. Any theory's a good one at the moment.
Well...when I stole your gamma radiation and forced you into chaos, *that's* when I knew I was finally out of control.
My last thought when I flew into space was...that I was so sorry.
So maybe I woke up thinking I should tell you so.

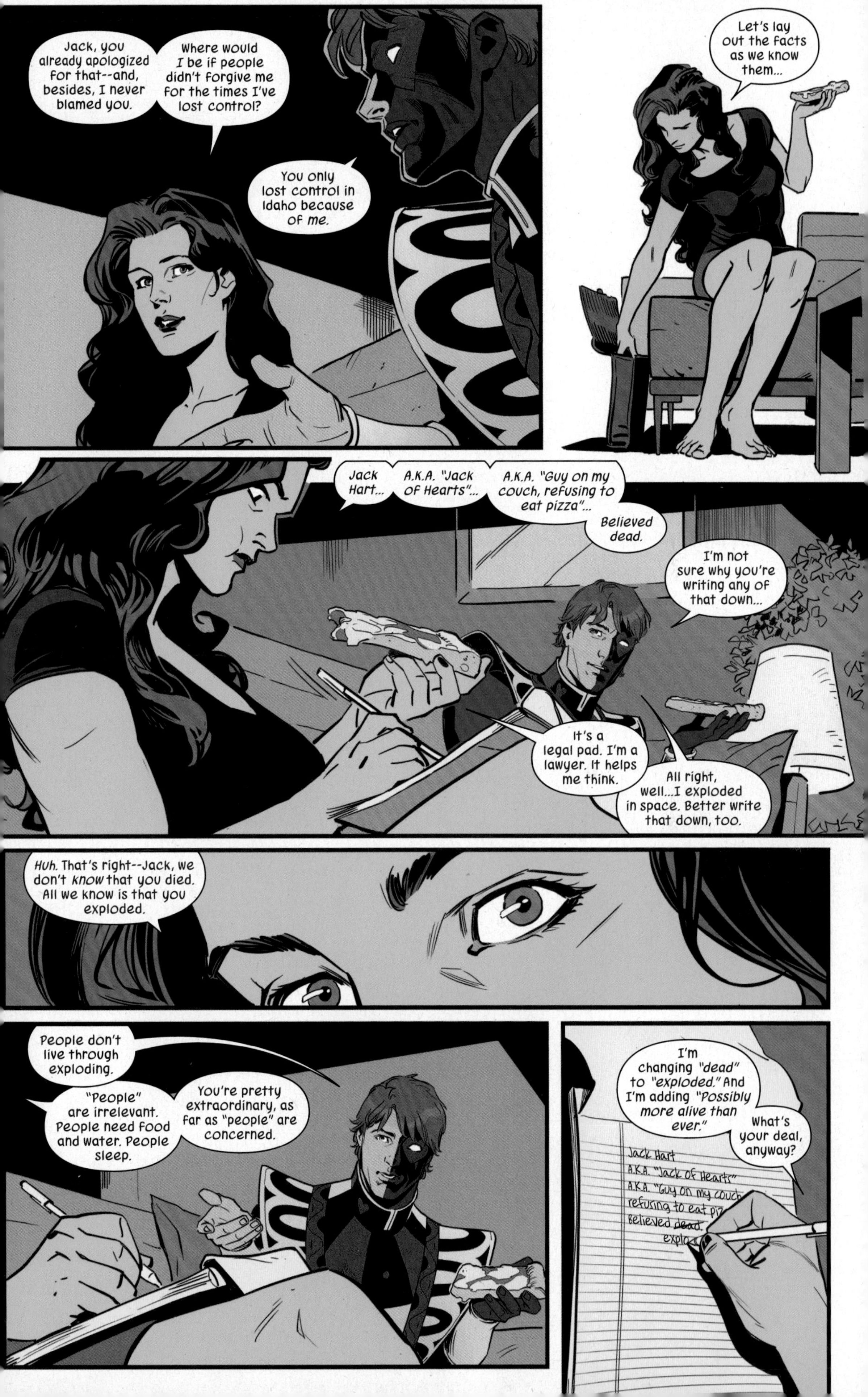

Jack, you already apologized for that--and, besides, I never blamed you.
Where would I be if people didn't forgive me for the times I've lost control?
You only lost control in Idaho because of me.
Let's lay out the facts as we know them...
Jack Hart...
A.K.A. "Jack of Hearts"...
A.K.A. "Guy on my couch, refusing to eat pizza"...
Believed dead.
I'm not sure why you're writing any of that down...
It's a legal pad. I'm a lawyer. It helps me think.
All right, well...I exploded in space. Better write that down, too.
Huh. That's right--Jack, we don't know that you died. All we know is that you exploded.
People don't live through exploding.
"People" are irrelevant. People need food and water. People sleep.
You're pretty extraordinary, as far as "people" are concerned.
I'm changing "dead" to "exploded." And I'm adding "Possibly more alive than ever."
What's your deal, anyway?
Jack Hart
A.K.A. "Jack of Hearts"
A.K.A. "Guy on my couch
refusing to eat pi
Believed dead.

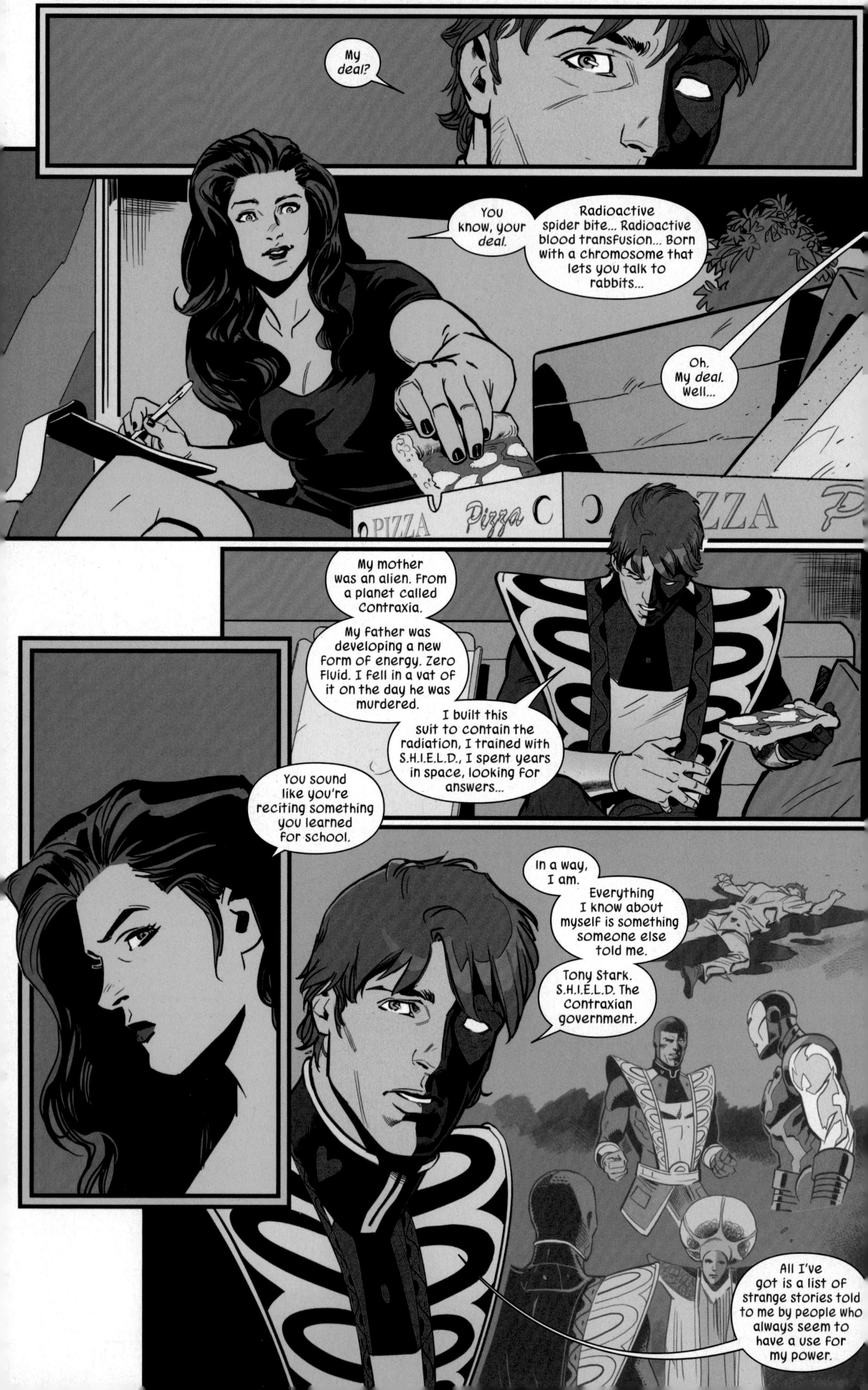

My deal?
You know, your deal.
Radioactive spider bite... Radioactive blood transfusion... Born with a chromosome that lets you talk to rabbits...
Oh. My deal. Well...
PIZZA
Pizza
ZZA
My mother was an alien. From a planet called Contraxia.
My father was developing a new form of energy. Zero Fluid. I fell in a vat of it on the day he was murdered.
I built this suit to contain the radiation, I trained with S.H.I.E.L.D., I spent years in space, looking for answers...
You sound like you're reciting something you learned for school.
In a way, I am.
Everything I know about myself is something someone else told me.
Tony Stark. S.H.I.E.L.D. The Contraxian government.
All I've got is a list of strange stories told to me by people who always seem to have a use for my power.

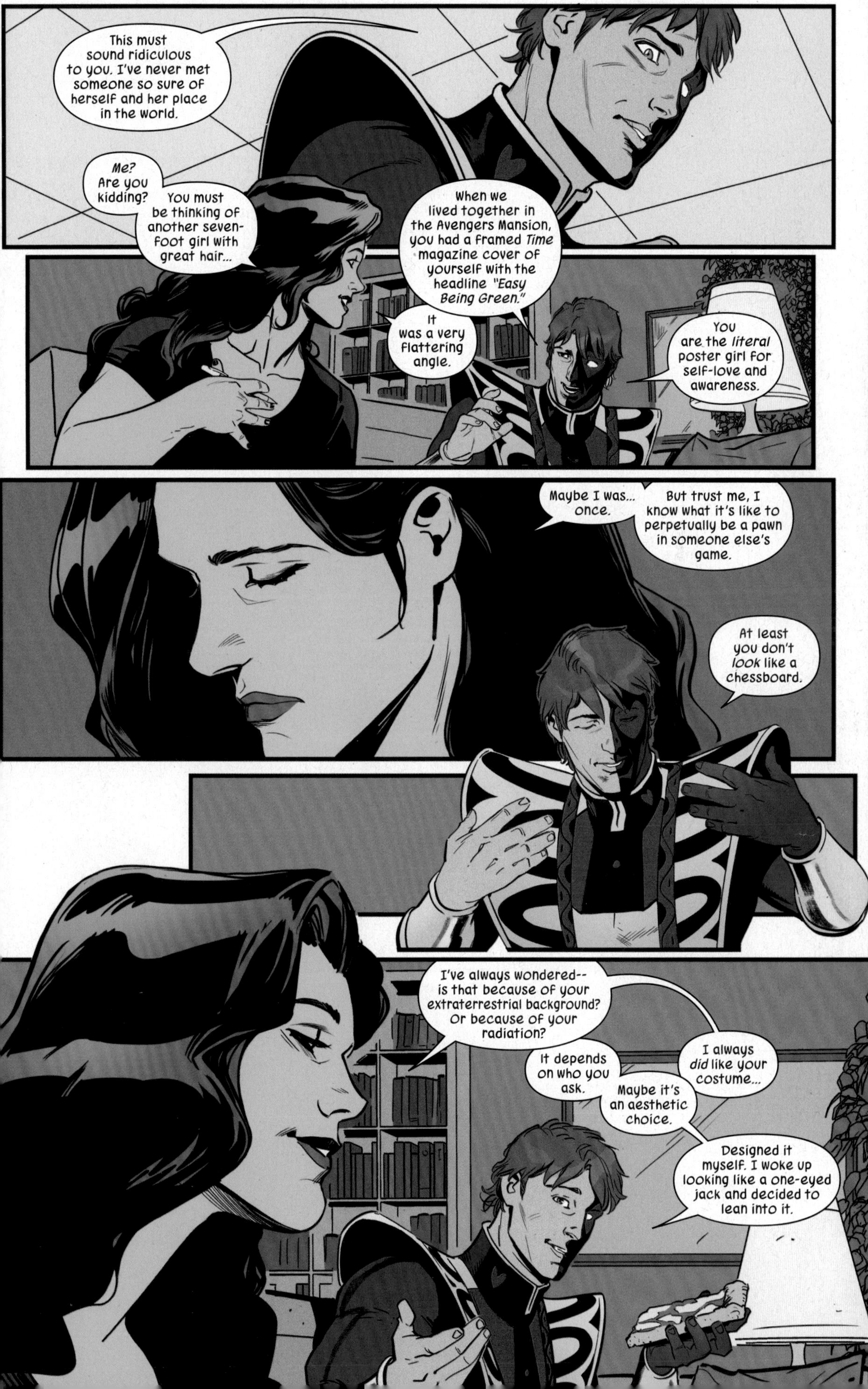

This must sound ridiculous to you. I've never met someone so sure of herself and her place in the world.
Me? Are you kidding?
You must be thinking of another seven-foot girl with great hair...
When we lived together in the Avengers Mansion, you had a framed *Time* magazine cover of yourself with the headline *"Easy Being Green."*
It was a very flattering angle.
You are the *literal* poster girl for self-love and awareness.
Maybe I was... once.
But trust me, I know what it's like to perpetually be a pawn in someone else's game.
At least you don't *look* like a chessboard.
I've always wondered-- is that because of your extraterrestrial background? Or because of your radiation?
It depends on who you ask.
I always *did* like your costume...
Maybe it's an aesthetic choice.
Designed it myself. I woke up looking like a one-eyed jack and decided to lean into it.

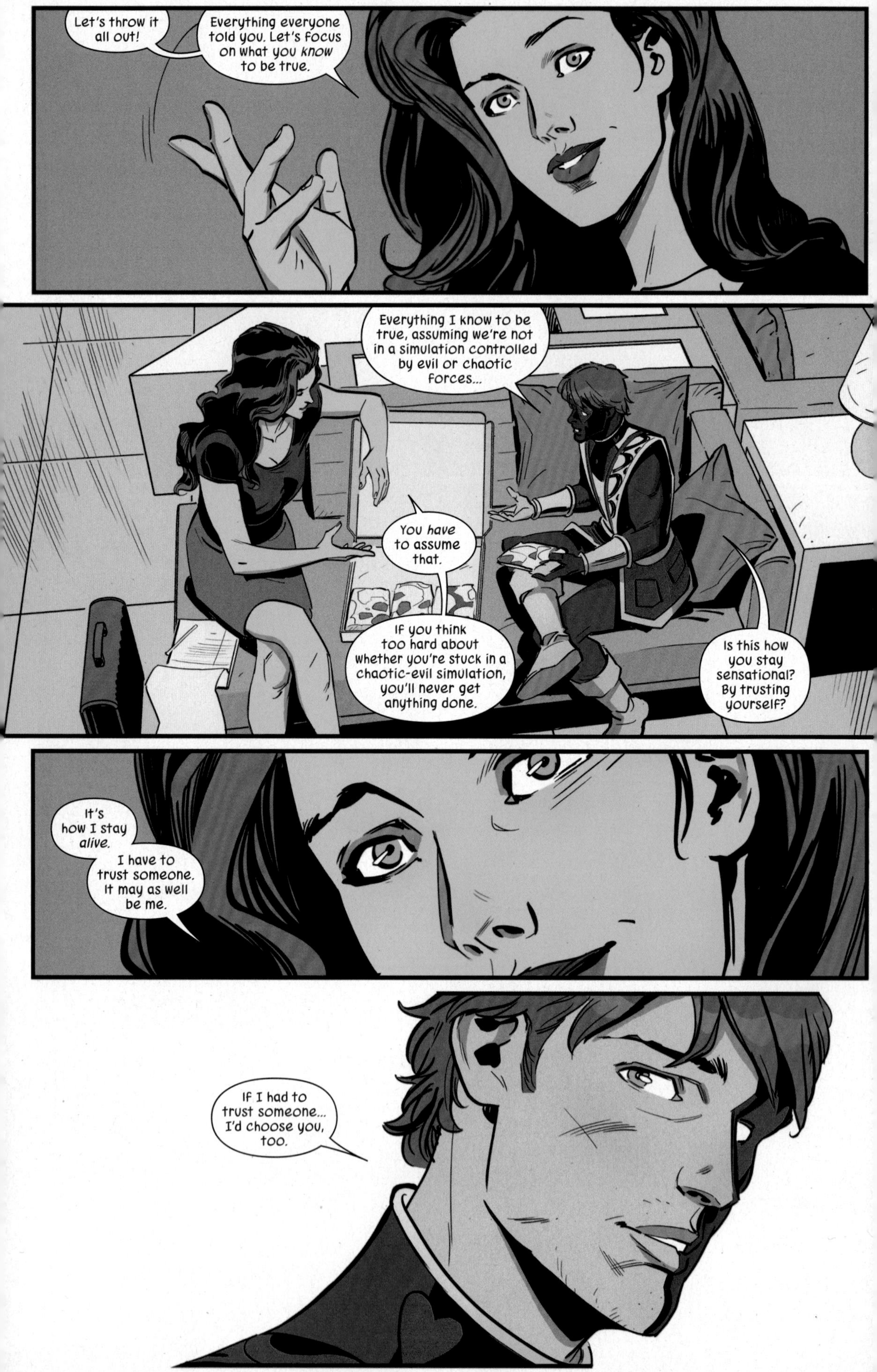

Let's throw it all out!
Everything everyone told you. Let's focus on what you *know* to be true.
Everything I know to be true, assuming we're not in a simulation controlled by evil or chaotic forces...
You *have* to assume that.
If you think too hard about whether you're stuck in a chaotic-evil simulation, you'll never get anything done.
Is this how you stay sensational? By trusting yourself?
It's how I stay *alive*.
I have to trust someone. It may as well be me.
If I had to trust someone... I'd choose you, too.

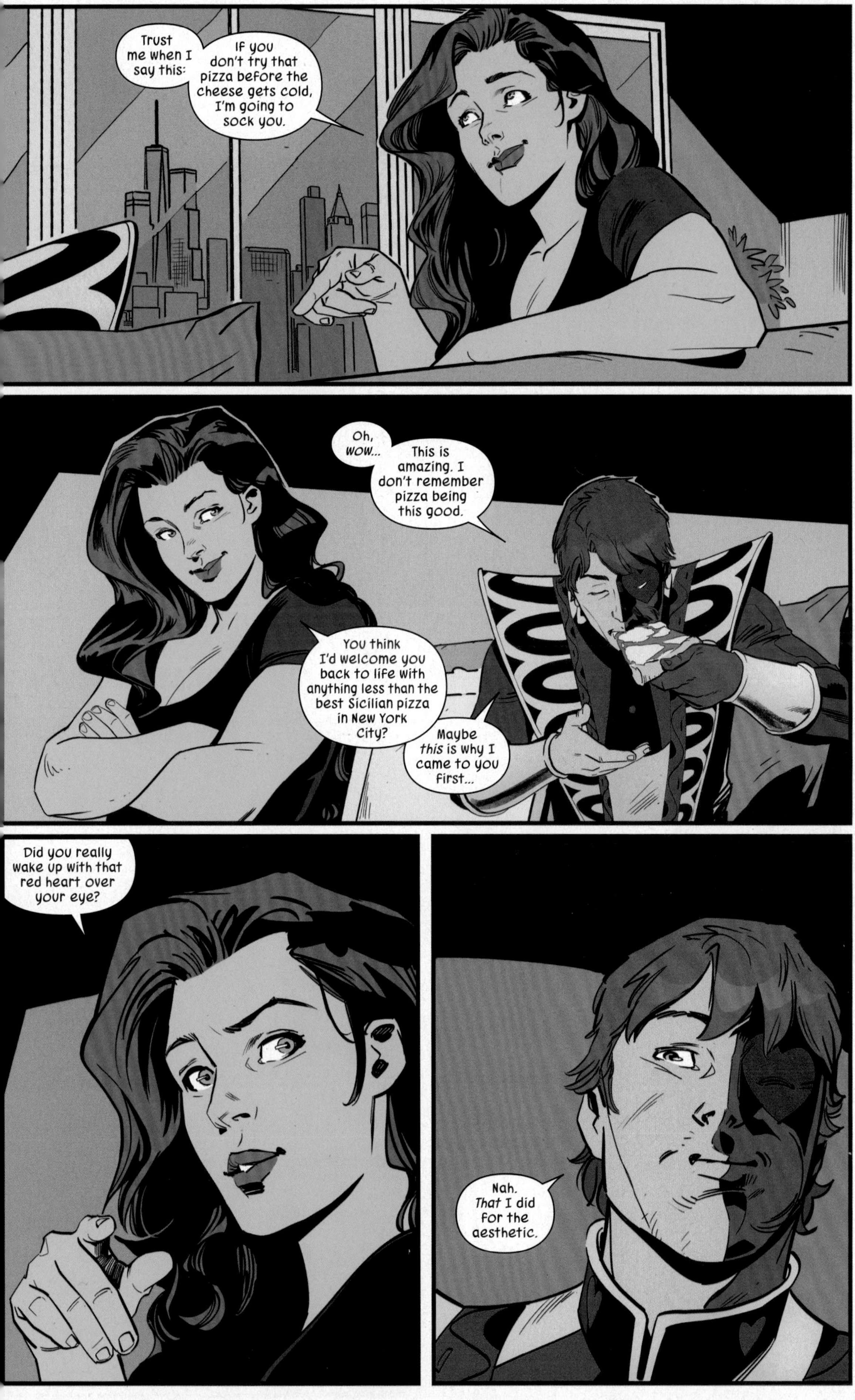
Trust me when I say this:
If you don't try that pizza before the cheese gets cold, I'm going to sock you.
Oh, wow...
This is amazing. I don't remember pizza being this good.
You think I'd welcome you back to life with anything less than the best Sicilian pizza in New York City?
Maybe *this* is why I came to you first...
Did you really wake up with that red heart over your eye?
Nah. *That* I did for the aesthetic.

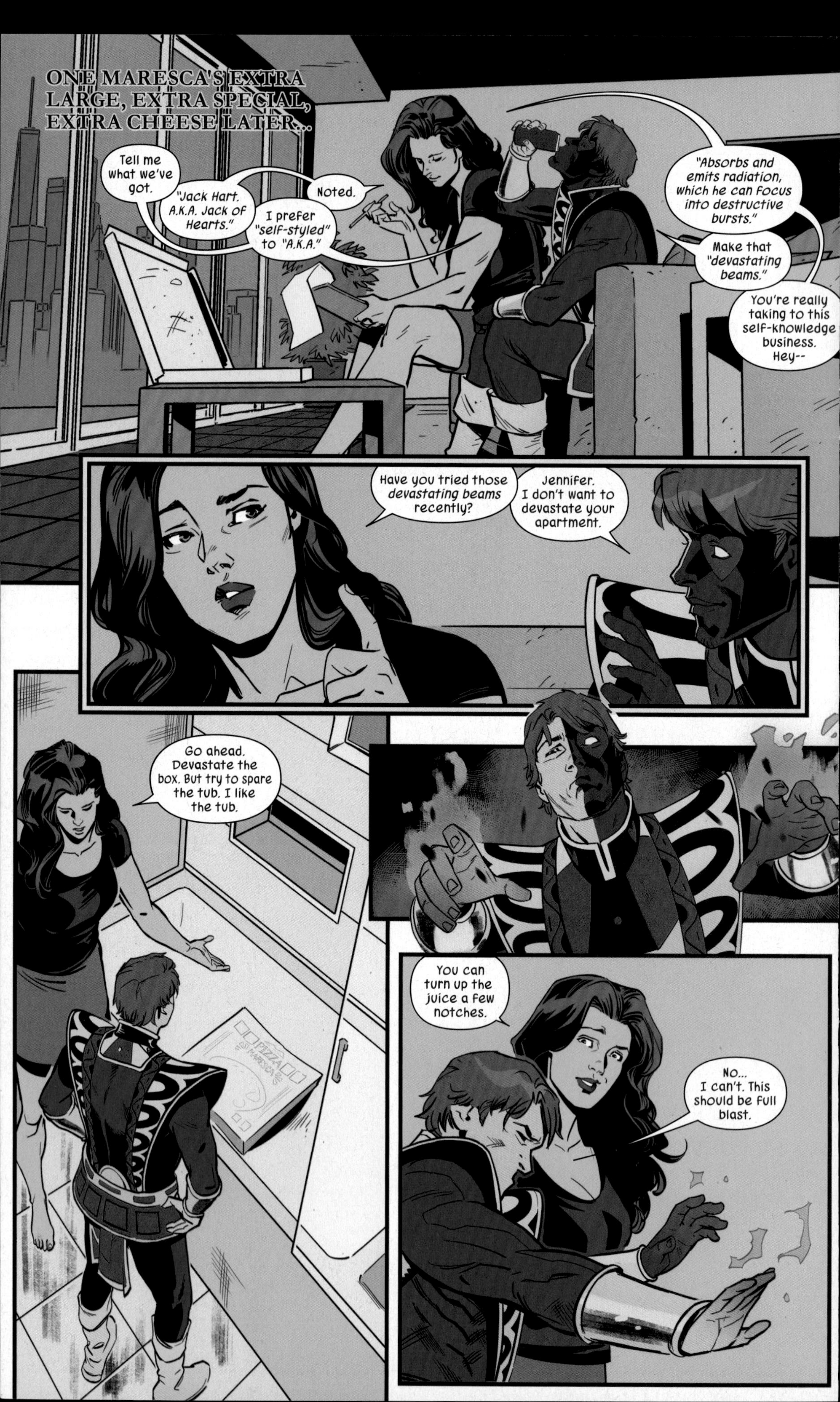
ONE MARESCA'S EXTRA LARGE, EXTRA SPECIAL, EXTRA CHEESE LATER...
Tell me what we've got.
"Jack Hart. A.K.A. Jack of Hearts."
Noted.
I prefer "self-styled" to "A.K.A."
"Absorbs and emits radiation, which he can focus into destructive bursts."
Make that "devastating beams."
You're really taking to this self-knowledge business. Hey--
Have you tried those devastating beams recently?
Jennifer. I don't want to devastate your apartment.
Go ahead. Devastate the box. But try to spare the tub. I like the tub.
You can turn up the juice a few notches.
No... I can't. This should be full blast.

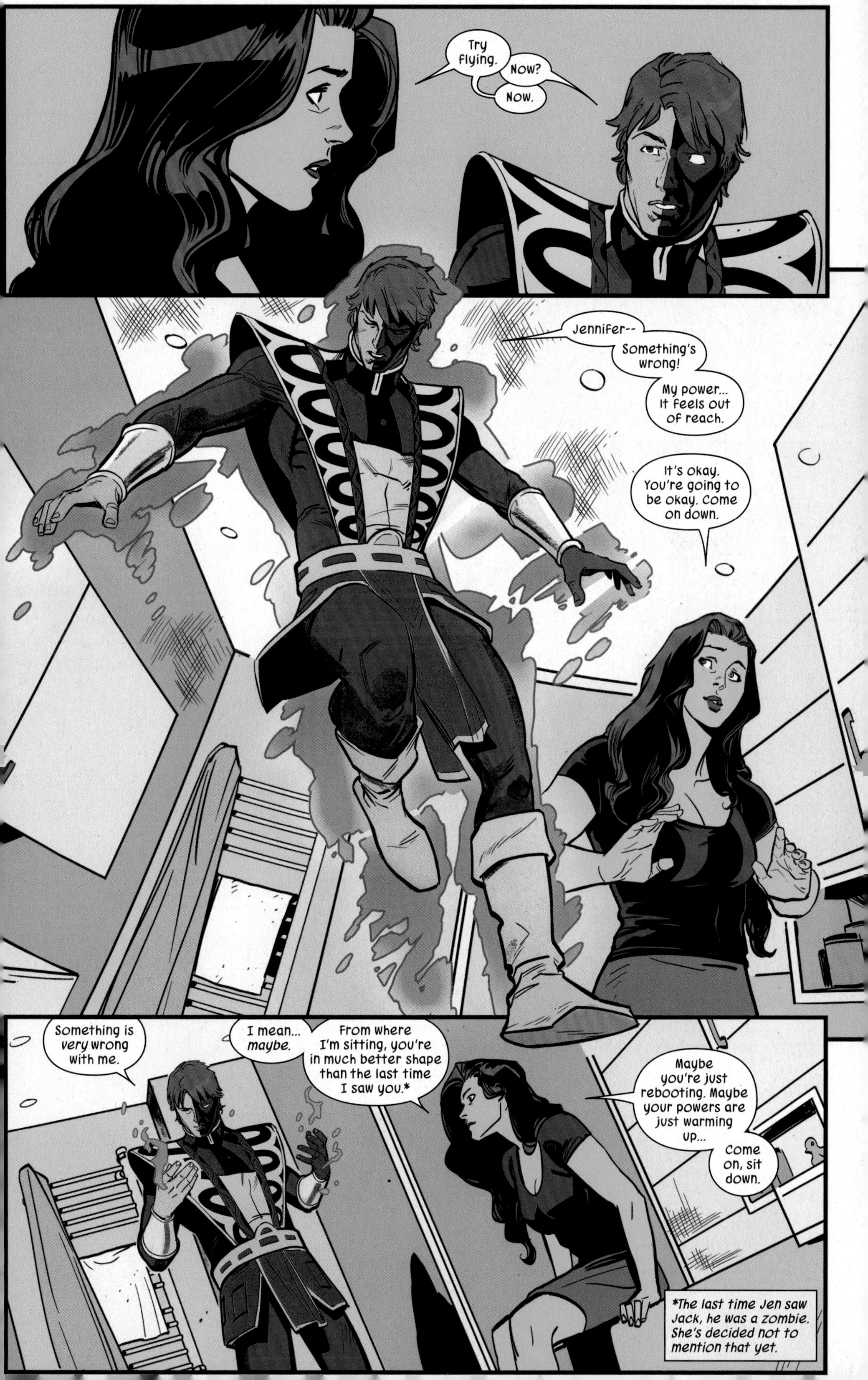
Try flying.
NOW?
Now.
Jennifer--
Something's wrong!
My power... It feels out of reach.
It's okay. You're going to be okay. Come on down.
Something is *very* wrong with me.
I mean... *maybe.*
From where I'm sitting, you're in much better shape than the last time I saw you.*
Maybe you're just rebooting. Maybe your powers are just warming up...
Come on, sit down.
*The last time Jen saw Jack, he was a zombie. She's decided not to mention that yet.

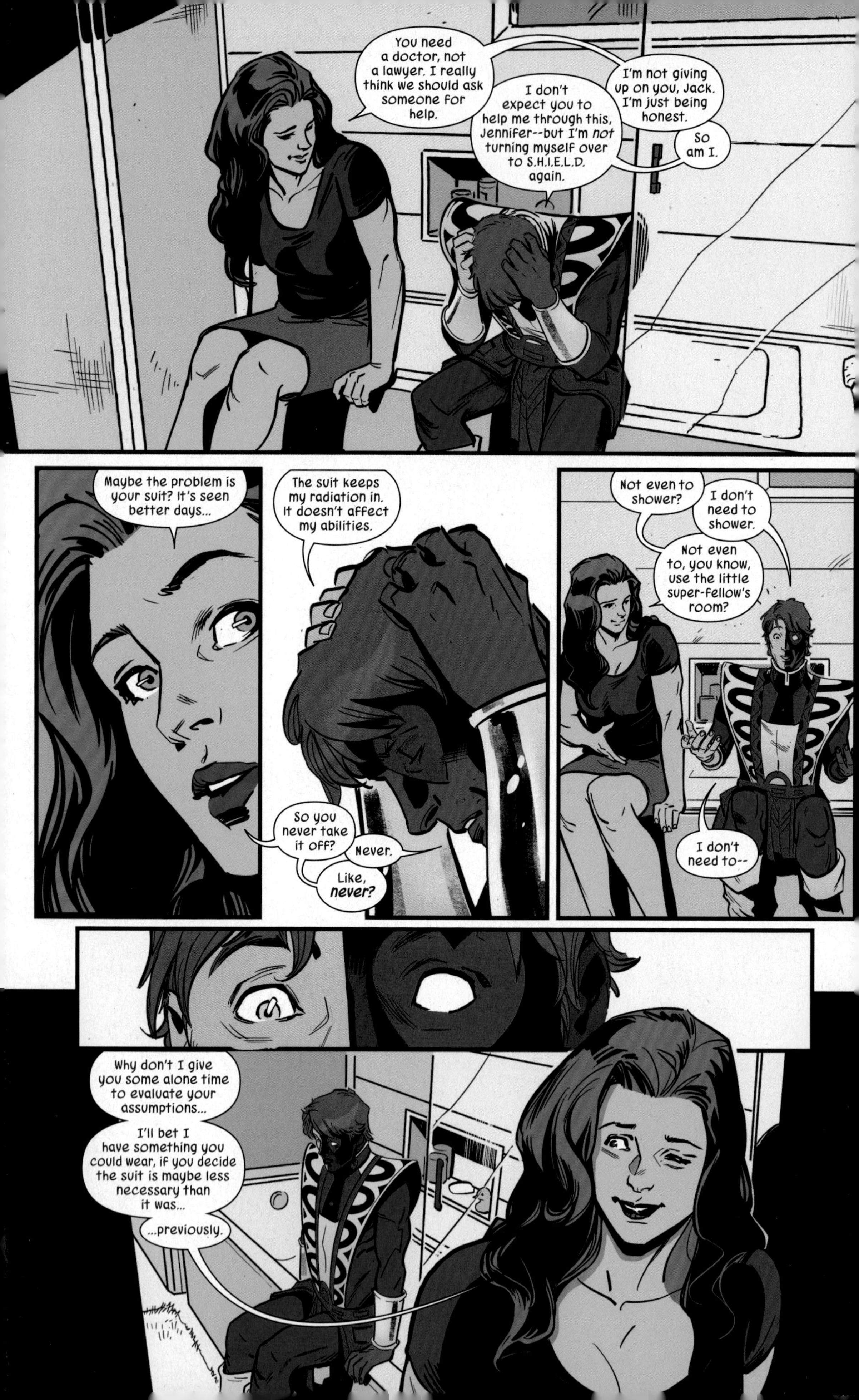

You need a doctor, not a lawyer. I really think we should ask someone for help.
I don't expect you to help me through this, Jennifer--but I'm *not* turning myself over to S.H.I.E.L.D. again.
I'm not giving up on you, Jack. I'm just being honest.
So am I.
Maybe the problem is your suit? It's seen better days...
The suit keeps my radiation in. It doesn't affect my abilities.
So you never take it off?
Never.
Like, ***never?***
Not even to shower?
I don't need to shower.
Not even to, you know, use the little super-fellow's room?
I don't need to--
Why don't I give you some alone time to evaluate your assumptions...
I'll bet I have something you could wear, if you decide the suit is maybe less necessary than it was...
...previously.

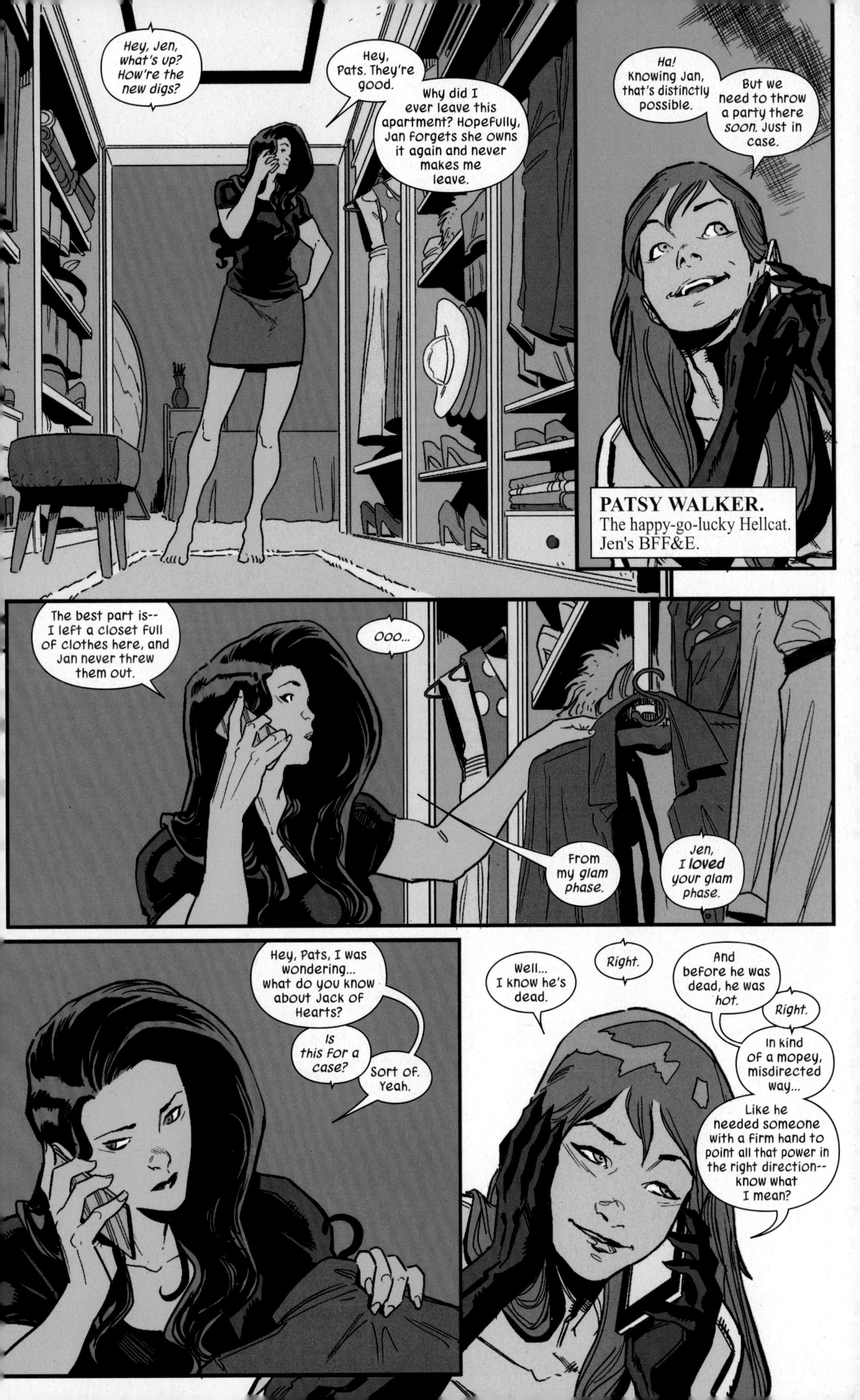
Hey, Jen, what's up? How're the new digs?
Hey, Pats. They're good.
Why did I ever leave this apartment? Hopefully, Jan forgets she owns it again and never makes me leave.
Ha! Knowing Jan, that's distinctly possible.
But we need to throw a party there soon. Just in case.
PATSY WALKER. The happy-go-lucky Hellcat. Jen's BFF&E.
The best part is-- I left a closet full of clothes here, and Jan never threw them out.
Ooo...
From my glam phase.
Jen, I loved your glam phase.
Hey, Pats, I was wondering... what do you know about Jack of Hearts?
Is this for a case?
Sort of. Yeah.
Well... I know he's dead.
Right.
And before he was dead, he was hot.
Right.
In kind of a mopey, misdirected way...
Like he needed someone with a firm hand to point all that power in the right direction-- know what I mean?

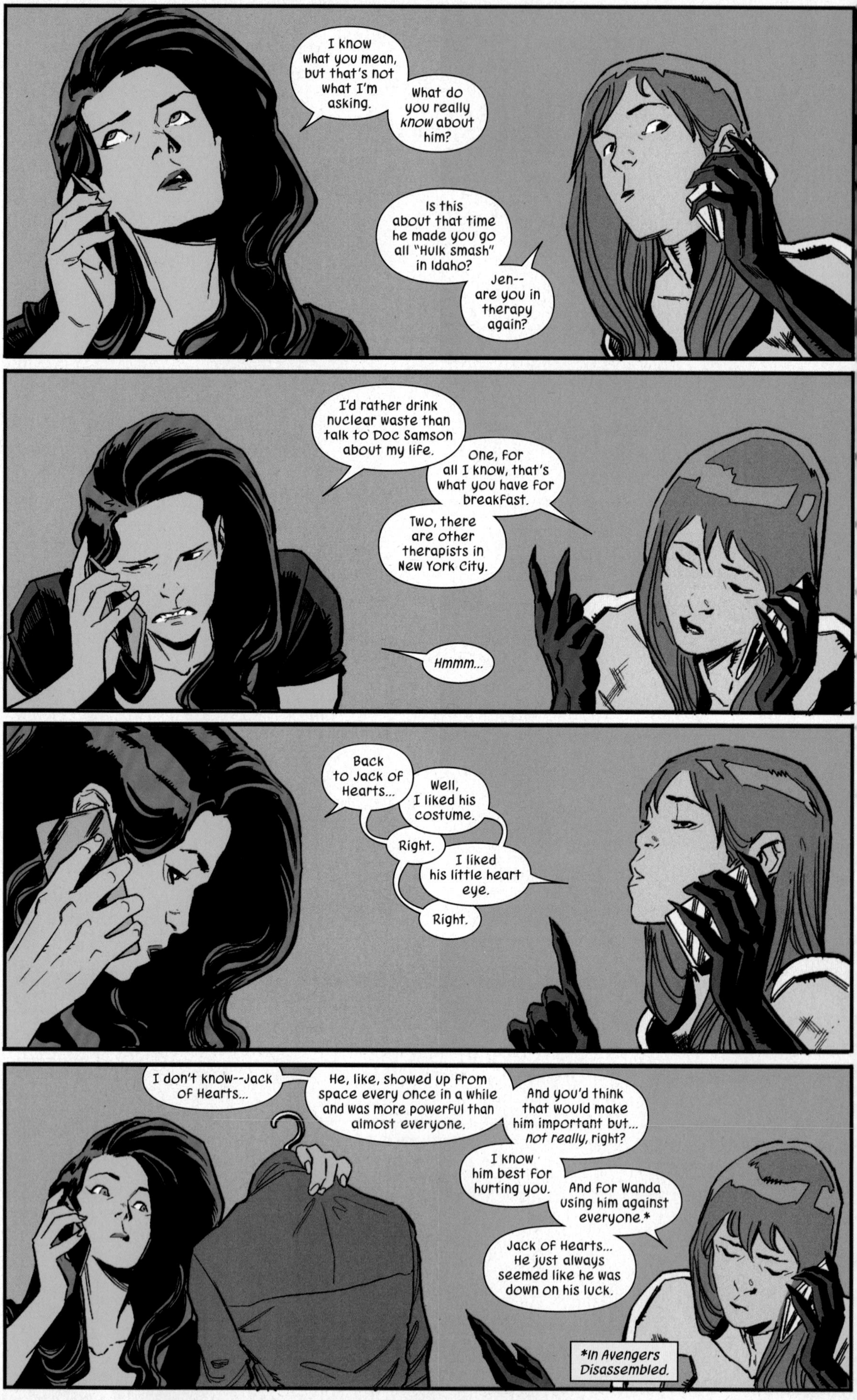

I know what you mean, but that's not what I'm asking.
What do you really *know* about him?
Is this about that time he made you go all "Hulk smash" in Idaho?
Jen-- are you in therapy again?
I'd rather drink nuclear waste than talk to Doc Samson about my life.
One, for all I know, that's what you have for breakfast.
Two, there are other therapists in New York City.
Hmmm...
Back to Jack of Hearts...
Well, I liked his costume.
Right.
I liked his little heart eye.
Right.
I don't know--Jack of Hearts...
He, like, showed up from space every once in a while and was more powerful than almost everyone.
And you'd think that would make him important but... *not really*, right?
I know him best for hurting you.
And for Wanda using him against everyone.*
Jack of Hearts... He just always seemed like he was down on his luck.
*In Avengers Disassembled.

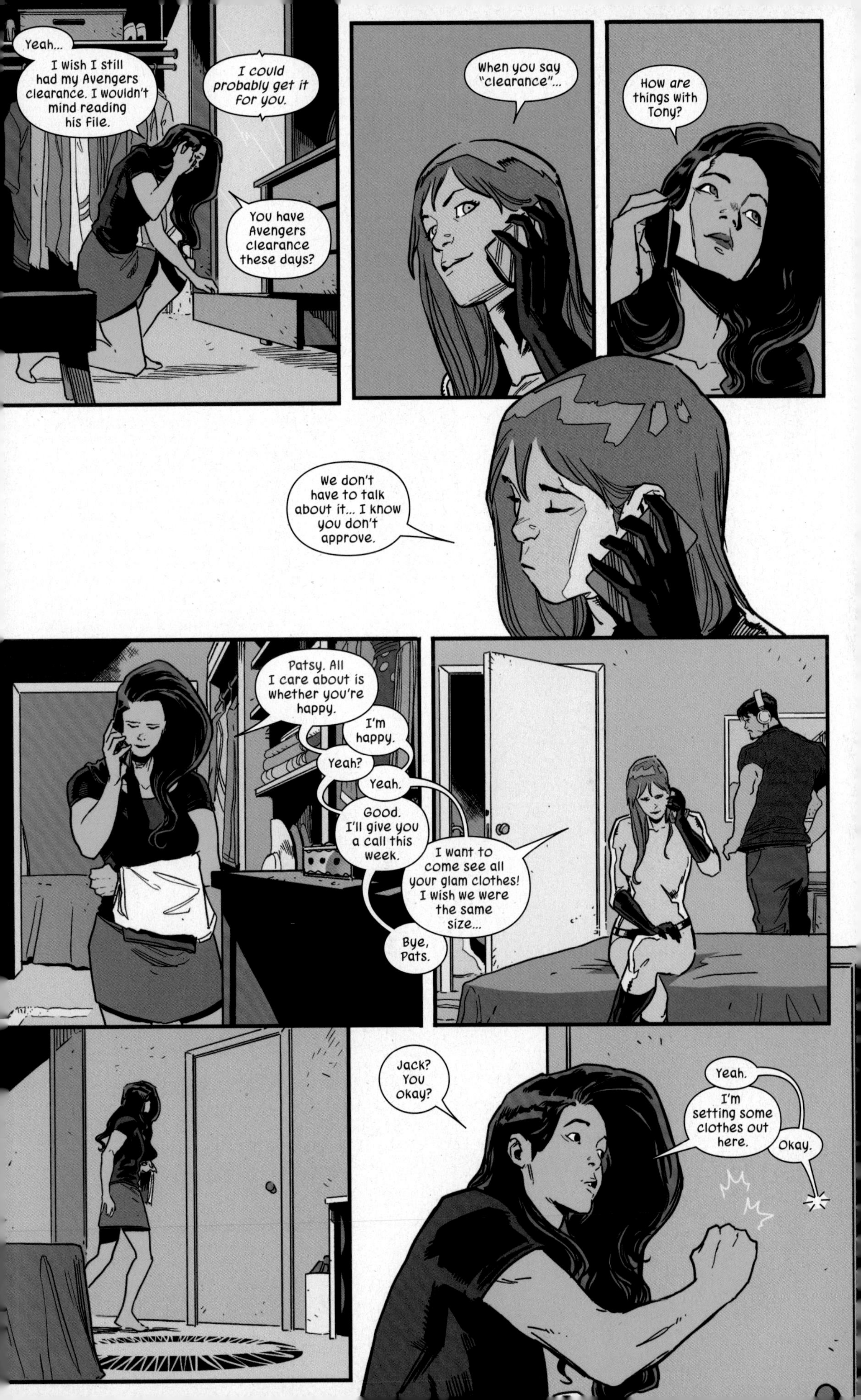
Yeah...
I wish I still had my Avengers clearance. I wouldn't mind reading his file.
I could probably get it for you.
You have Avengers clearance these days?
When you say "clearance"...
How are things with Tony?
We don't have to talk about it... I know you don't approve.
Patsy. All I care about is whether you're happy.
I'm happy.
Yeah?
Yeah.
Good. I'll give you a call this week.
I want to come see all your glam clothes! I wish we were the same size...
Bye, Pats.
Jack? You okay?
Yeah.
I'm setting some clothes out here.
Okay.

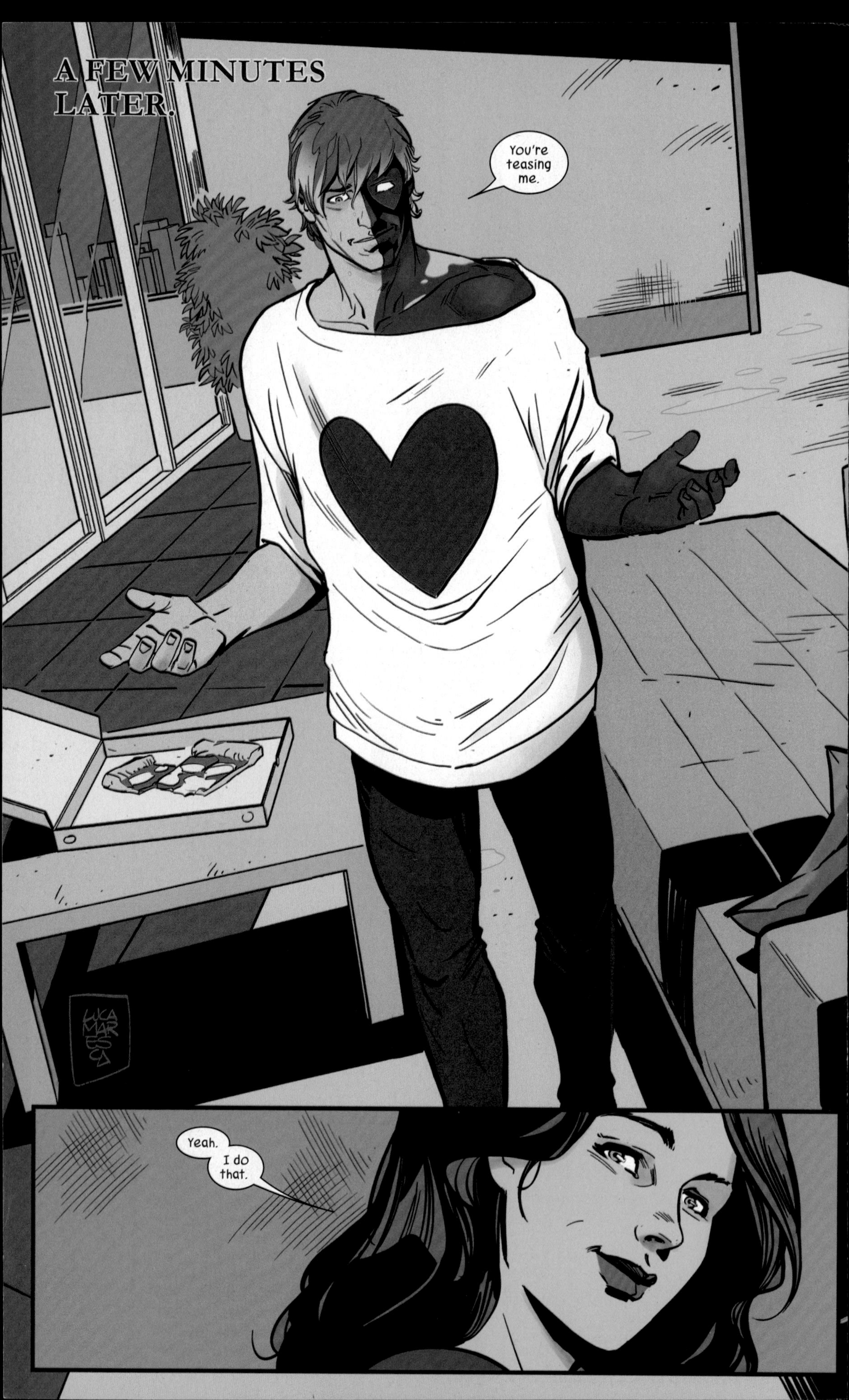
A FEW MINUTES LATER.
You're teasing me.
Yeah. I do that.
LUCA MARESCA

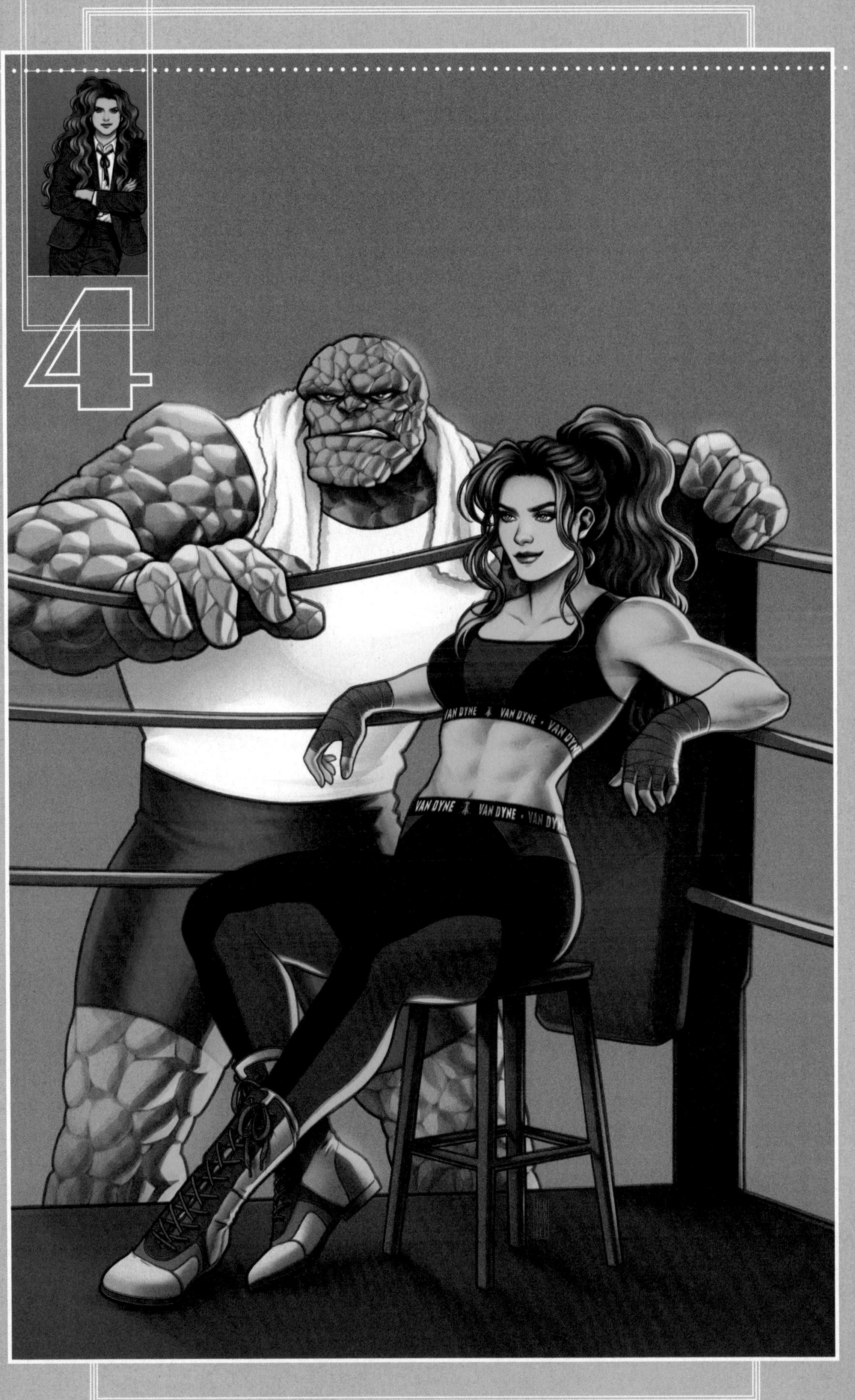
4
VAN DYNE
VAN DYNE

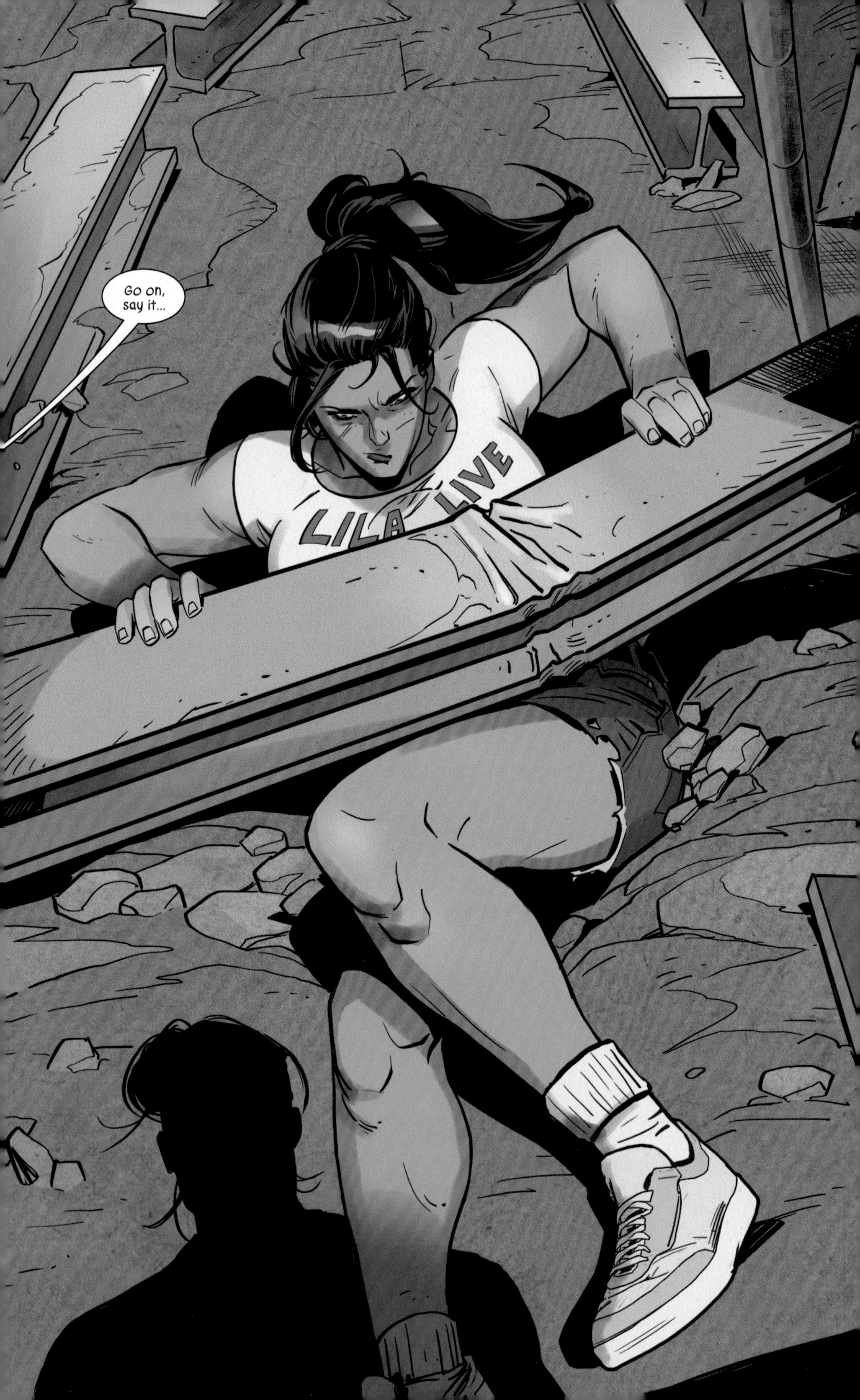
Go on, say it...
LILA LIVE

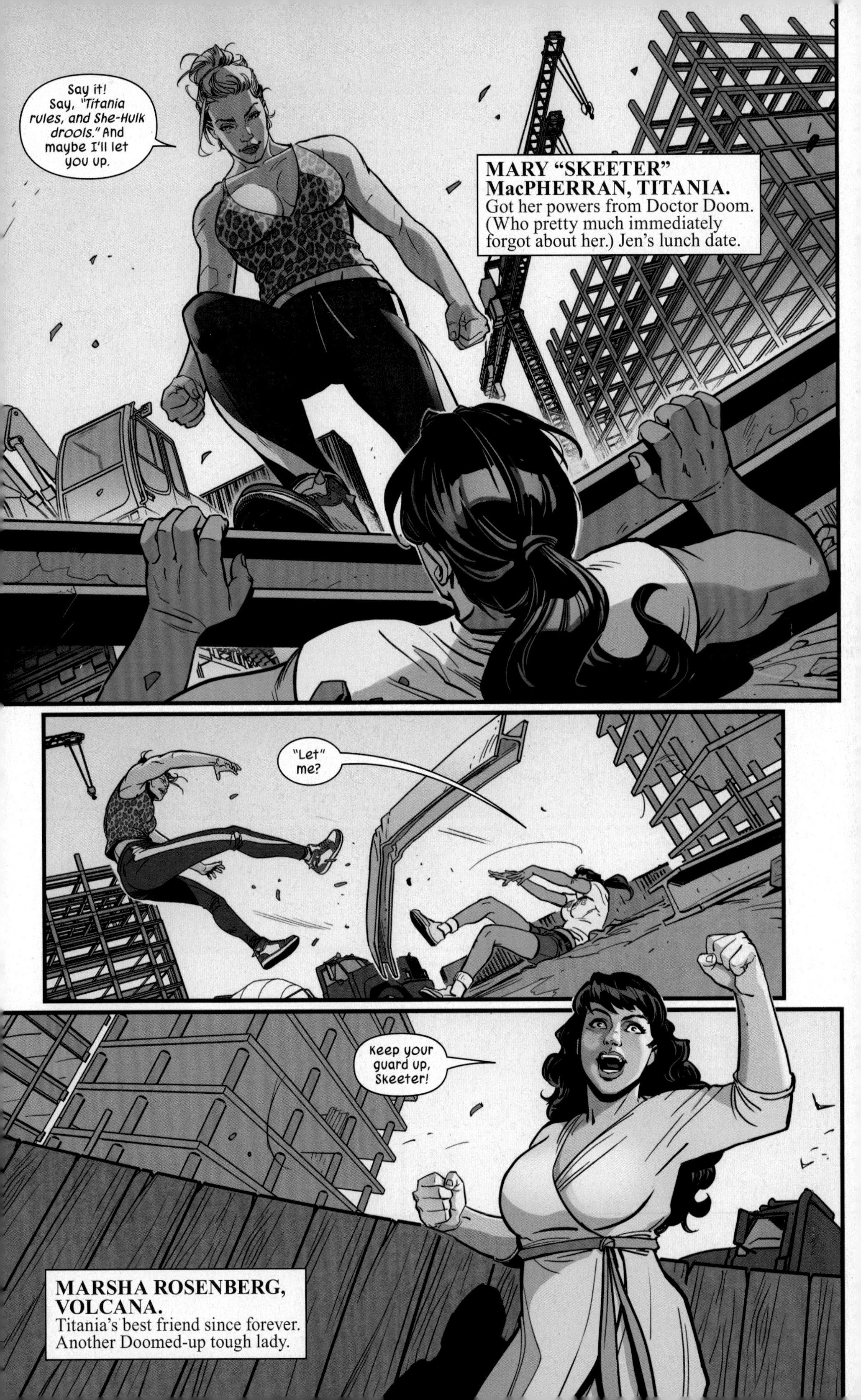

Say it! Say, "Titania rules, and She-Hulk drools." And maybe I'll let you up.
MARY "SKEETER" MacPHERRAN, TITANIA.
Got her powers from Doctor Doom. (Who pretty much immediately forgot about her.) Jen's lunch date.
"Let" me?
Keep your guard up, Skeeter!
MARSHA ROSENBERG, VOLCANA.
Titania's best friend since forever. Another Doomed-up tough lady.

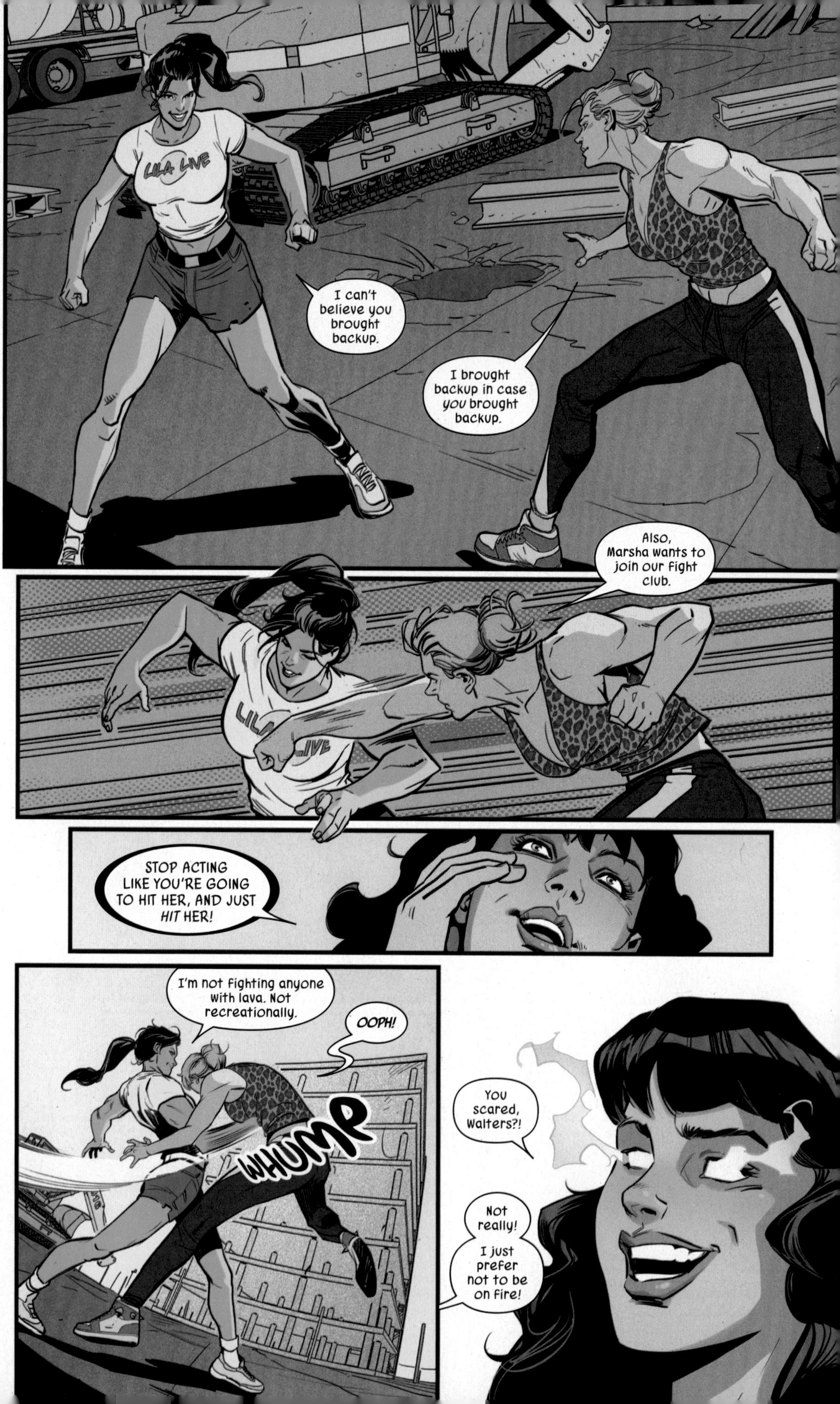
LILA LIVE
I can't believe you brought backup.
I brought backup in case *you* brought backup.
Also, Marsha wants to join our fight club.
STOP ACTING LIKE YOU'RE GOING TO HIT HER, AND JUST *HIT HER!*
I'm not fighting anyone with lava. Not recreationally.
OOPH!
WHUMP
You scared, Walters?!
Not really!
I just prefer not to be on fire!

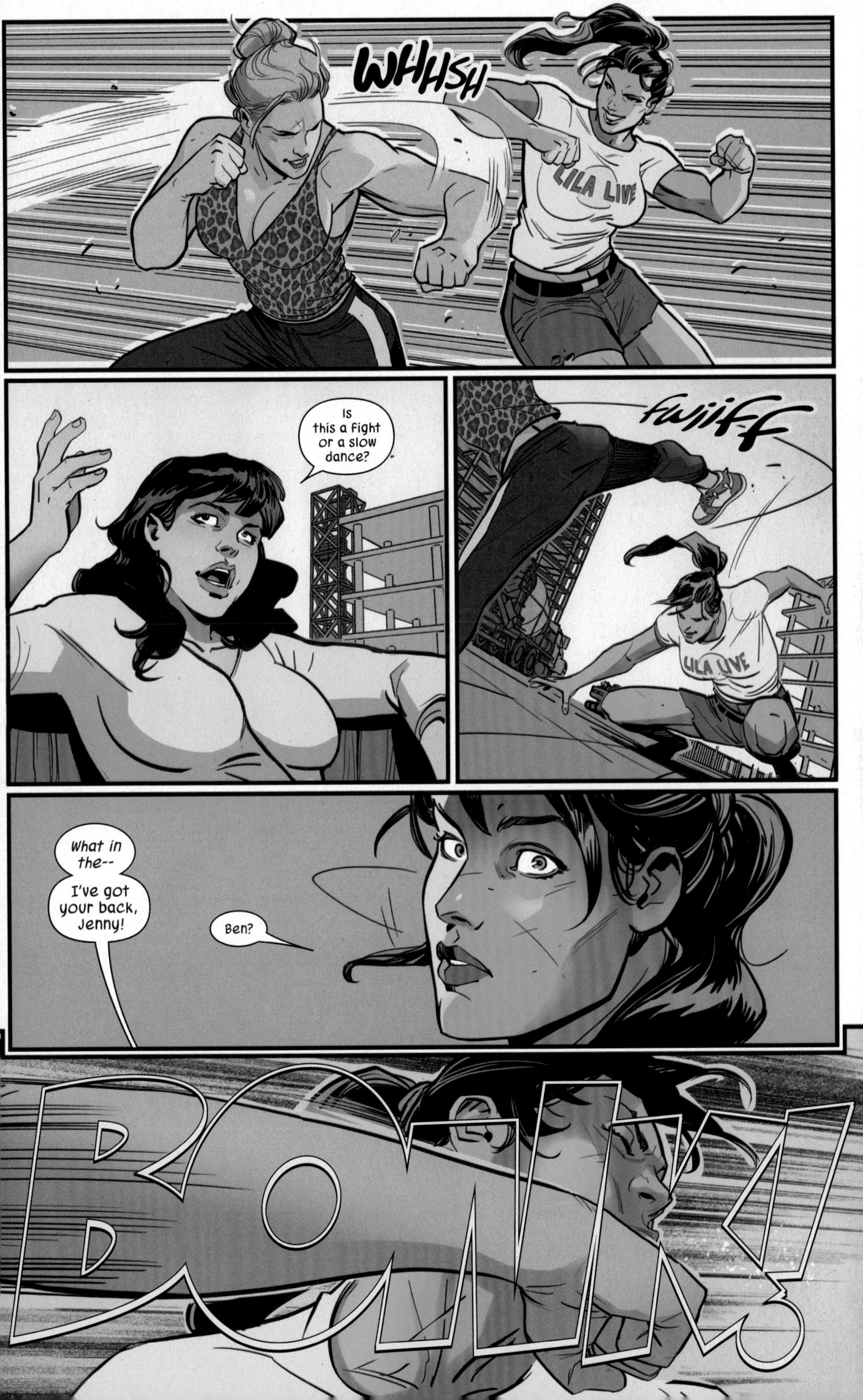
WHHSH
Is this a fight or a slow dance?
fwiiff
What in the--
I've got your back, Jenny!
Ben?
BOINK!

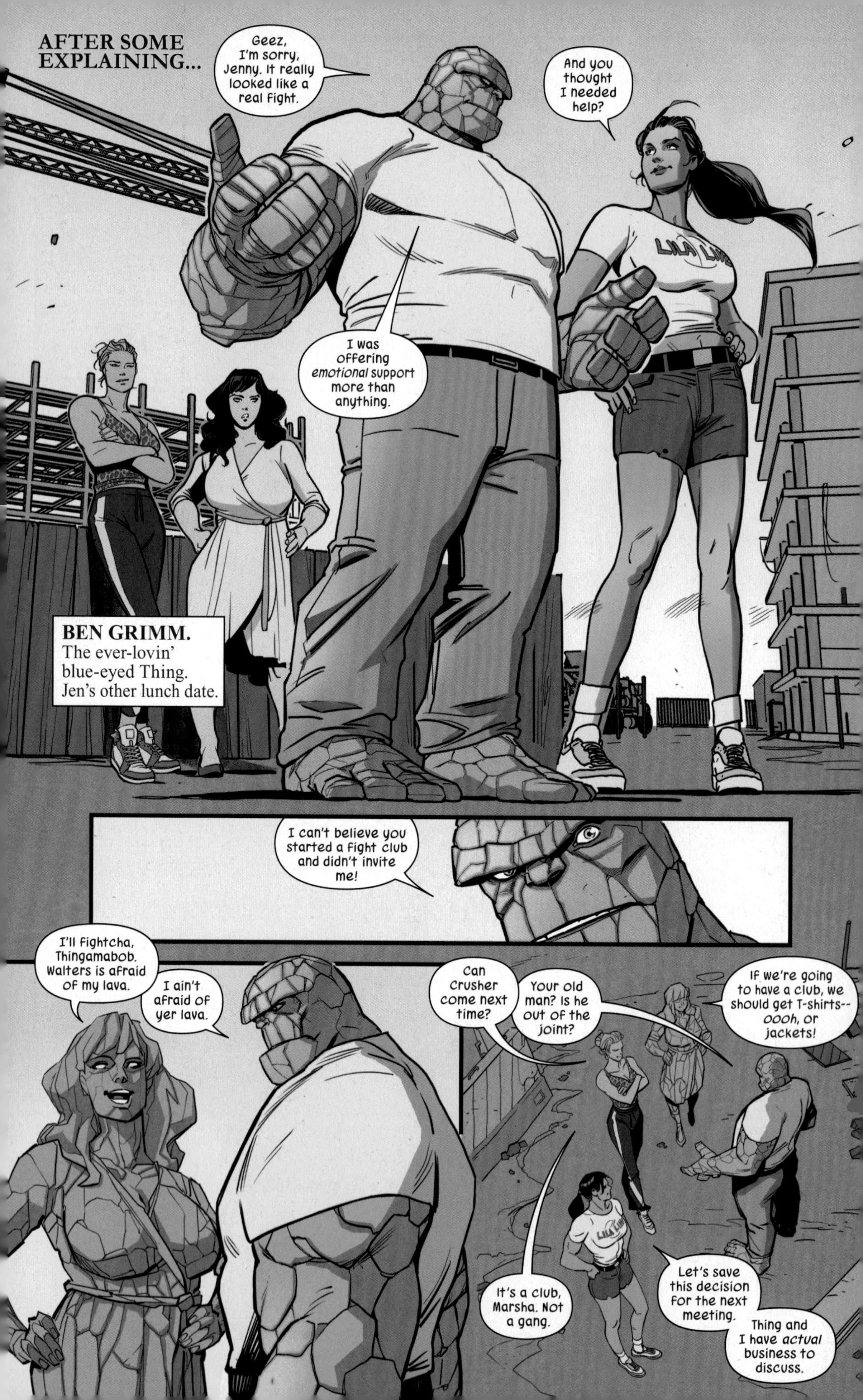
AFTER SOME EXPLAINING...
Geez, I'm sorry, Jenny. It really looked like a real fight.
And you thought I needed help?
I was offering *emotional* support more than anything.
BEN GRIMM.
The ever-lovin' blue-eyed Thing.
Jen's other lunch date.
I can't believe you started a fight club and didn't invite me!
I'll fightcha, Thingamabob. Walters is afraid of my lava.
I ain't afraid of yer lava.
Can Crusher come next time?
Your old man? Is he out of the joint?
If we're going to have a club, we should get T-shirts-- *oooh*, or jackets!
It's a club, Marsha. Not a gang.
Let's save this decision for the next meeting.
Thing and I have *actual* business to discuss.

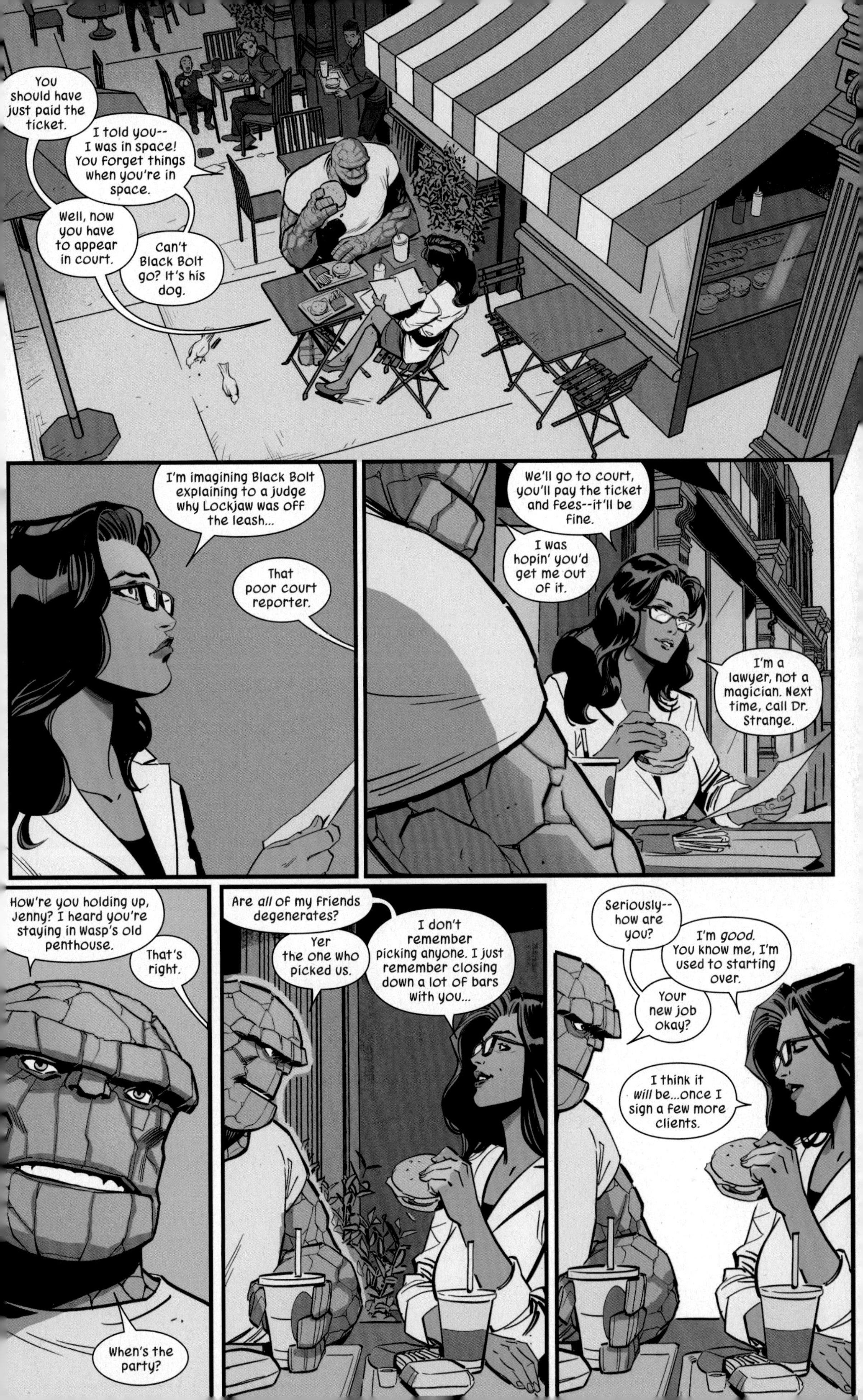

You should have just paid the ticket.
I told you-- I was in space! You forget things when you're in space.
Well, now you have to appear in court.
Can't Black Bolt go? It's his dog.
I'm imagining Black Bolt explaining to a judge why Lockjaw was off the leash...
That poor court reporter.
We'll go to court, you'll pay the ticket and fees--it'll be fine.
I was hopin' you'd get me out of it.
I'm a lawyer, not a magician. Next time, call Dr. Strange.
How're you holding up, Jenny? I heard you're staying in Wasp's old penthouse.
That's right.
When's the party?
Are *all* of my friends degenerates?
Yer the one who picked us.
I don't remember picking anyone. I just remember closing down a lot of bars with you...
Seriously-- how are you?
I'm *good.* You know me, I'm used to starting over.
Your new job okay?
I think it *will* be...once I sign a few more clients.

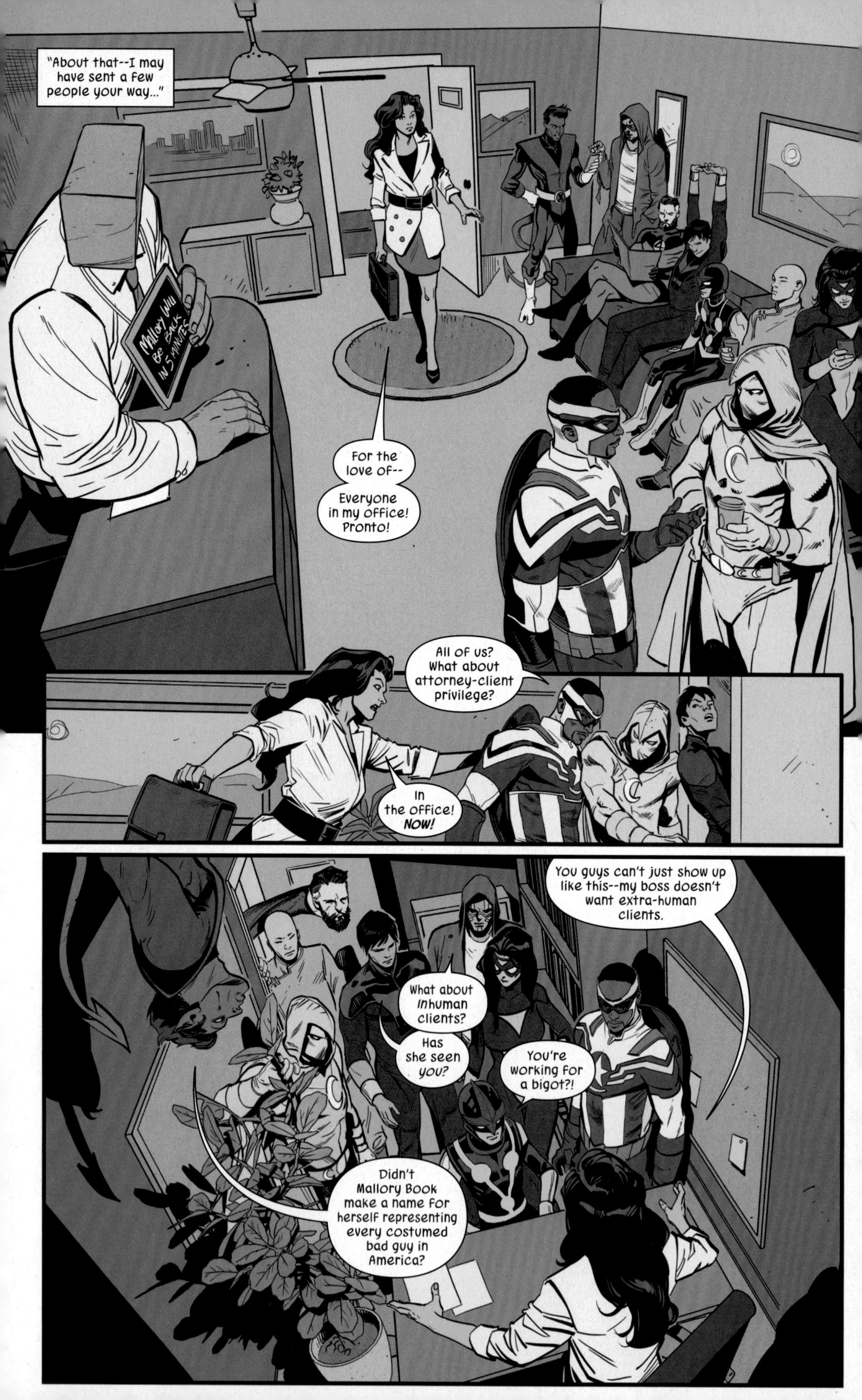
"About that--I may have sent a few people your way..."
Mallory will be back in 5 minutes
For the love of--
Everyone in my office! Pronto!
All of us? What about attorney-client privilege?
In the office! NOW!
You guys can't just show up like this--my boss doesn't want extra-human clients.
What about inhuman clients?
Has she seen you?
You're working for a bigot?!
Didn't Mallory Book make a name for herself representing every costumed bad guy in America?

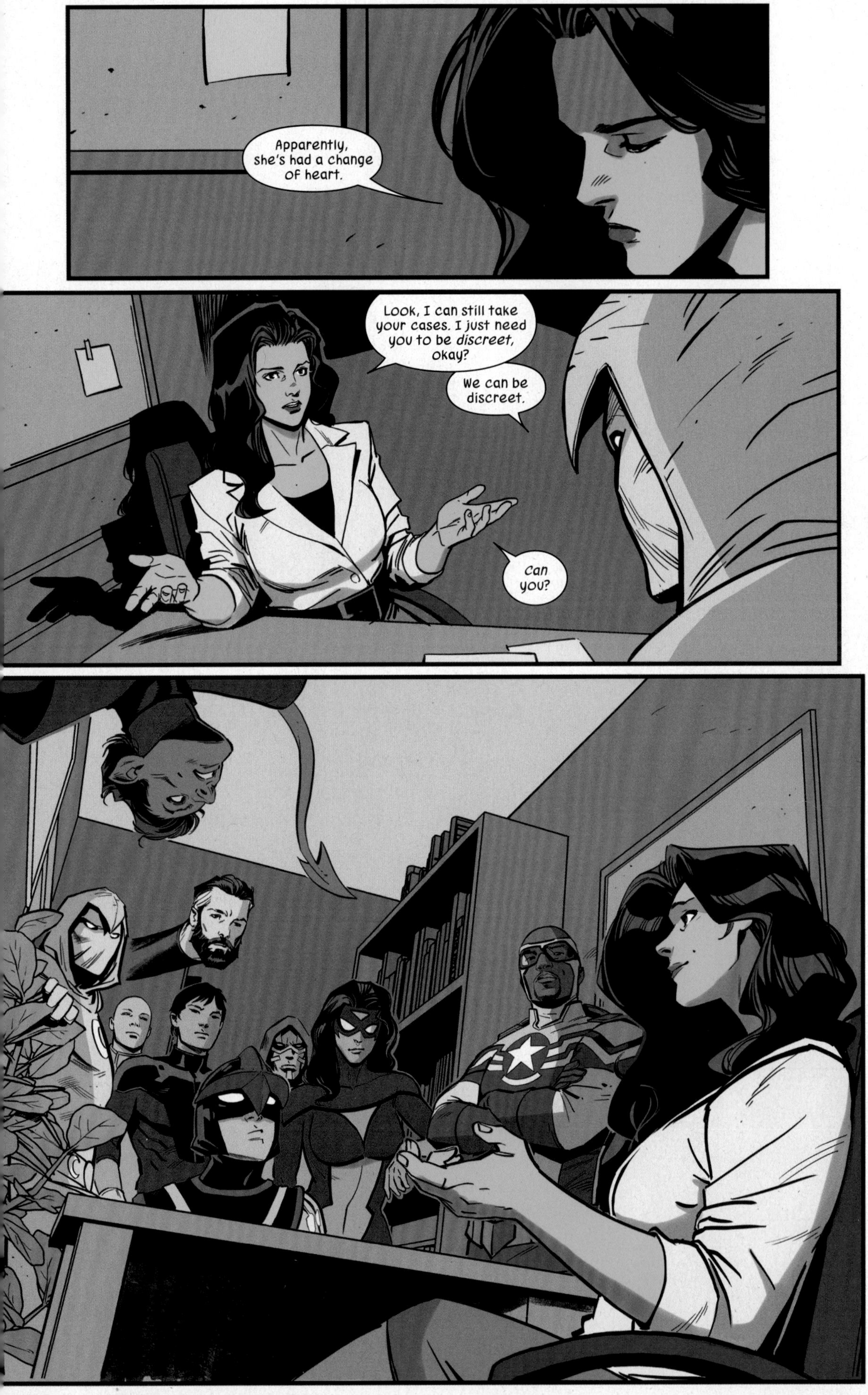
Apparently, she's had a change of heart.
Look, I can still take your cases. I just need you to be *discreet*, okay?
We can be discreet.
Can you?

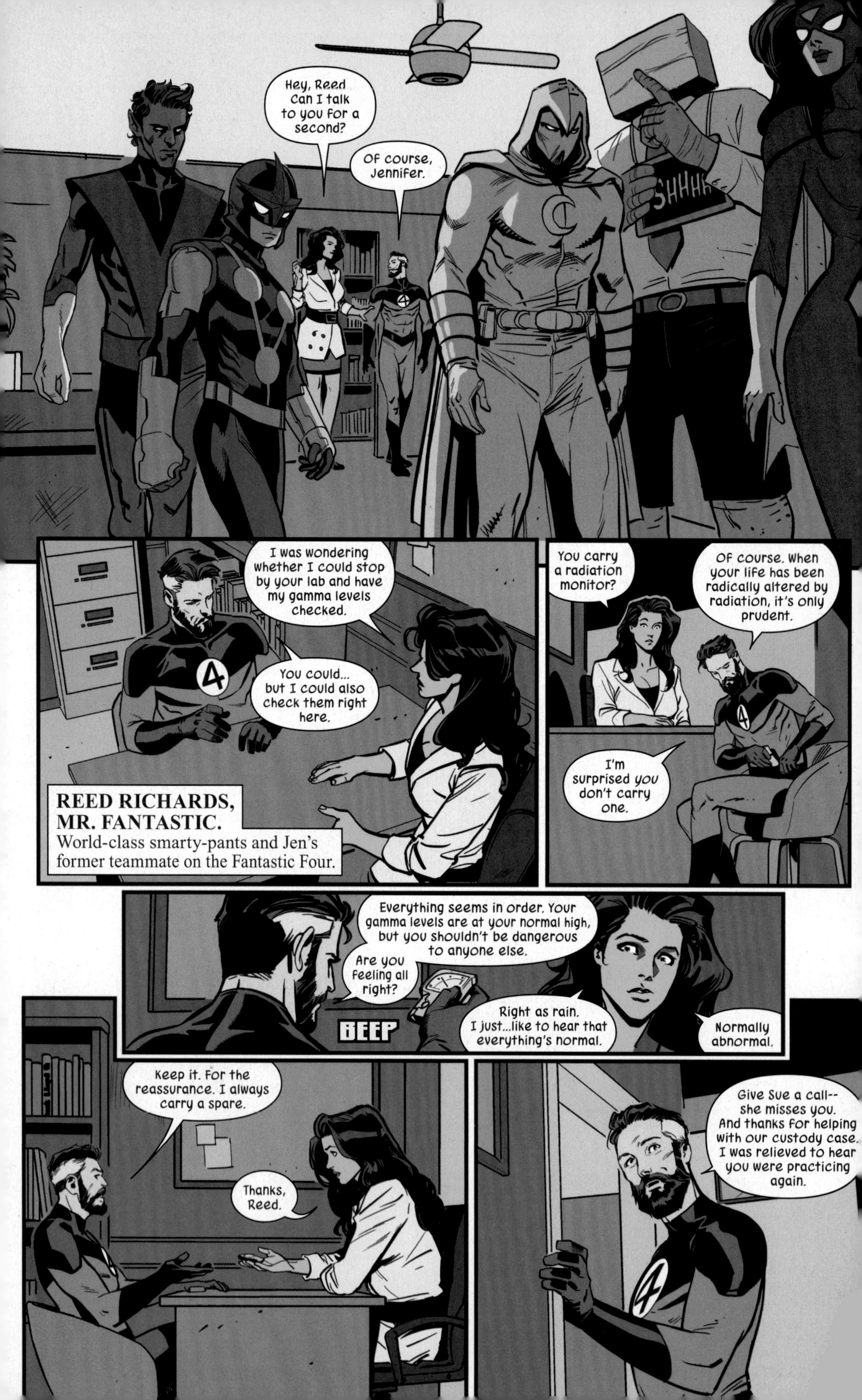
Hey, Reed Can I talk to you for a second?
Of course, Jennifer.
SHHHH
I was wondering whether I could stop by your lab and have my gamma levels checked.
You could... but I could also check them right here.
REED RICHARDS, MR. FANTASTIC.
World-class smarty-pants and Jen's former teammate on the Fantastic Four.
You carry a radiation monitor?
Of course. When your life has been radically altered by radiation, it's only prudent.
I'm surprised you don't carry one.
Everything seems in order. Your gamma levels are at your normal high, but you shouldn't be dangerous to anyone else.
Are you feeling all right?
BEEP
Right as rain. I just...like to hear that everything's normal.
Normally abnormal.
Keep it. For the reassurance. I always carry a spare.
Thanks, Reed.
Give Sue a call-- she misses you. And thanks for helping with our custody case. I was relieved to hear you were practicing again.

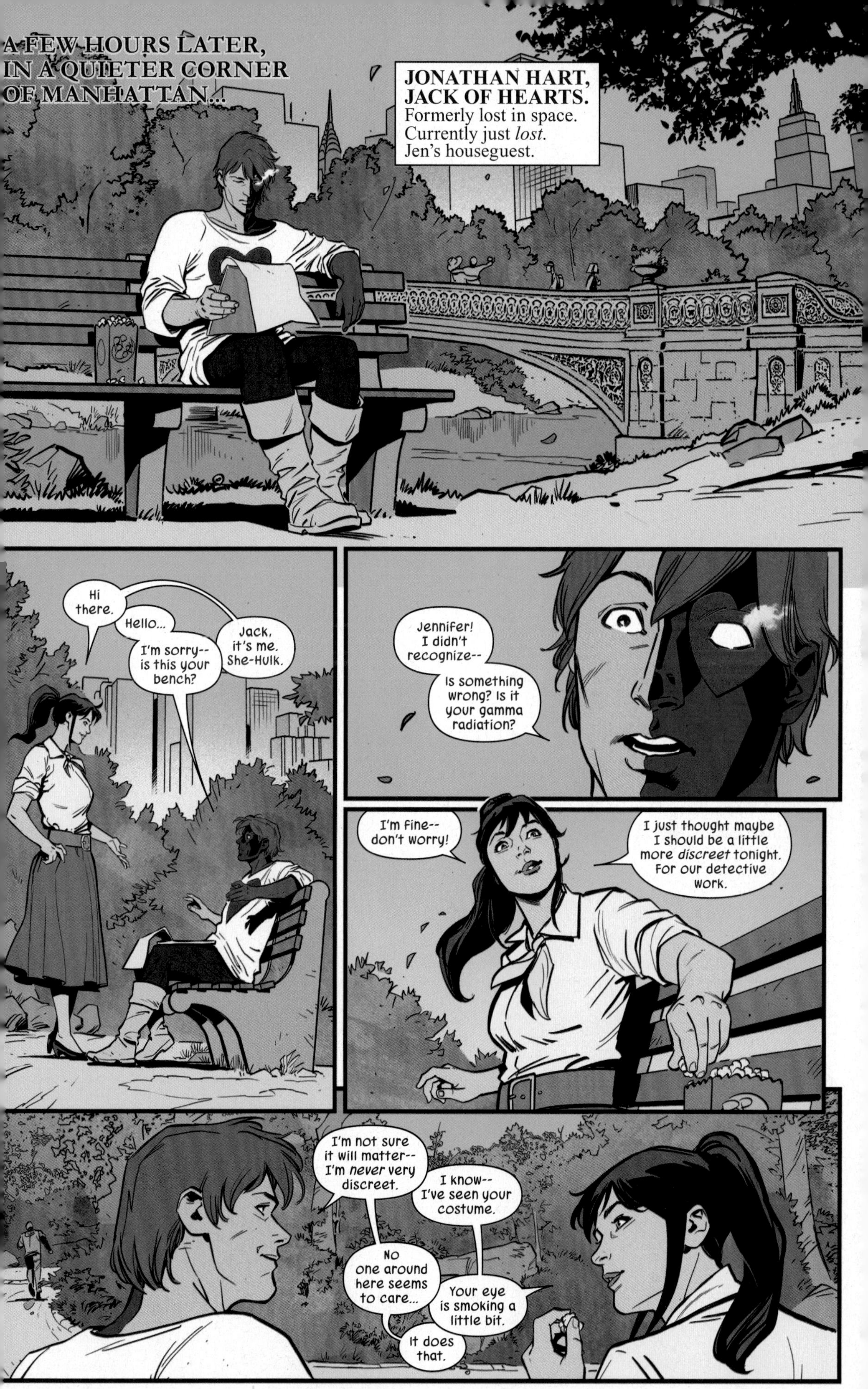
A FEW HOURS LATER, IN A QUIETER CORNER OF MANHATTAN...
JONATHAN HART, JACK OF HEARTS. Formerly lost in space. Currently just *lost*. Jen's houseguest.
Hi there.
Hello...
I'm sorry--is this your bench?
Jack, it's me. She-Hulk.
Jennifer! I didn't recognize--
Is something wrong? Is it your gamma radiation?
I'm fine--don't worry!
I just thought maybe I should be a little more *discreet* tonight. For our detective work.
I'm not sure it will matter--I'm *never* very discreet.
I know--I've seen your costume.
No one around here seems to care...
Your eye is smoking a little bit.
It does that.

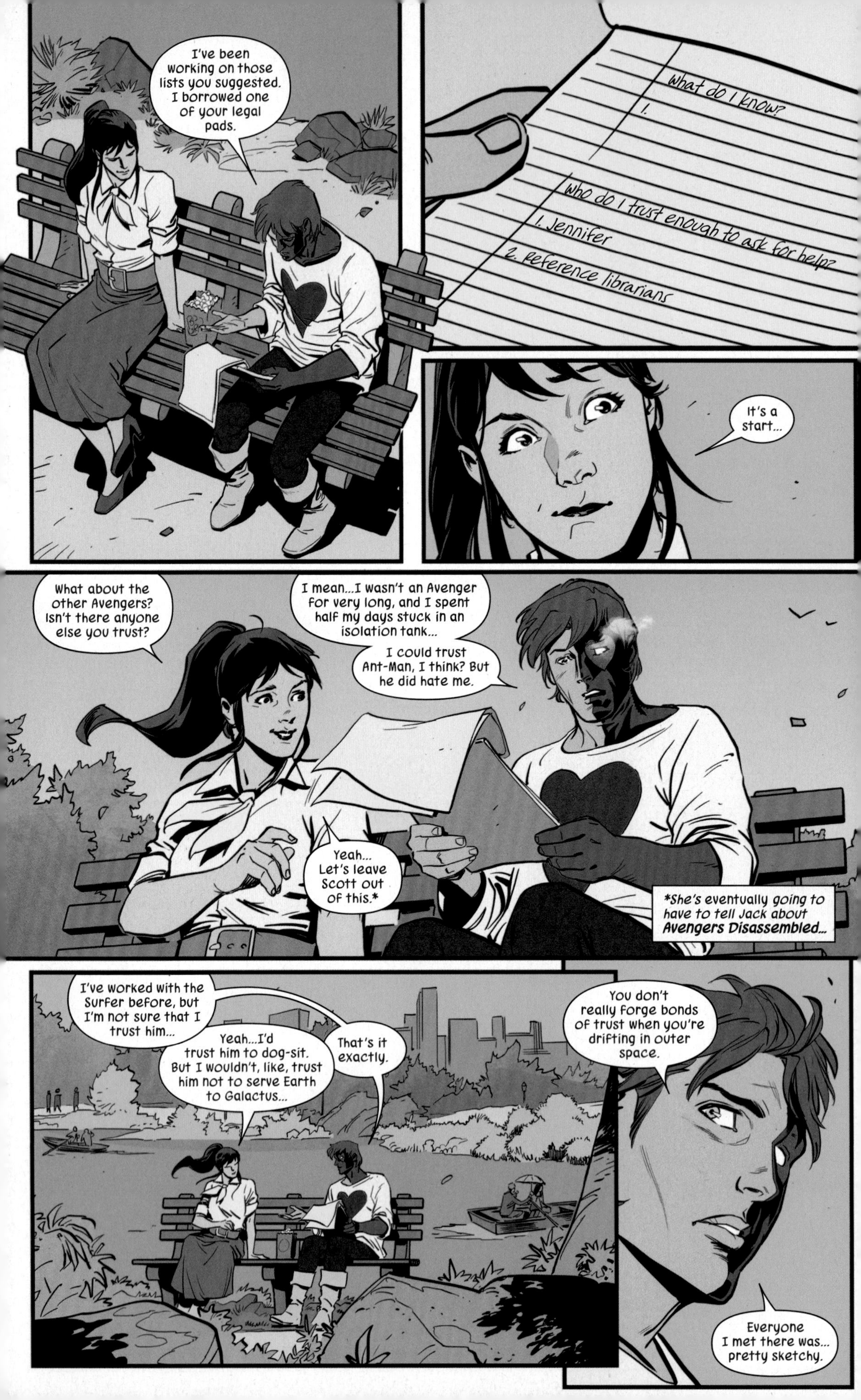
I've been working on those lists you suggested. I borrowed one of your legal pads.
What do I know?
1.
Who do I trust enough to ask for help?
1. Jennifer
2. Reference librarians
It's a start...
What about the other Avengers? Isn't there anyone else you trust?
I mean...I wasn't an Avenger for very long, and I spent half my days stuck in an isolation tank...
I could trust Ant-Man, I think? But he did hate me.
Yeah... Let's leave Scott out of this.*
*She's eventually going to have to tell Jack about Avengers Disassembled...
I've worked with the Surfer before, but I'm not sure that I trust him...
Yeah...I'd trust him to dog-sit. But I wouldn't, like, trust him not to serve Earth to Galactus...
That's it exactly.
You don't really forge bonds of trust when you're drifting in outer space.
Everyone I met there was... pretty sketchy.

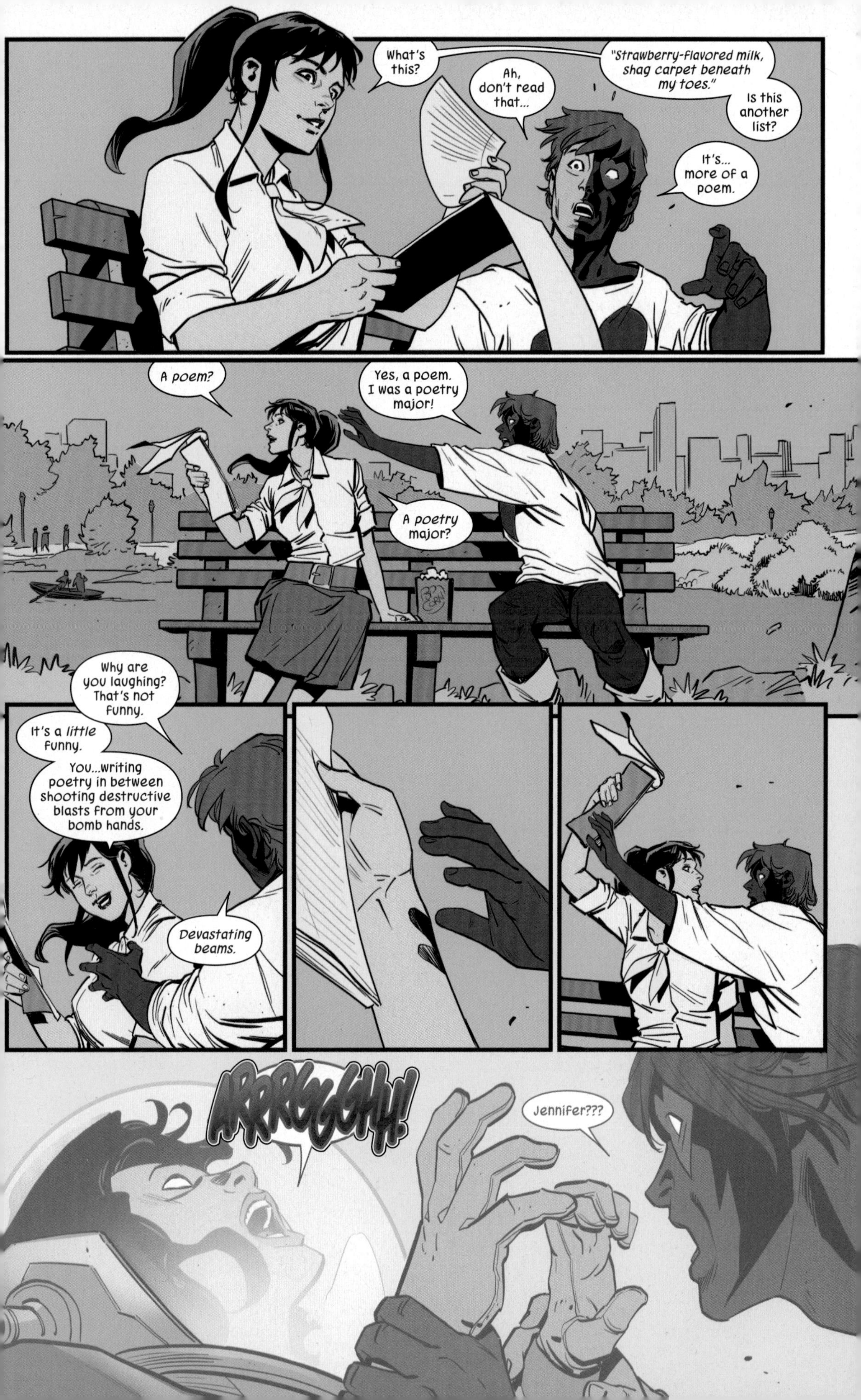
What's this?
Ah, don't read that...
"Strawberry-flavored milk, shag carpet beneath my toes."
Is this another list?
It's... more of a poem.
A poem?
Yes, a poem. I was a poetry major!
A poetry major?
Why are you laughing? That's not funny.
It's a little funny.
You...writing poetry in between shooting destructive blasts from your bomb hands.
Devastating beams.
ARRRGGGH!
Jennifer???

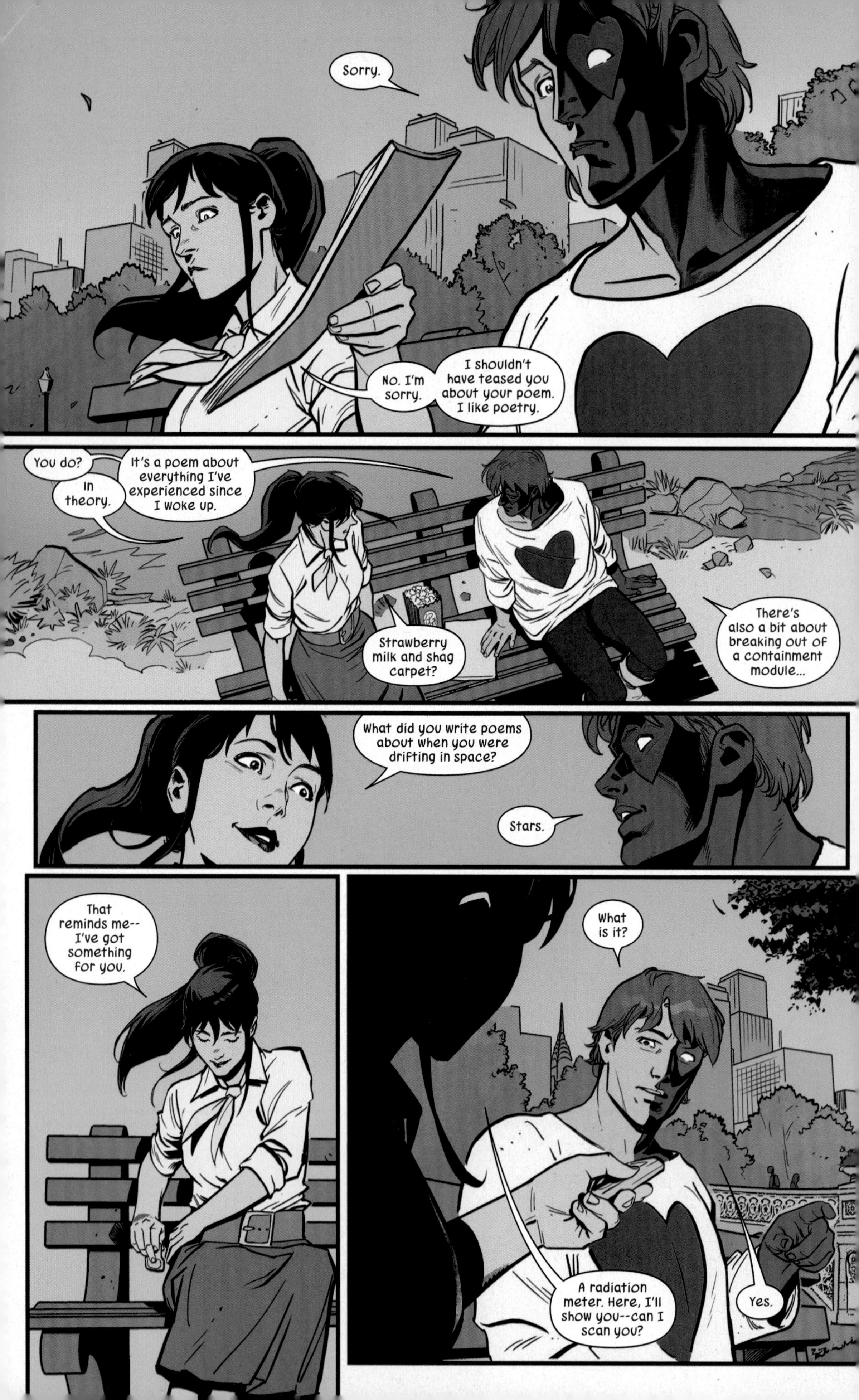
Sorry.
No. I'm sorry.
I shouldn't have teased you about your poem. I like poetry.
You do?
In theory.
It's a poem about everything I've experienced since I woke up.
Strawberry milk and shag carpet?
There's also a bit about breaking out of a containment module...
What did you write poems about when you were drifting in space?
Stars.
That reminds me-- I've got something for you.
What is it?
A radiation meter. Here, I'll show you--can I scan you?
Yes.

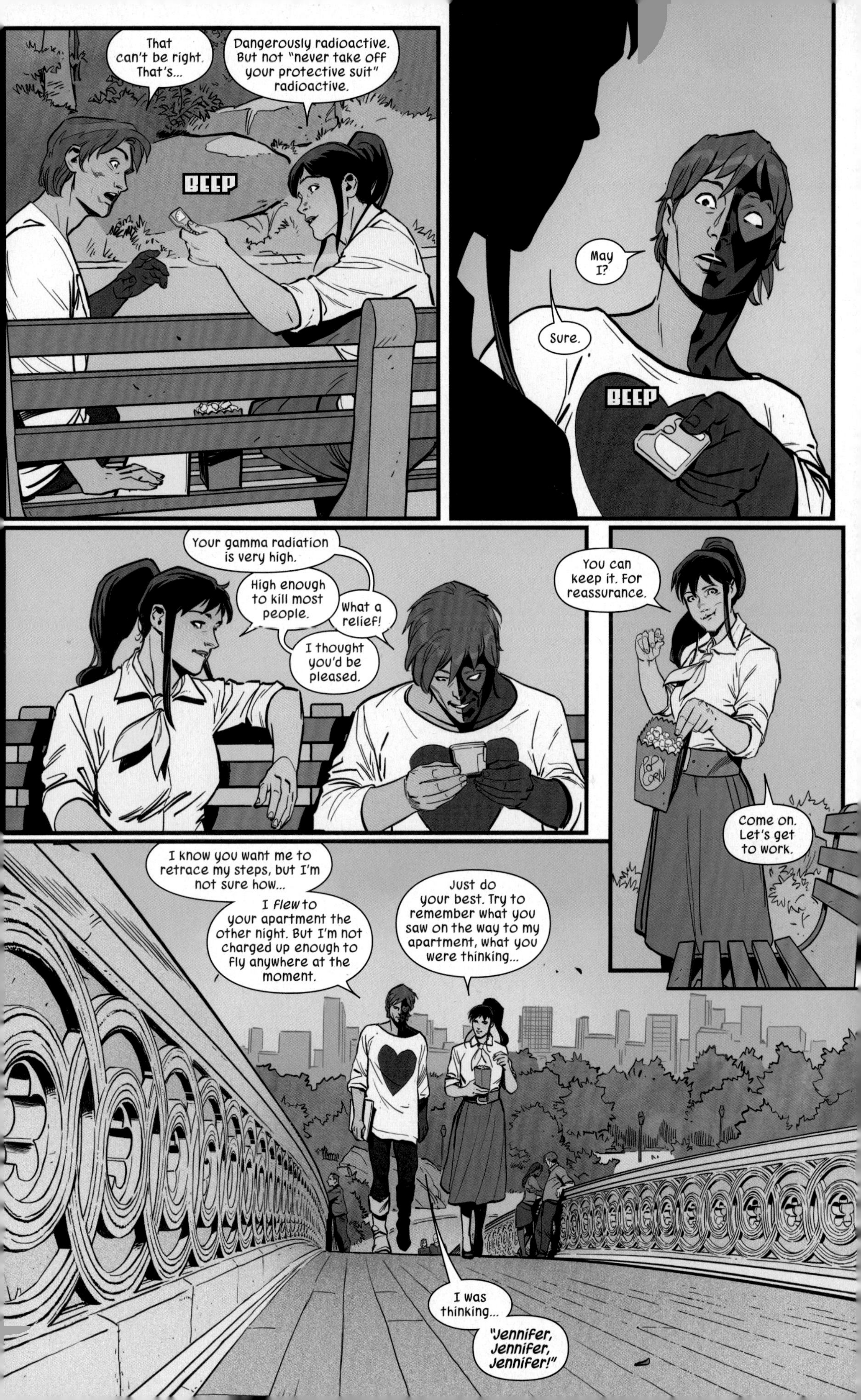
That can't be right. That's...
Dangerously radioactive. But not "never take off your protective suit" radioactive.
BEEP
May I?
Sure.
BEEP
Your gamma radiation is very high.
High enough to kill most people.
What a relief!
I thought you'd be pleased.
You can keep it. For reassurance.
Come on. Let's get to work.
I know you want me to retrace my steps, but I'm not sure how...
I *flew* to your apartment the other night. But I'm not charged up enough to fly anywhere at the moment.
Just do your best. Try to remember what you saw on the way to my apartment, what you were thinking...
I was thinking...
"Jennifer, Jennifer, Jennifer!"

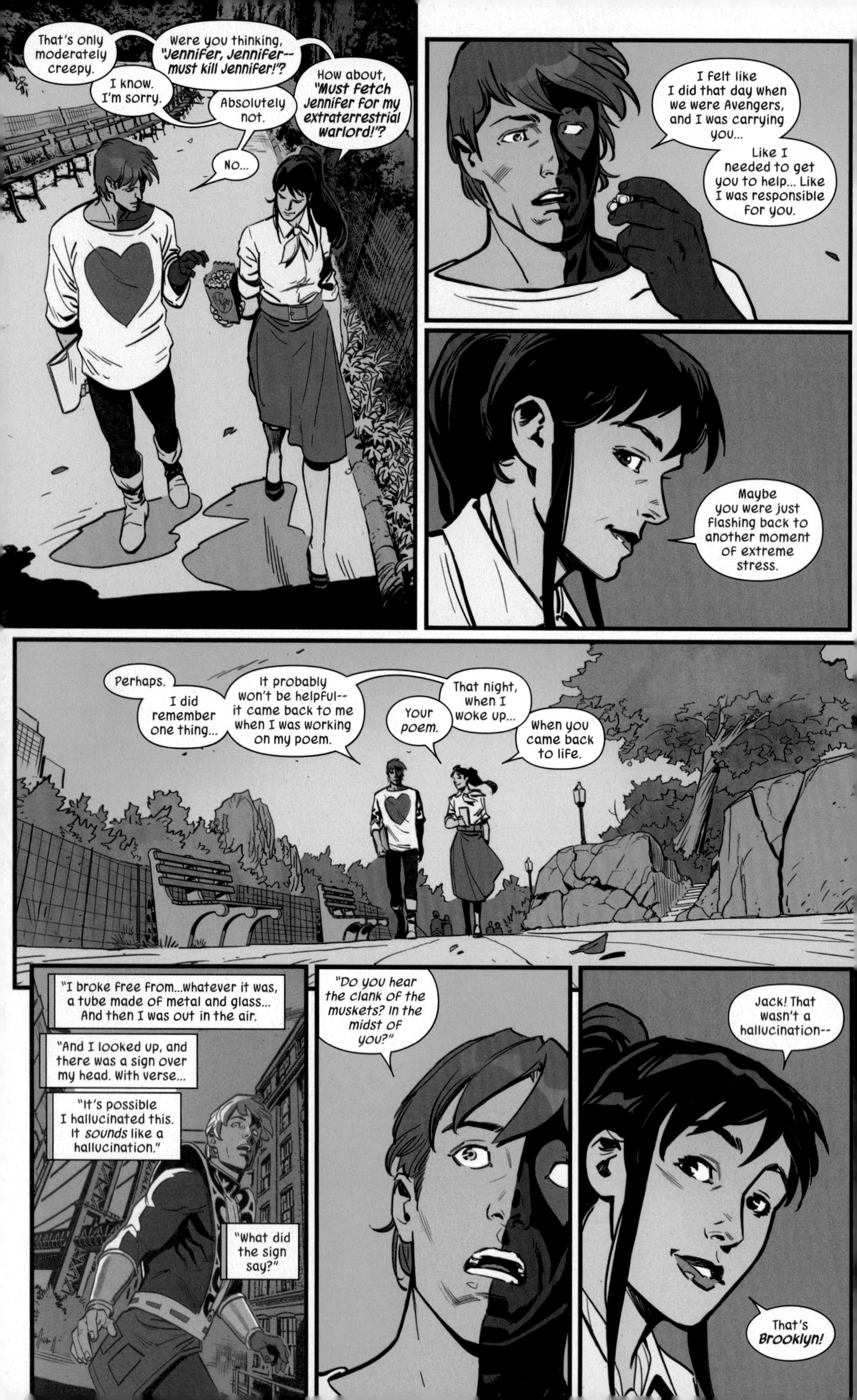
That's only moderately creepy.
Were you thinking, "Jennifer, Jennifer-- must kill Jennifer!"?
I know. I'm sorry.
Absolutely not.
How about, "Must fetch Jennifer for my extraterrestrial warlord!"?
No...
I felt like I did that day when we were Avengers, and I was carrying you...
Like I needed to get you to help... Like I was responsible for you.
Maybe you were just flashing back to another moment of extreme stress.
Perhaps.
I did remember one thing...
It probably won't be helpful-- it came back to me when I was working on my poem.
Your poem.
That night, when I woke up...
When you came back to life.
"I broke free from...whatever it was, a tube made of metal and glass... And then I was out in the air.
"And I looked up, and there was a sign over my head. With verse...
"It's possible I hallucinated this. It sounds like a hallucination."
"What did the sign say?"
"Do you hear the clank of the muskets? In the midst of you?"
Jack! That wasn't a hallucination--
That's Brooklyn!

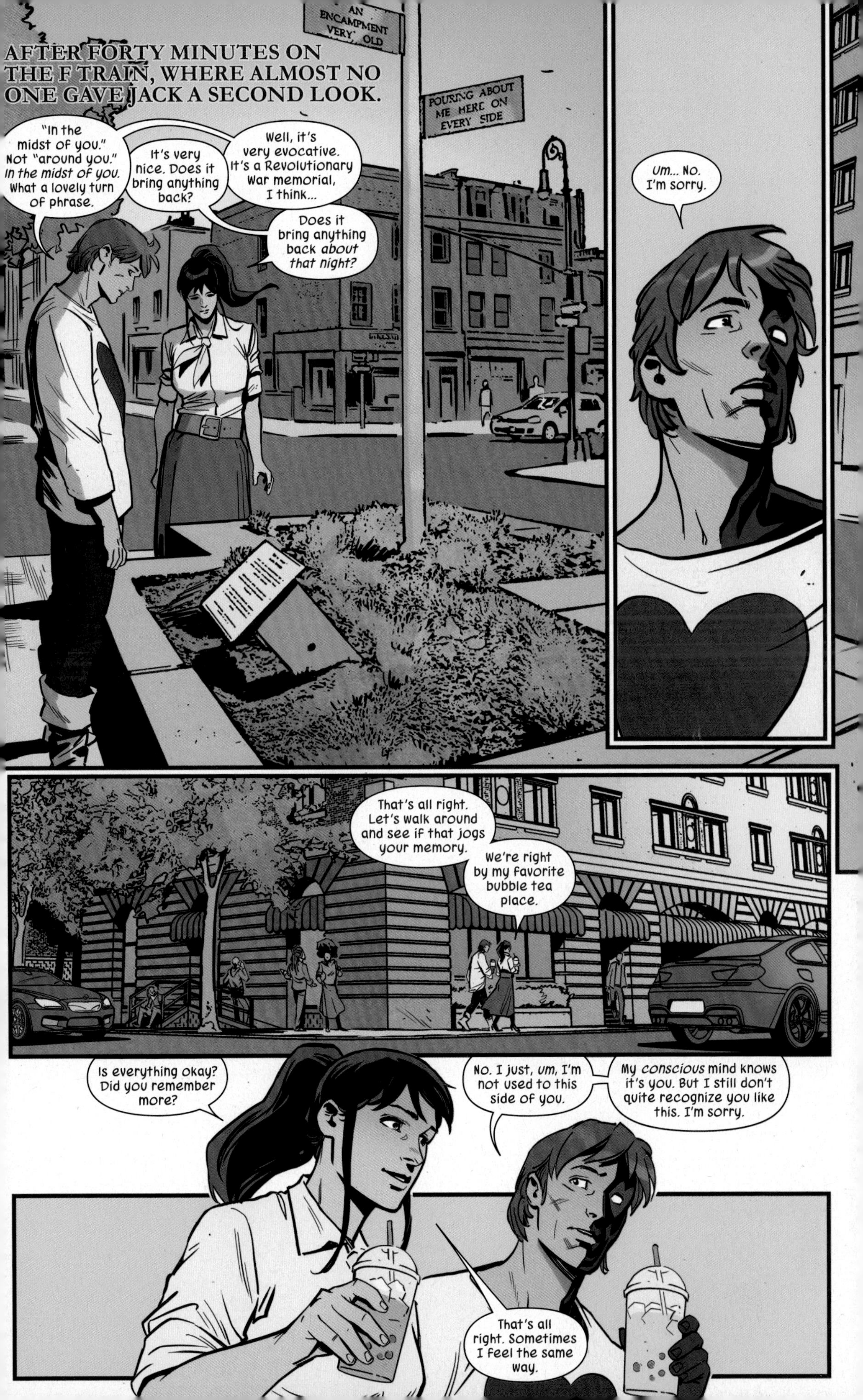
AN ENCAMPMENT VERY OLD
AFTER FORTY MINUTES ON THE F TRAIN, WHERE ALMOST NO ONE GAVE JACK A SECOND LOOK.
POURING ABOUT ME HERE ON EVERY SIDE
"In the midst of you." Not "around you." *In the midst of you.* What a lovely turn of phrase.
It's very nice. Does it bring anything back?
Well, it's very evocative. It's a Revolutionary War memorial, I think...
Does it bring anything back *about that night?*
Um... No. I'm sorry.
That's all right. Let's walk around and see if that jogs your memory.
We're right by my favorite bubble tea place.
Is everything okay? Did you remember more?
No. I just, *um*, I'm not used to this side of you.
My *conscious* mind knows it's you. But I still don't quite recognize you like this. I'm sorry.
That's all right. Sometimes I feel the same way.

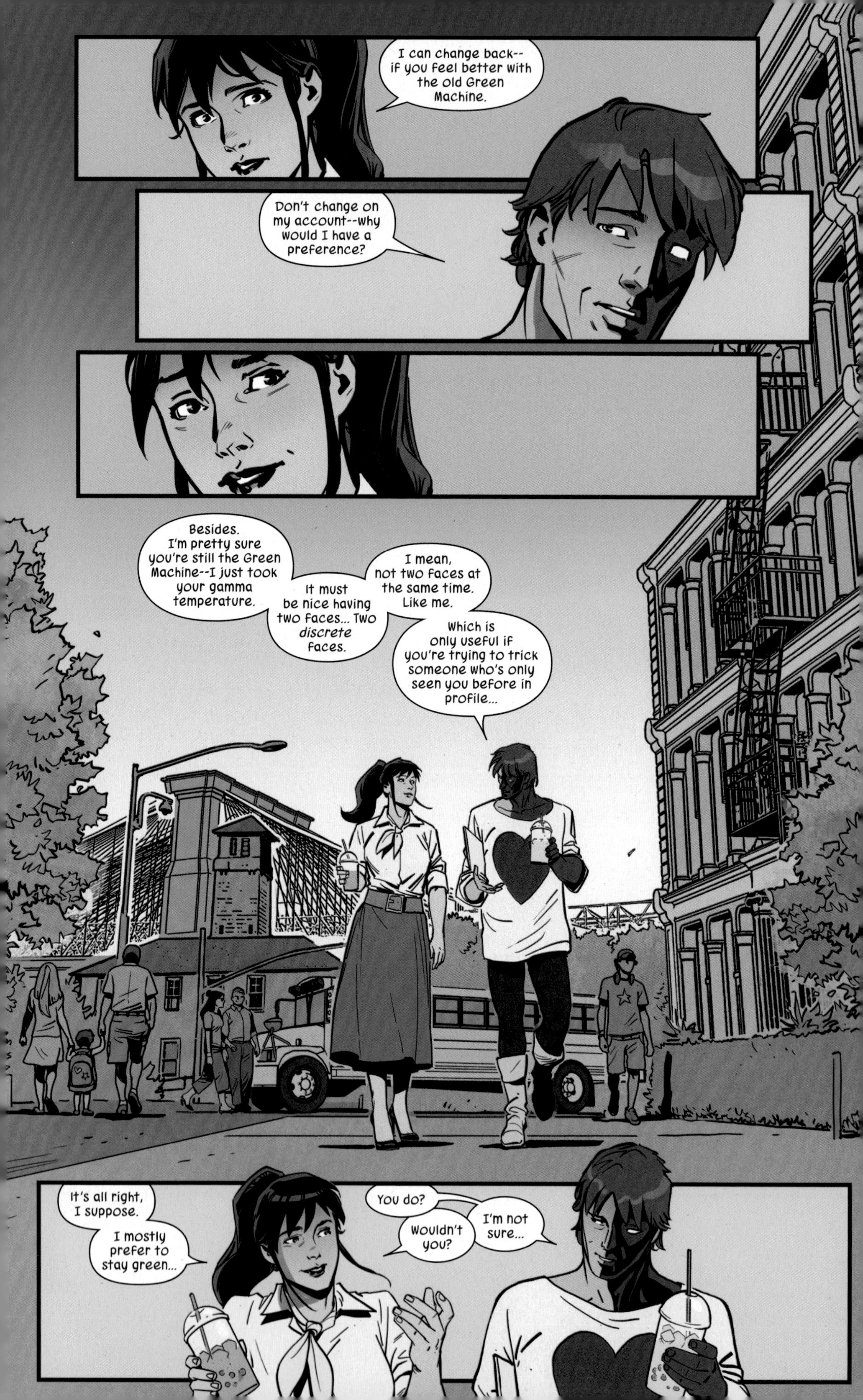
I can change back--if you feel better with the old Green Machine.
Don't change on my account--why would I have a preference?
Besides. I'm pretty sure you're still the Green Machine--I just took your gamma temperature.
It must be nice having two faces... Two *discrete* faces.
I mean, not two faces at the same time. Like me.
Which is only useful if you're trying to trick someone who's only seen you before in profile...
It's all right, I suppose.
I mostly prefer to stay green...
You do?
Wouldn't you?
I'm not sure...

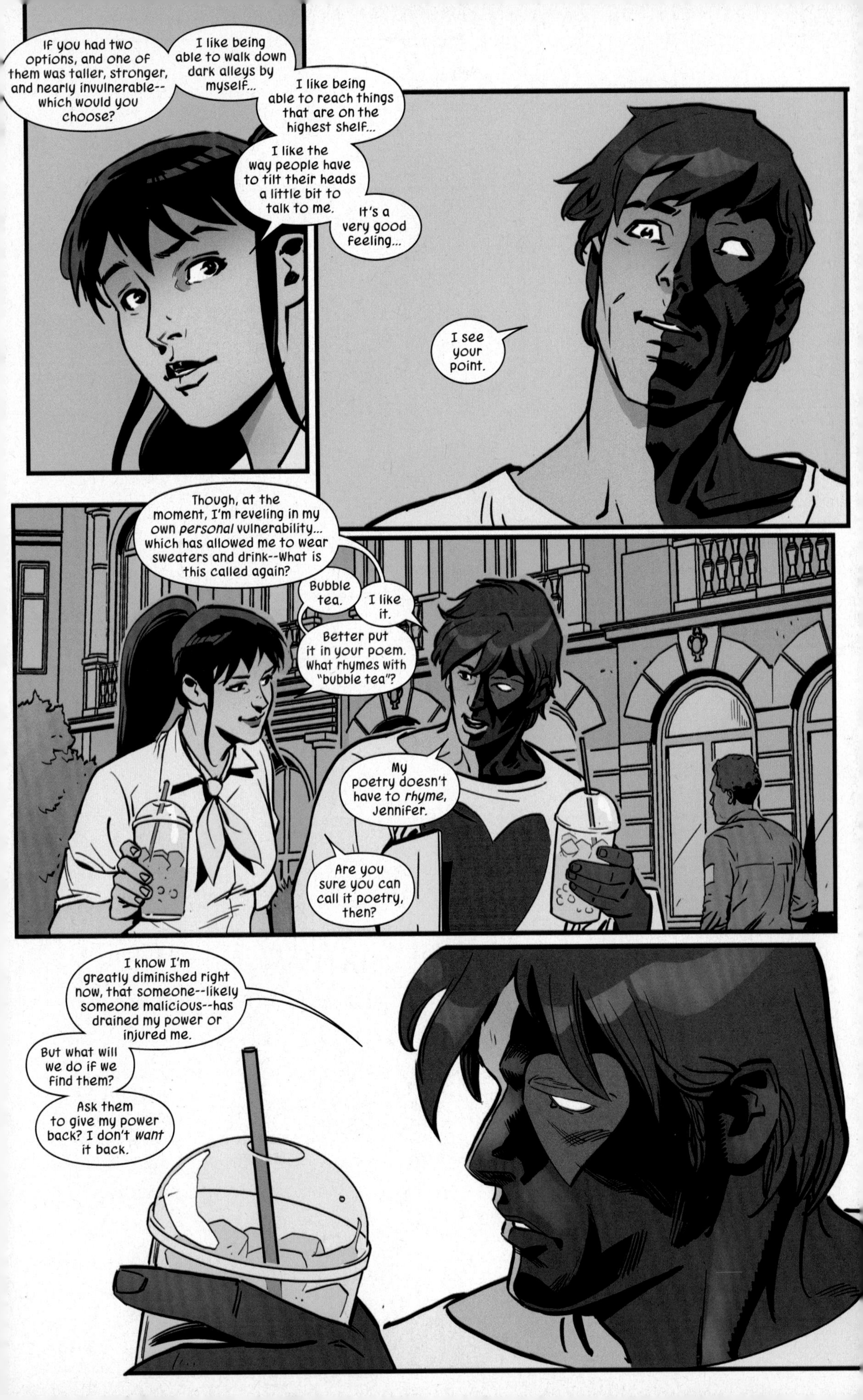
If you had two options, and one of them was taller, stronger, and nearly invulnerable--which would you choose?
I like being able to walk down dark alleys by myself...
I like being able to reach things that are on the highest shelf...
I like the way people have to tilt their heads a little bit to talk to me.
It's a very good feeling...
I see your point.
Though, at the moment, I'm reveling in my own *personal* vulnerability... which has allowed me to wear sweaters and drink--What is this called again?
Bubble tea.
I like it.
Better put it in your poem. What rhymes with "bubble tea"?
My poetry doesn't have to *rhyme*, Jennifer.
Are you sure you can call it poetry, then?
I know I'm greatly diminished right now, that someone--likely someone malicious--has drained my power or injured me.
But what will we do if we find them?
Ask them to give my power back? I don't *want* it back.

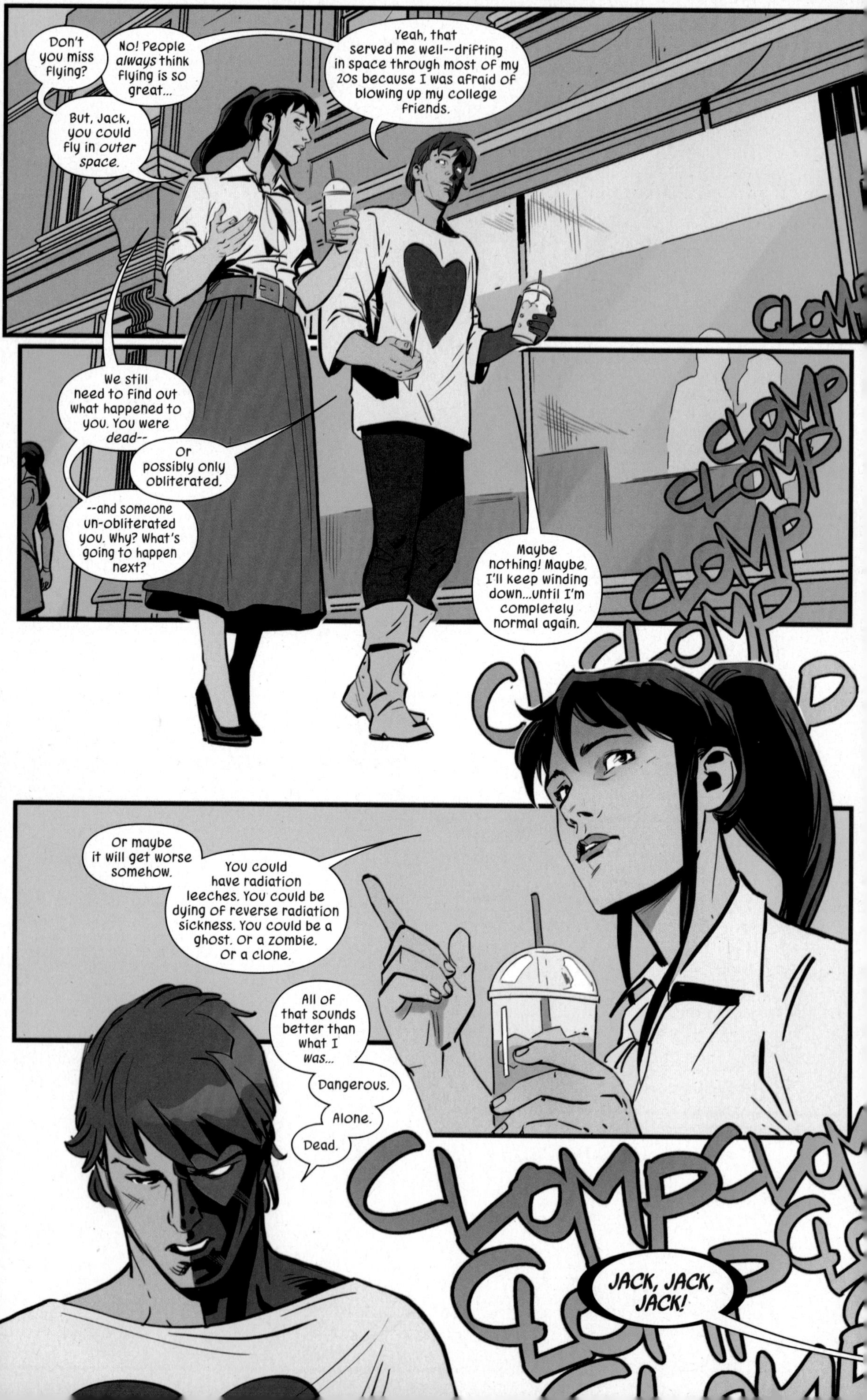

Don't you miss flying?
No! People *always* think flying is so great...
Yeah, that served me well--drifting in space through most of my 20s because I was afraid of blowing up my college friends.
But, Jack, you could fly in *outer space*.
CLOMP
We still need to find out what happened to you. You were *dead*--
Or possibly only obliterated.
--and someone un-obliterated you. Why? What's going to happen next?
CLOMP CLOMP CLOMP CLOMP
Maybe nothing! Maybe I'll keep winding down...until I'm completely normal again.
Or maybe it will get worse somehow.
You could have radiation leeches. You could be dying of reverse radiation sickness. You could be a ghost. Or a zombie. Or a clone.
All of that sounds better than what I was...
Dangerous.
Alone.
Dead.
CLOMP
JACK, JACK, JACK!

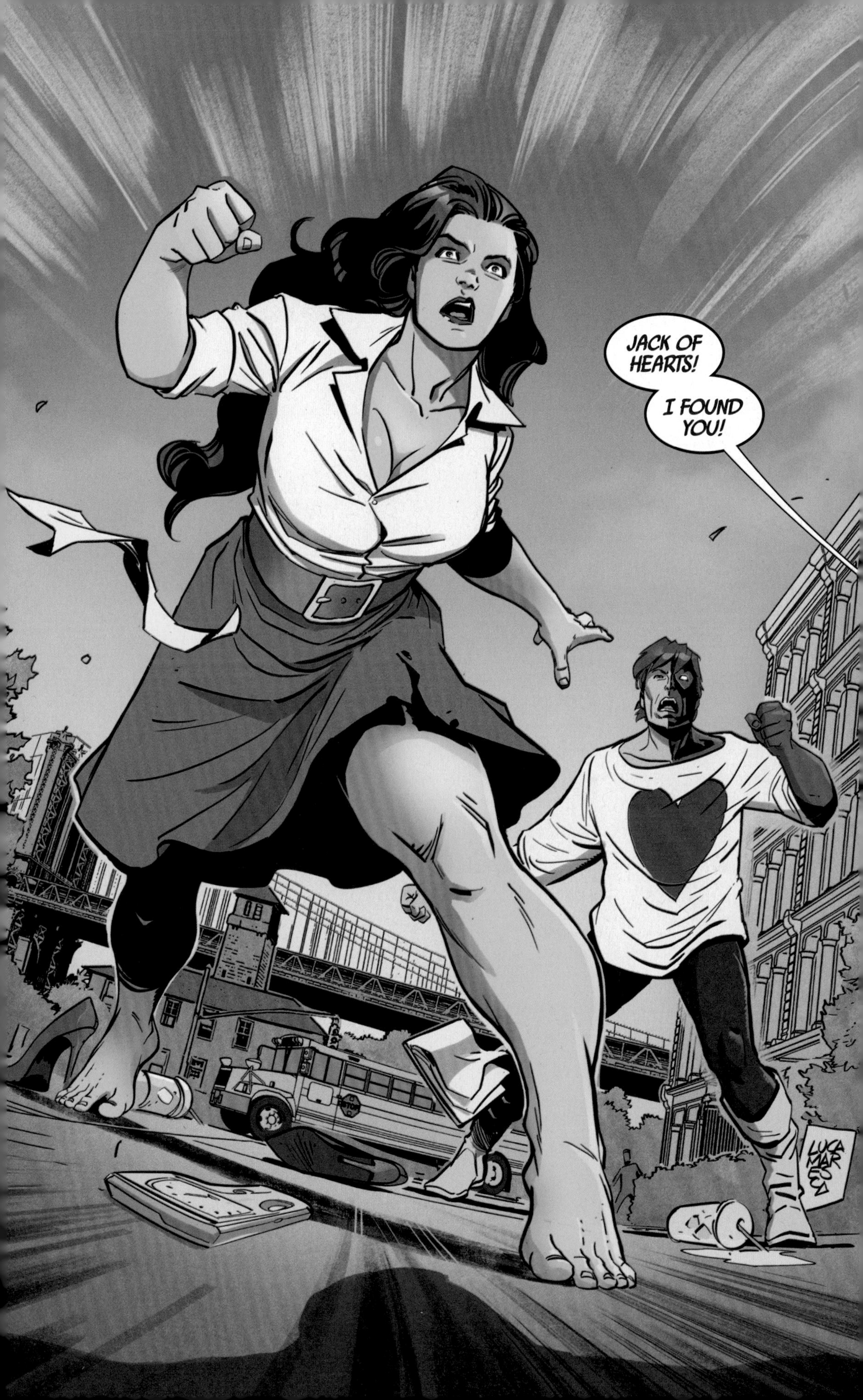
JACK OF HEARTS!
I FOUND YOU!

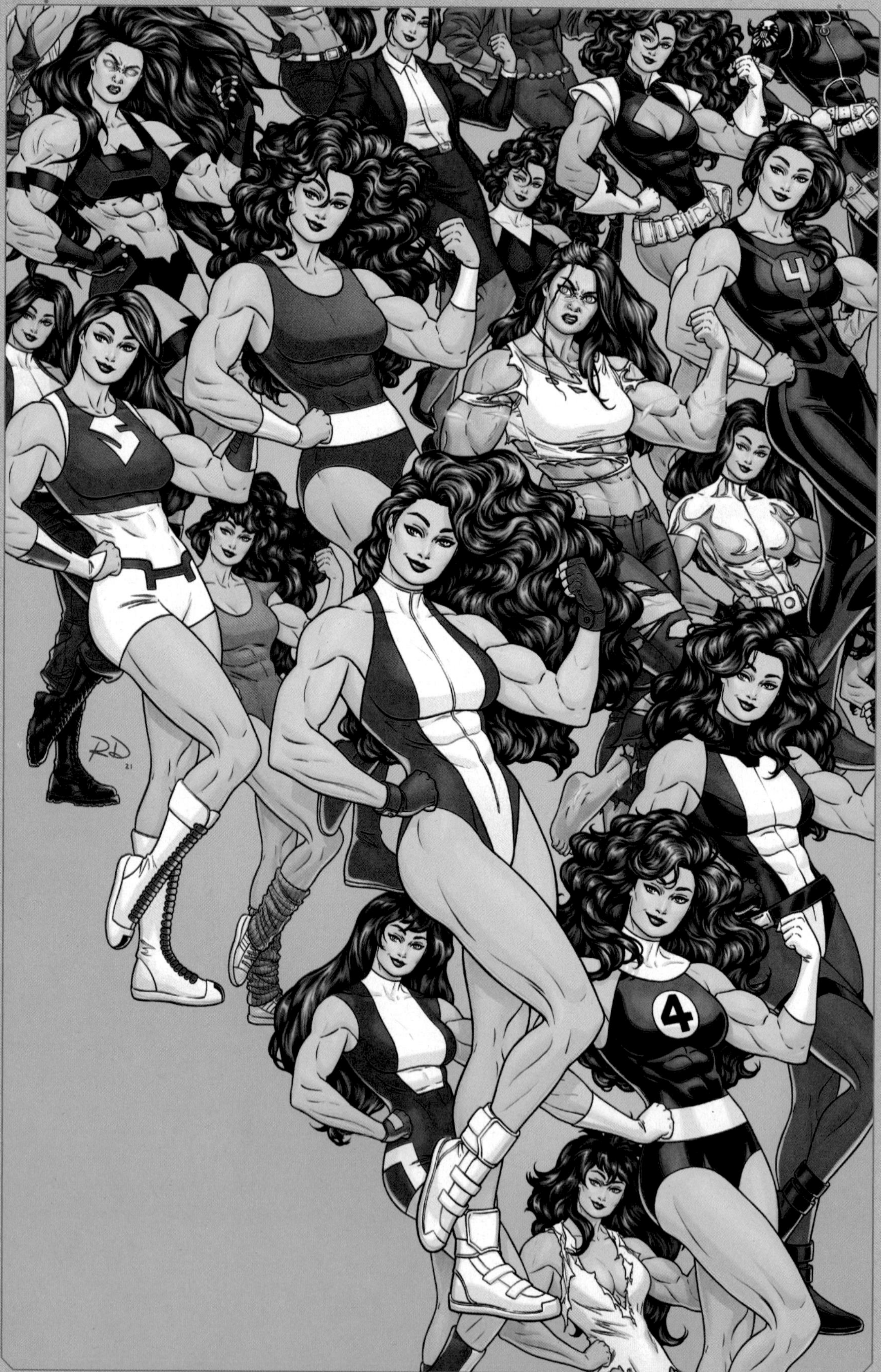

#4 VARIANT BY **RUSSELL DAUTERMAN**

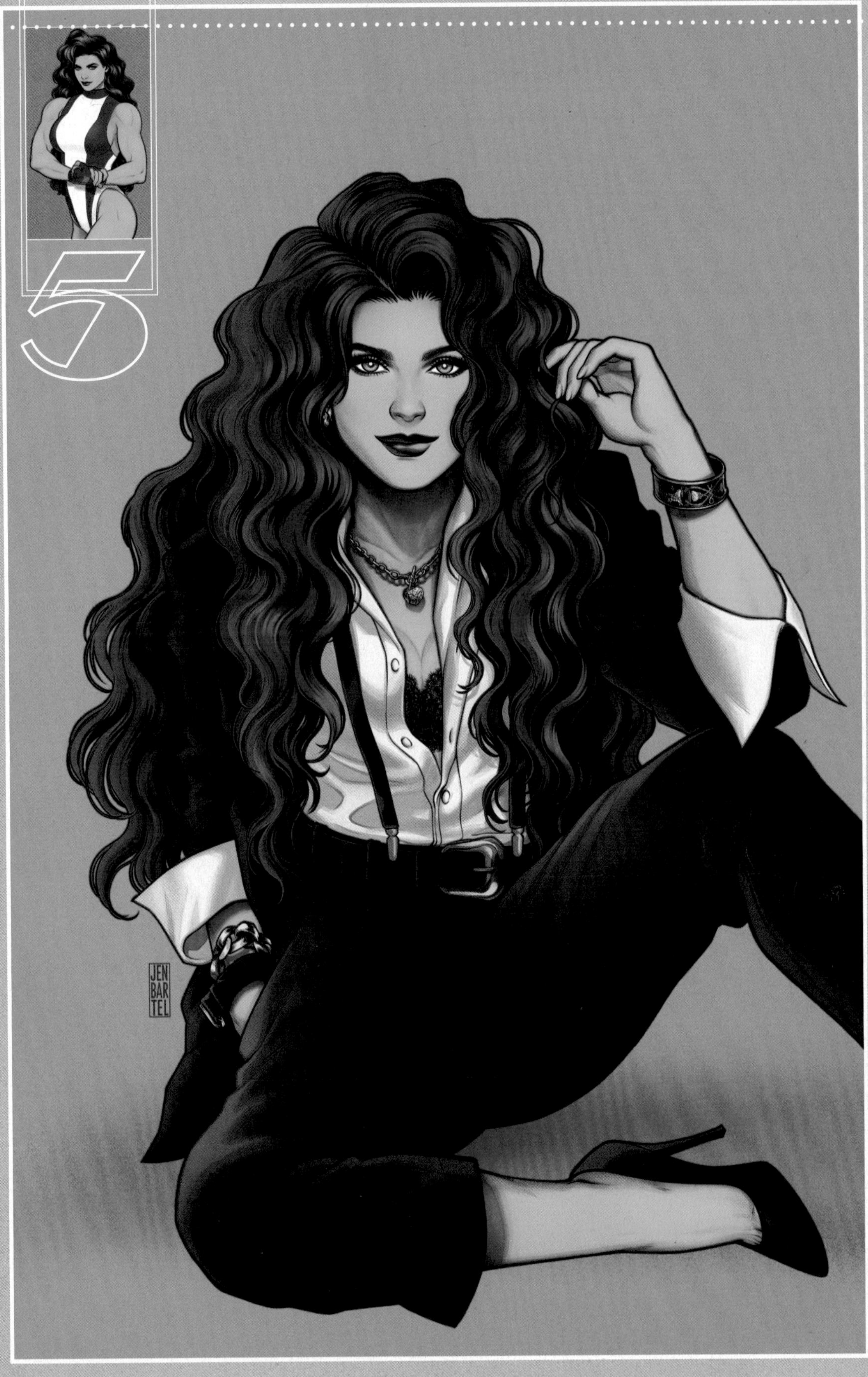
5
JEN BARTEL

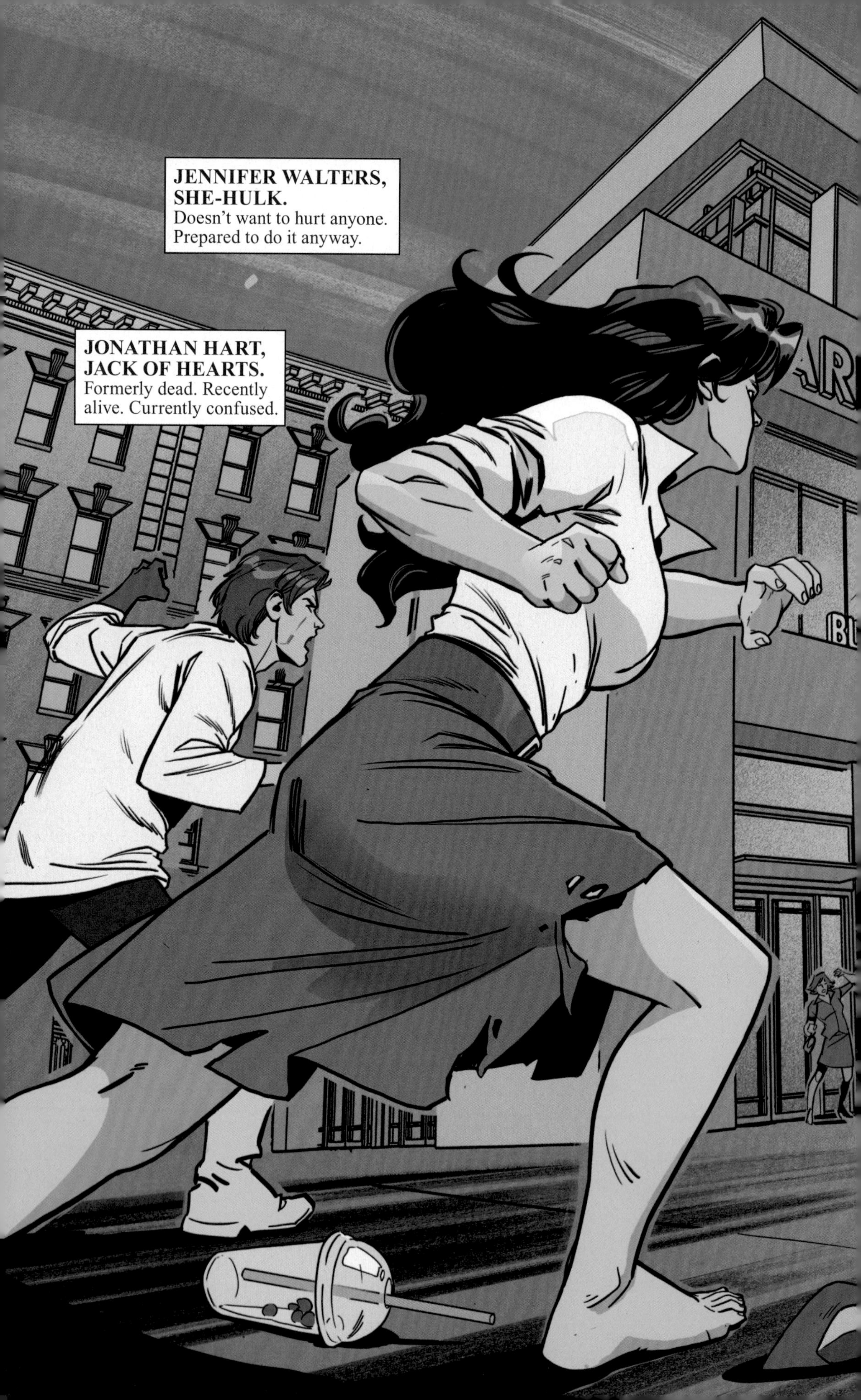
JENNIFER WALTERS, SHE-HULK.
Doesn't want to hurt anyone. Prepared to do it anyway.
JONATHAN HART, JACK OF HEARTS.
Formerly dead. Recently alive. Currently confused.

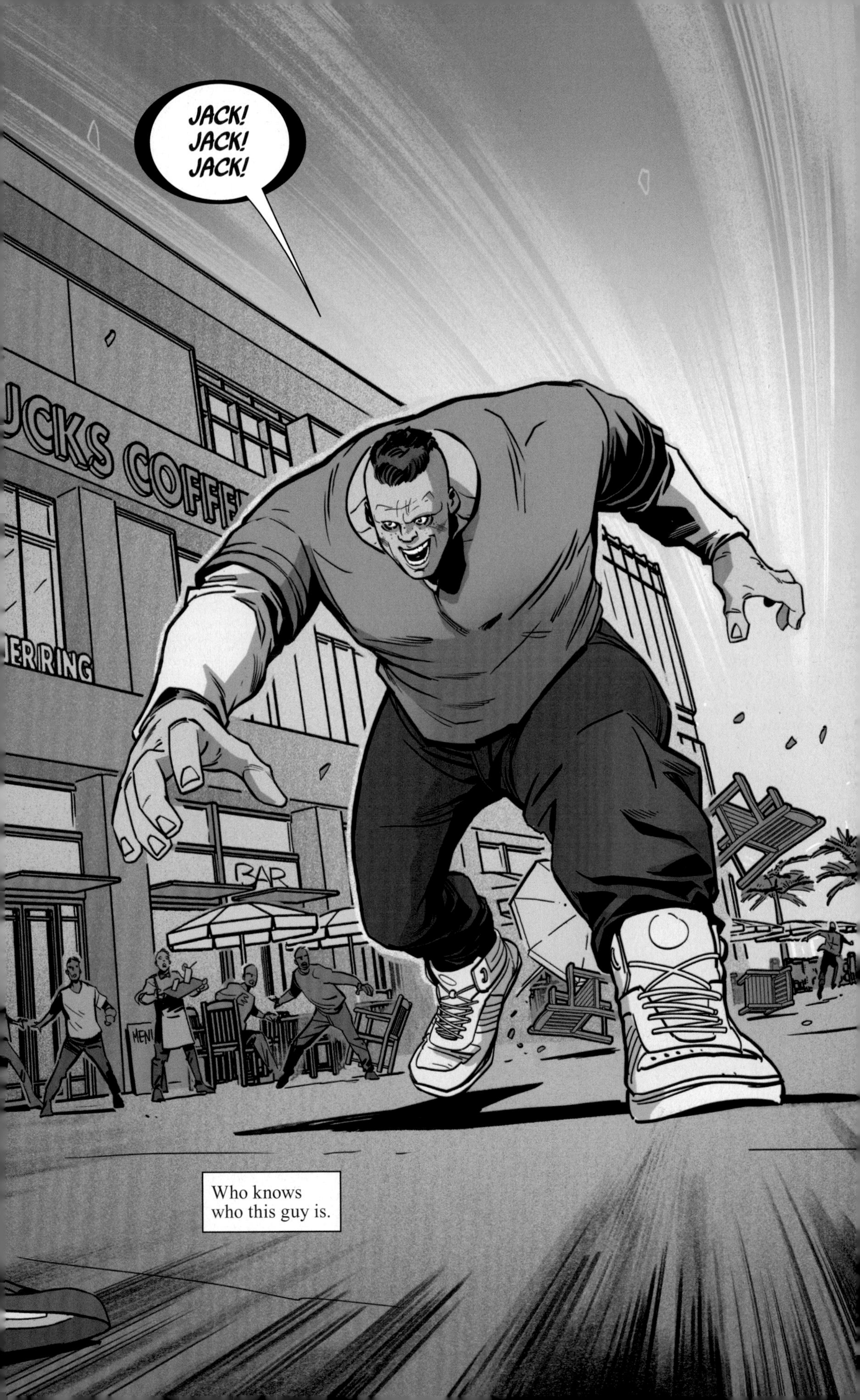
JACK! JACK! JACK!
UCKS COFFE
ERRING
BAR
MENU
Who knows who this guy is.

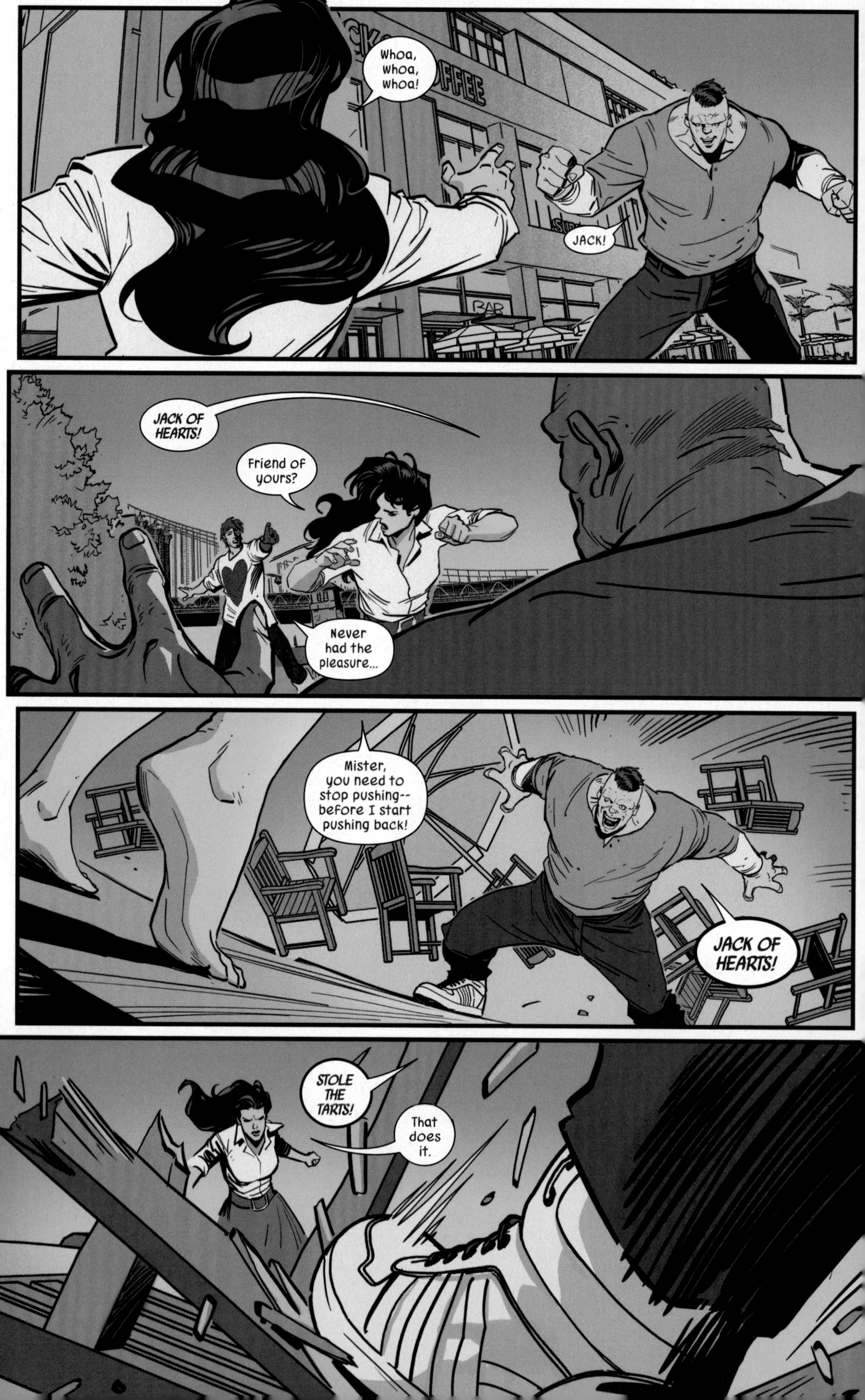
Whoa, whoa, whoa!
JACK!
JACK OF HEARTS!
Friend of yours?
Never had the pleasure...
Mister, you need to stop pushing-- before I start pushing back!
JACK OF HEARTS!
STOLE THE TARTS!
That does it.

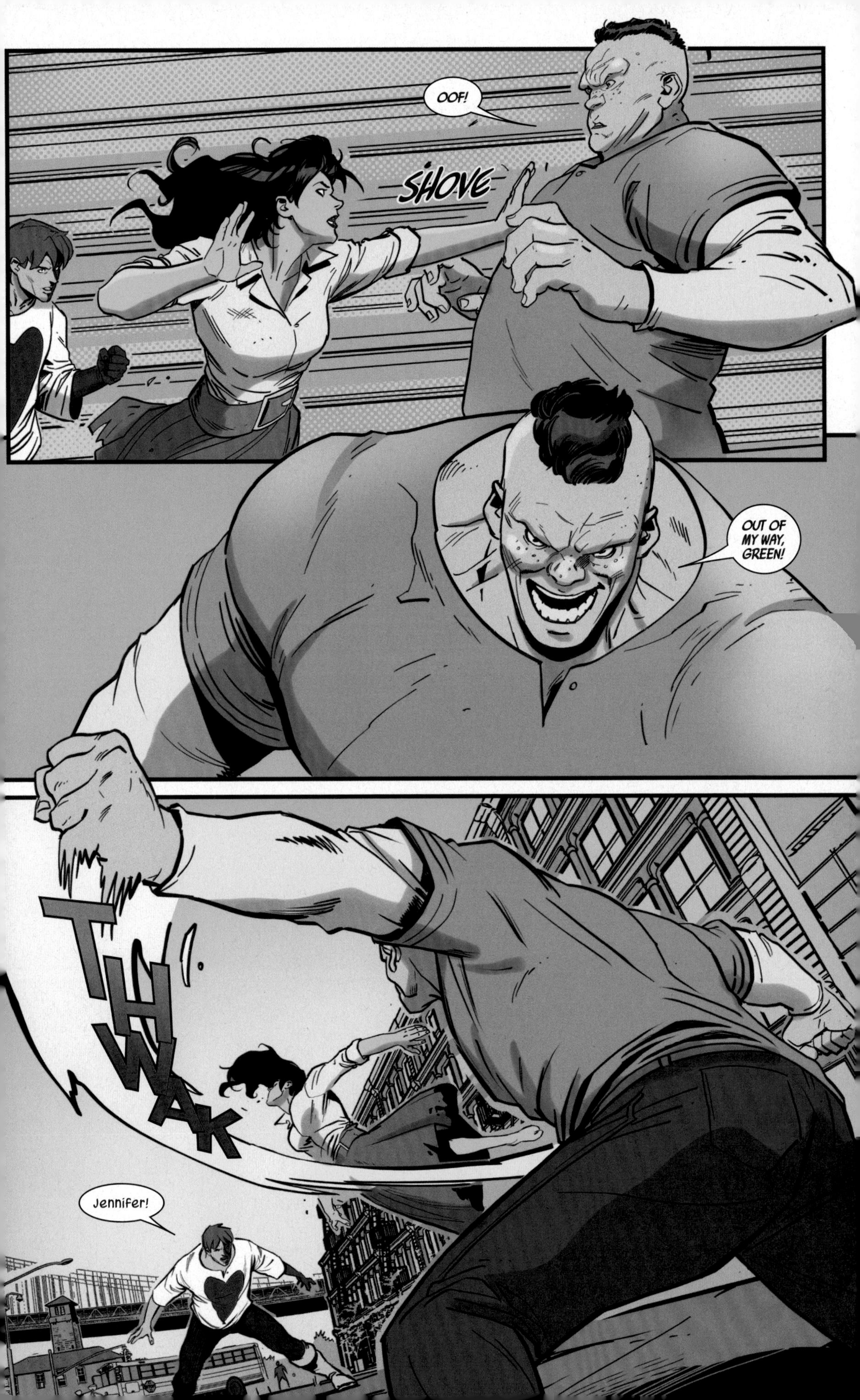
OOF!
SHOVE
OUT OF MY WAY, GREEN!
THWAK
Jennifer!

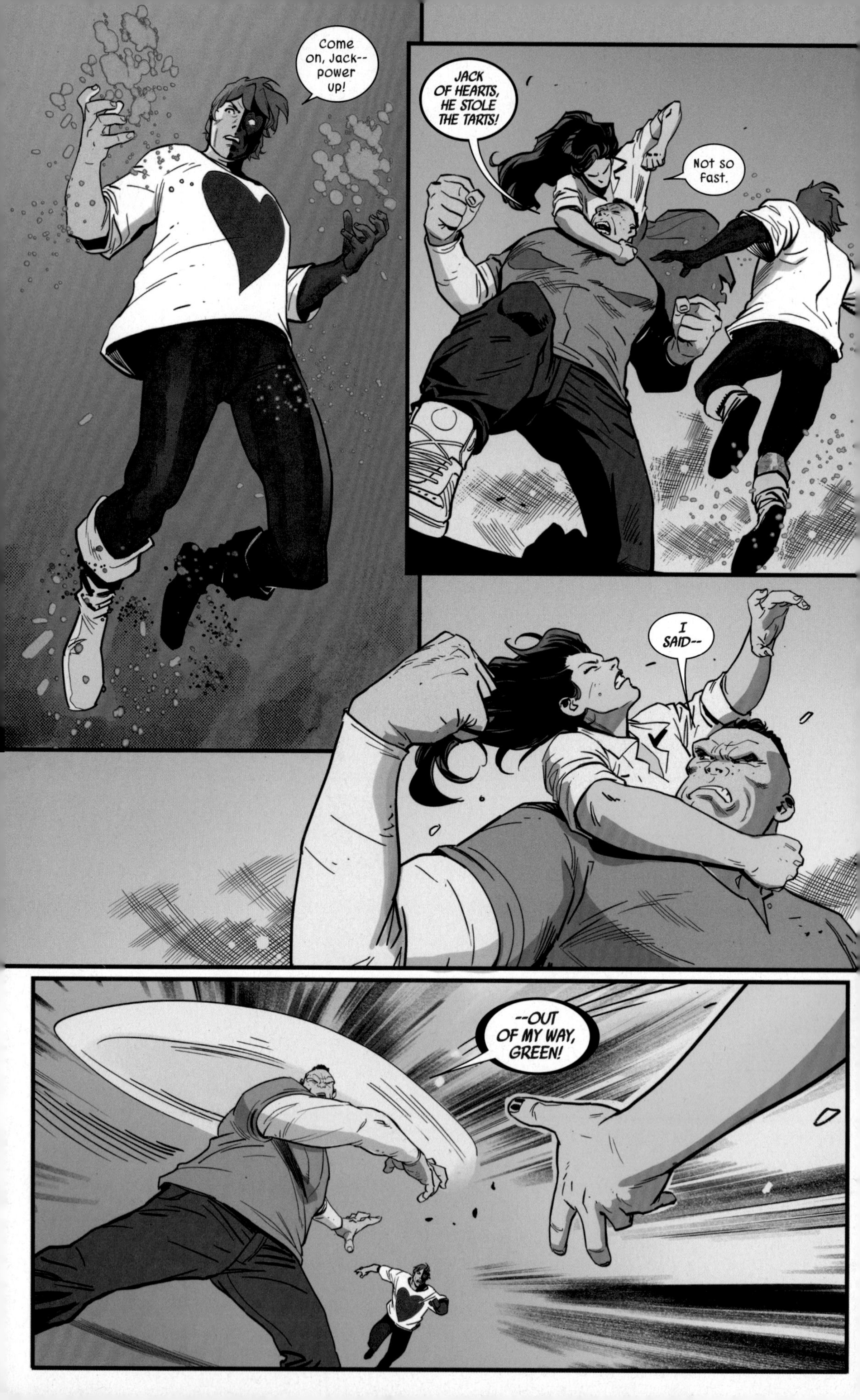
Come on, Jack-- power up!
JACK OF HEARTS, HE STOLE THE TARTS!
Not so fast.
I SAID--
--OUT OF MY WAY, GREEN!

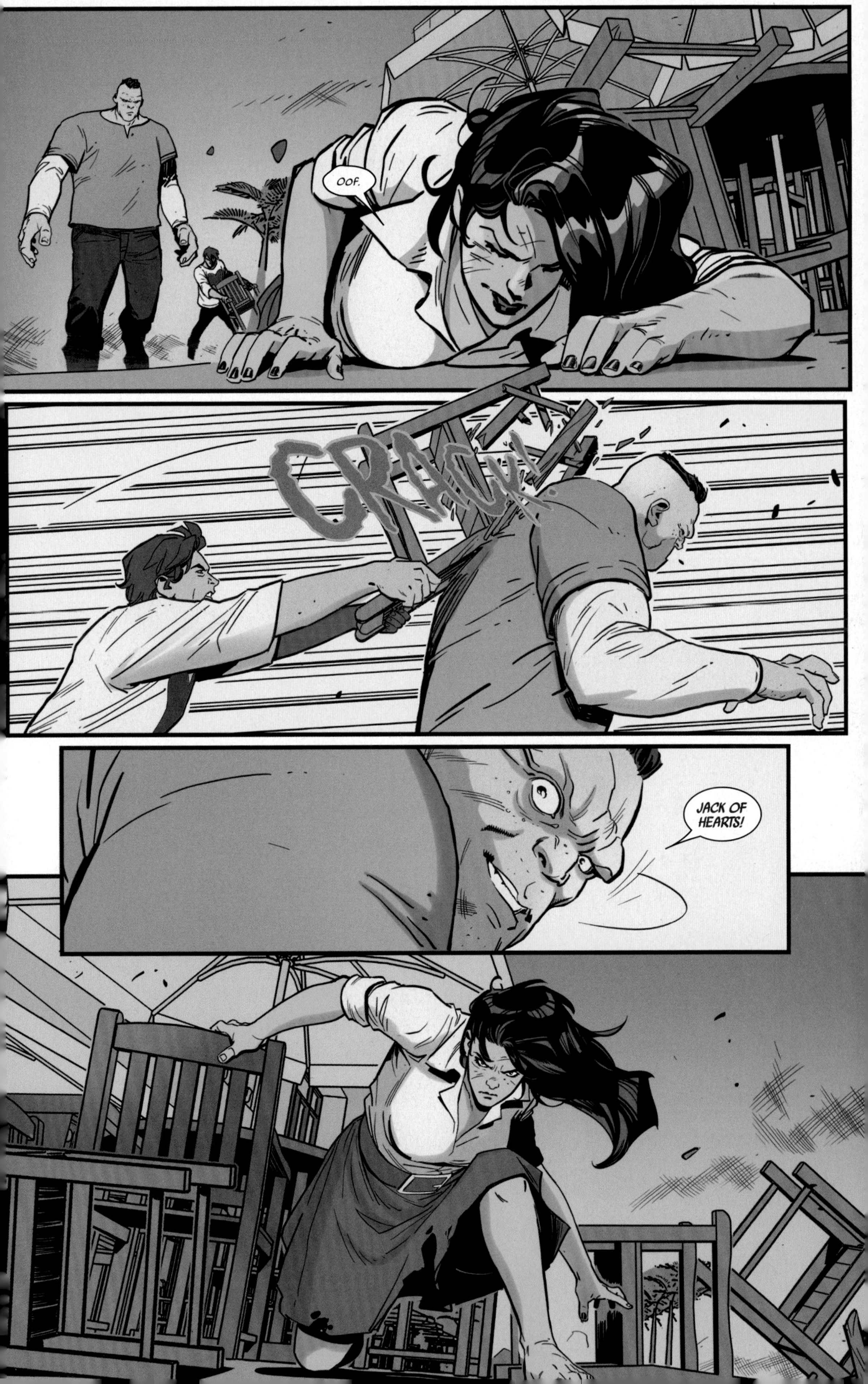
OOF.
CRACK!
JACK OF HEARTS!

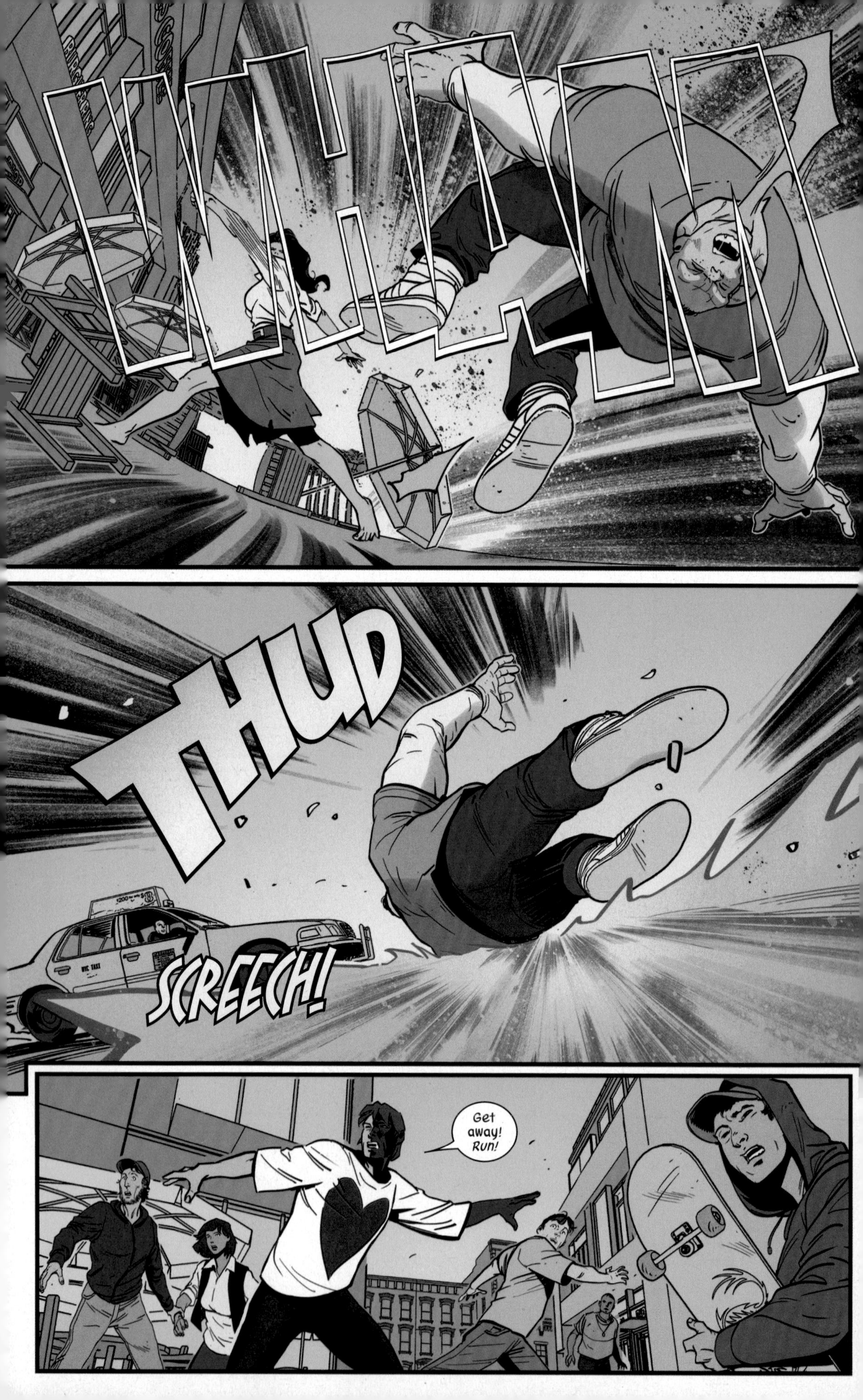
WHAM
THUD
SCREECH!
Get away! Run!

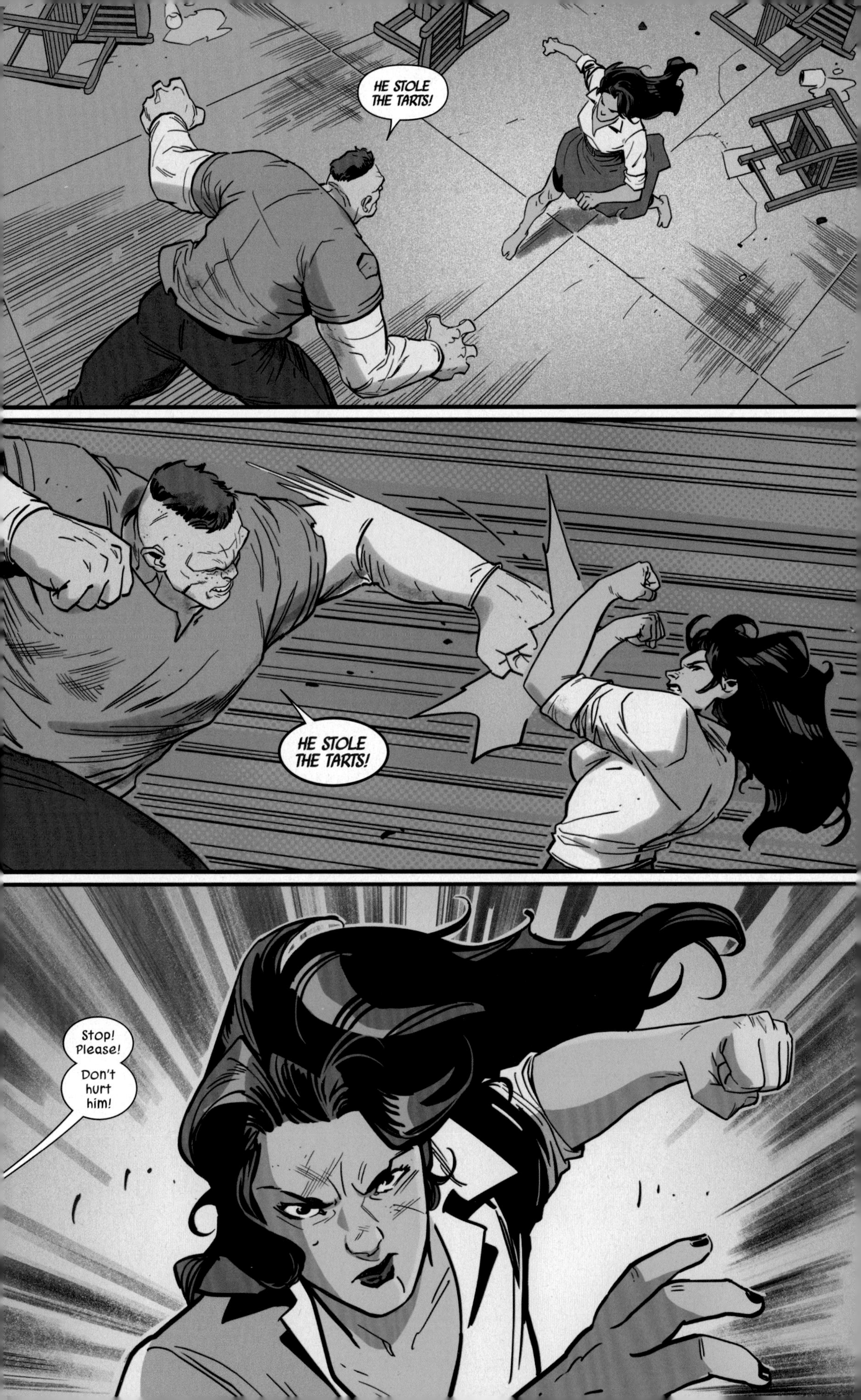
HE STOLE THE TARTS!
HE STOLE THE TARTS!
Stop! Please!
Don't hurt him!

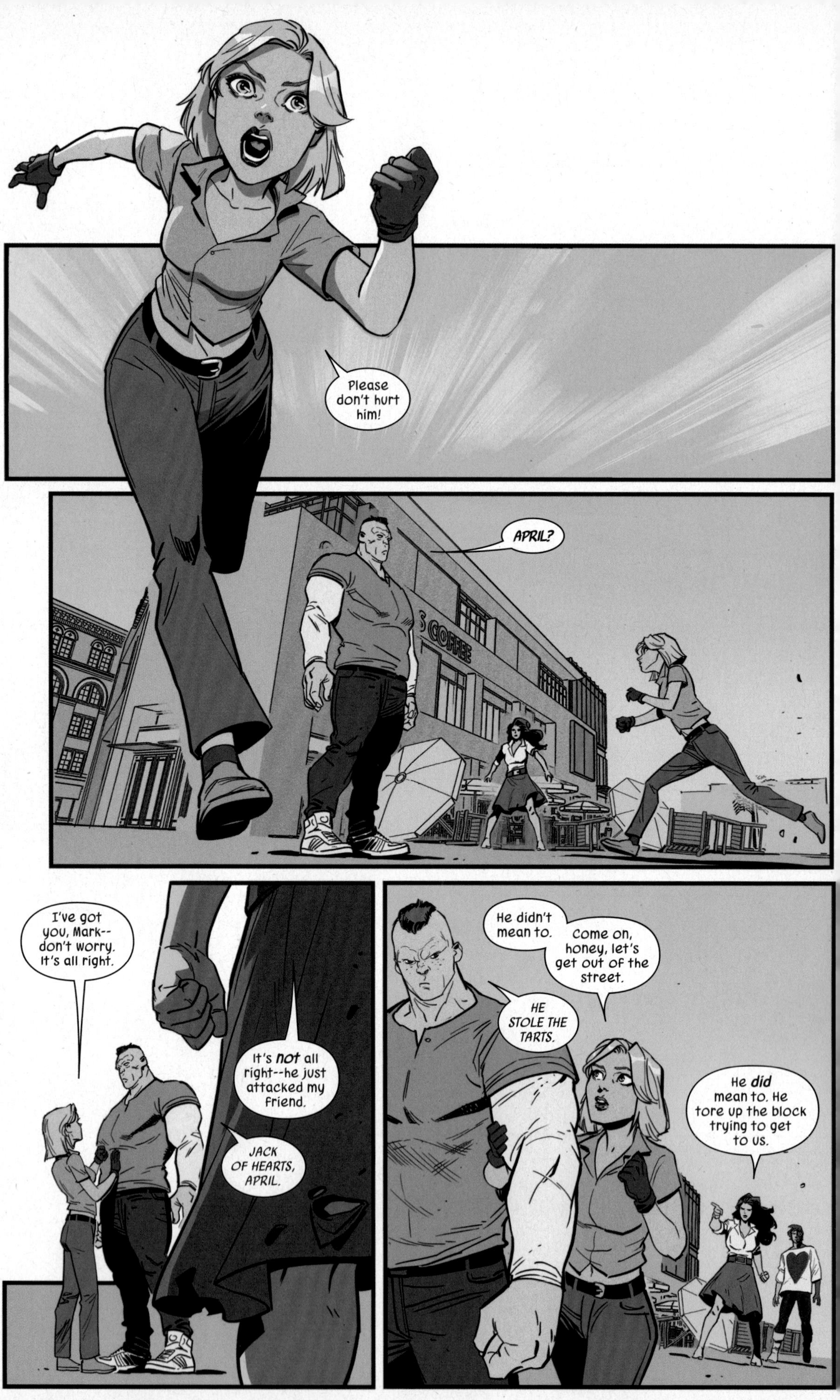
Please don't hurt him!
APRIL?
I've got you, Mark-- don't worry. It's all right.
It's *not* all right--he just attacked my friend.
JACK OF HEARTS, APRIL.
He didn't mean to.
Come on, honey, let's get out of the street.
HE STOLE THE TARTS.
He *did* mean to. He tore up the block trying to get to us.
S COFFEE

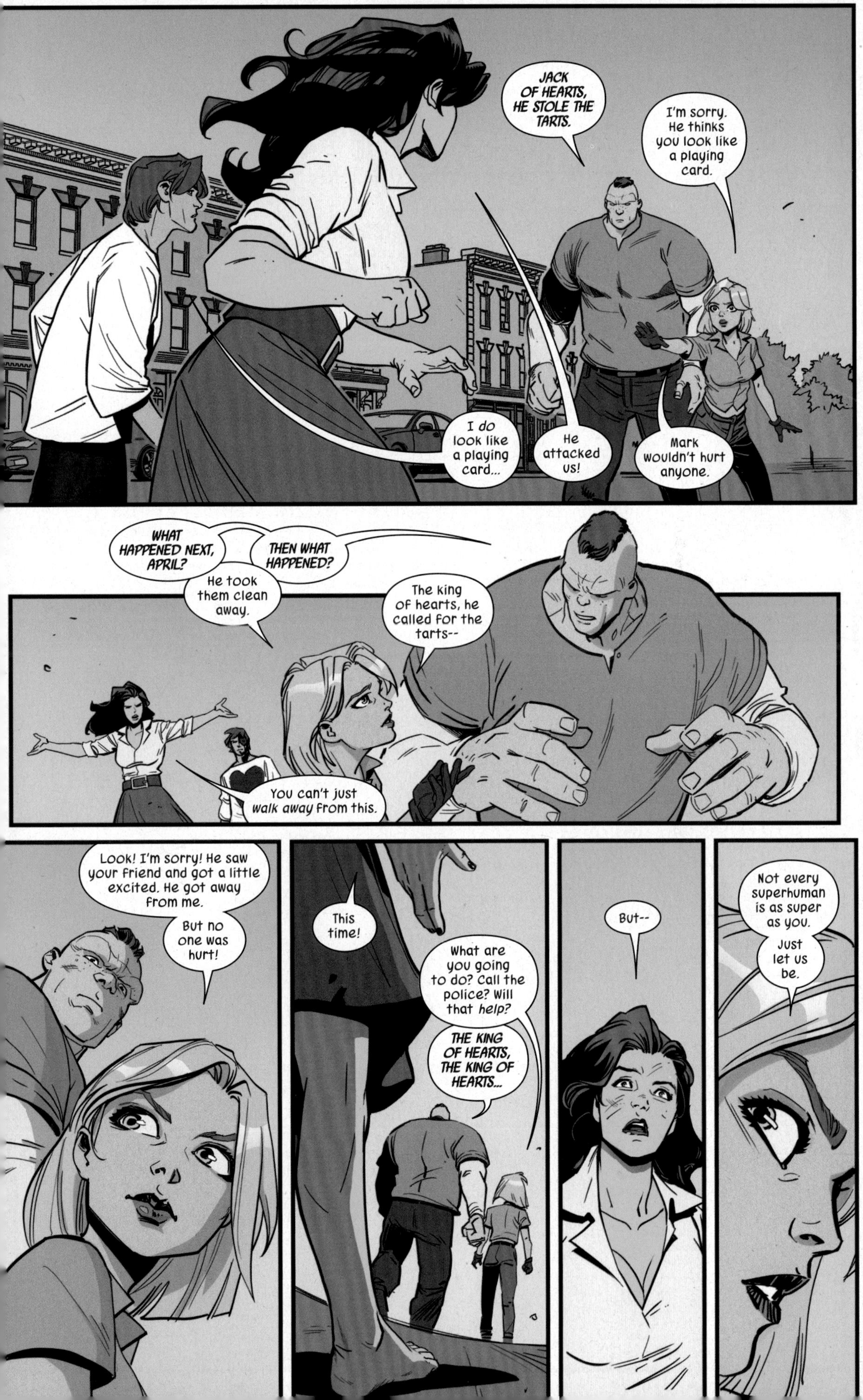
JACK OF HEARTS, HE STOLE THE TARTS.
I'm sorry. He thinks you look like a playing card.
I do look like a playing card...
He attacked us!
Mark wouldn't hurt anyone.
WHAT HAPPENED NEXT, APRIL?
THEN WHAT HAPPENED?
He took them clean away.
The king of hearts, he called for the tarts--
You can't just walk away from this.
Look! I'm sorry! He saw your friend and got a little excited. He got away from me.
But no one was hurt!
This time!
What are you going to do? Call the police? Will that help?
THE KING OF HEARTS, THE KING OF HEARTS...
But--
Not every superhuman is as super as you.
Just let us be.

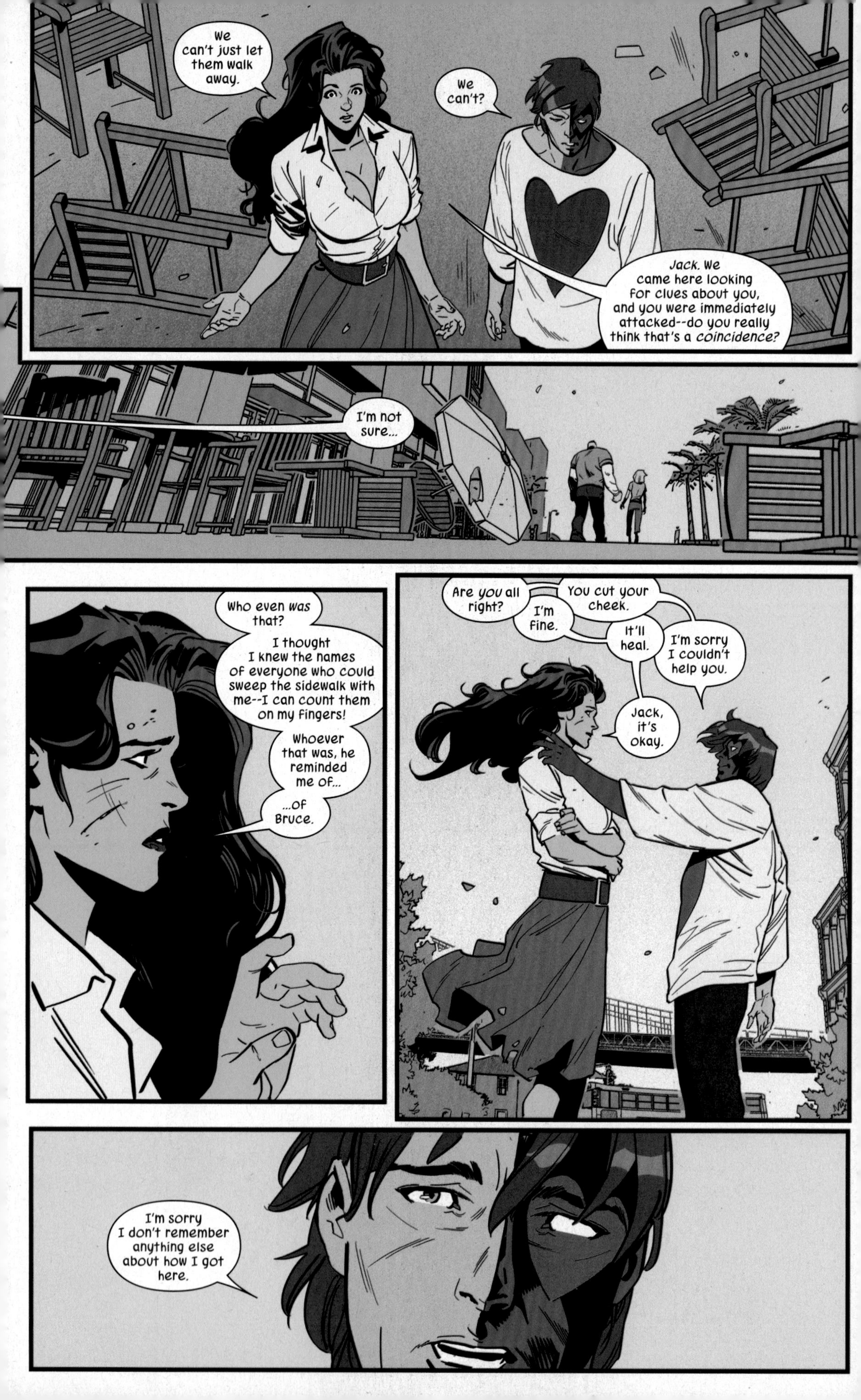
We can't just let them walk away.
We can't?
Jack. We came here looking for clues about you, and you were immediately attacked--do you really think that's a coincidence?
I'm not sure...
Who even was that?
I thought I knew the names of everyone who could sweep the sidewalk with me--I can count them on my fingers!
Whoever that was, he reminded me of...
...of Bruce.
Are you all right?
I'm fine.
You cut your cheek.
It'll heal.
I'm sorry I couldn't help you.
Jack, it's okay.
I'm sorry I don't remember anything else about how I got here.

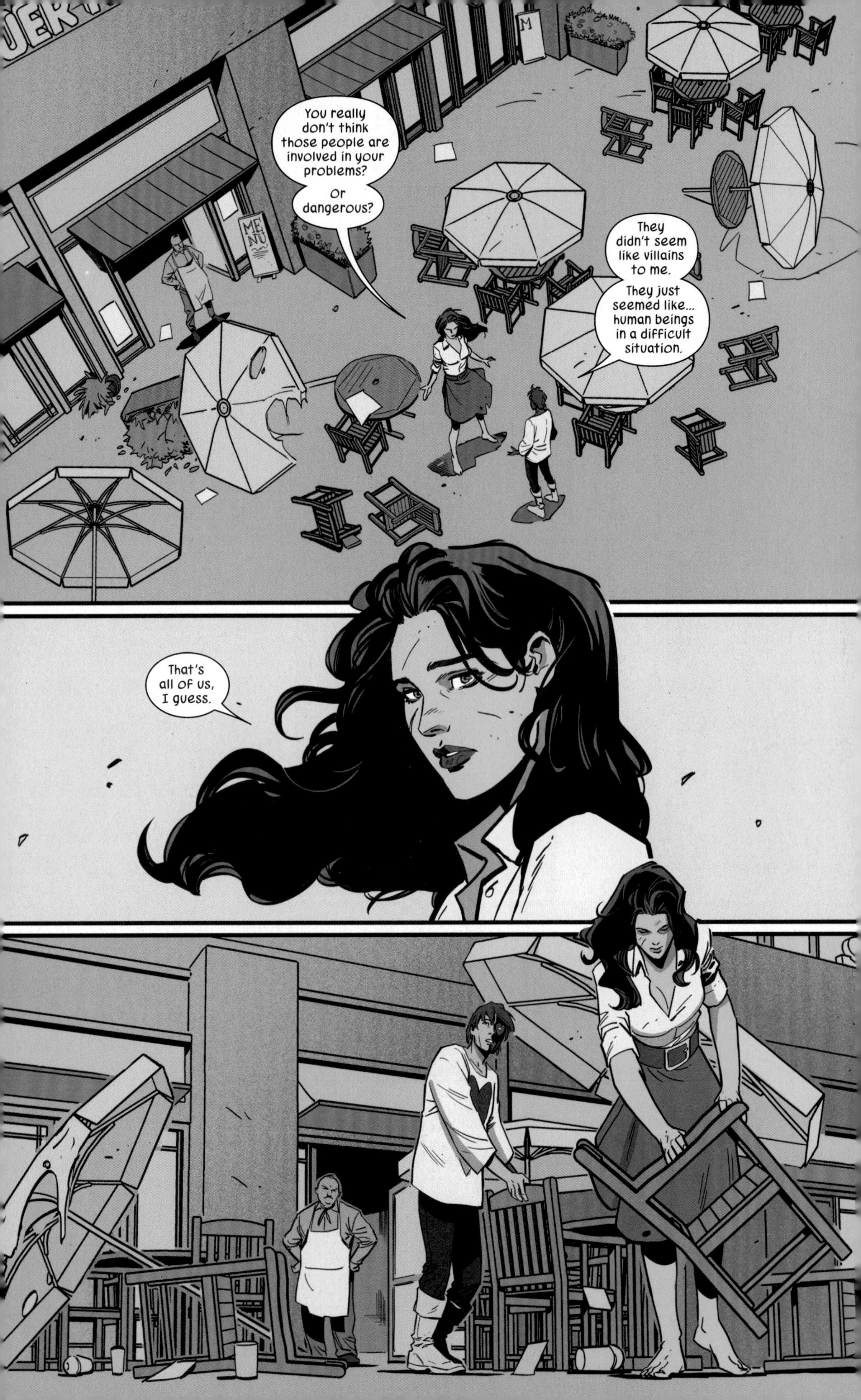
You really don't think those people are involved in your problems?
Or dangerous?
They didn't seem like villains to me.
They just seemed like... human beings in a difficult situation.
That's all of us, I guess.

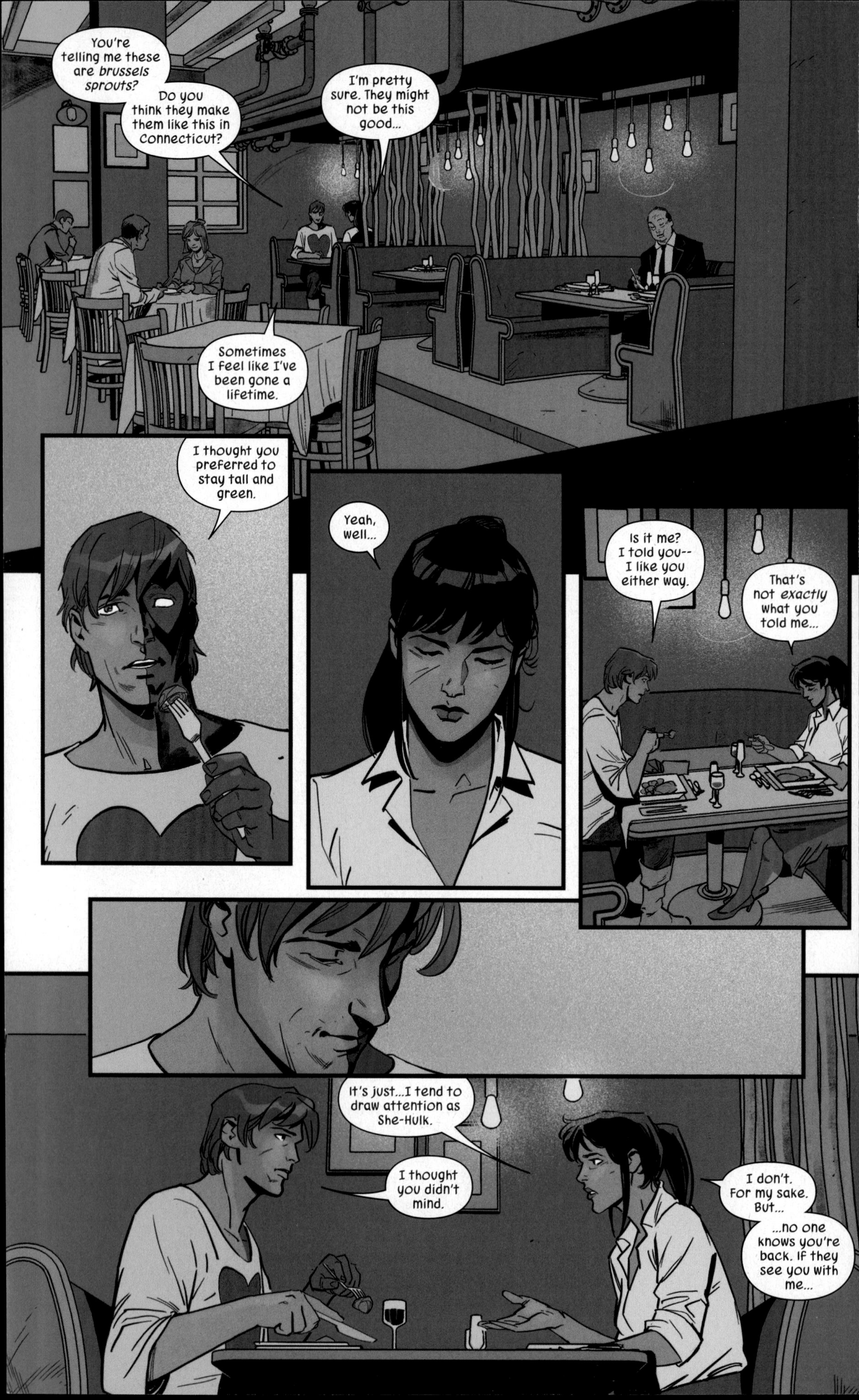
You're telling me these are *brussels sprouts?*
Do you think they make them like this in Connecticut?
I'm pretty sure. They might not be this good...
Sometimes I feel like I've been gone a lifetime.
I thought you preferred to stay tall and green.
Yeah, well...
Is it me? I told you-- I like you either way.
That's not *exactly* what you told me...
It's just...I tend to draw attention as She-Hulk.
I thought you didn't mind.
I don't. For my sake. But...
...no one knows you're back. If they see you with me...

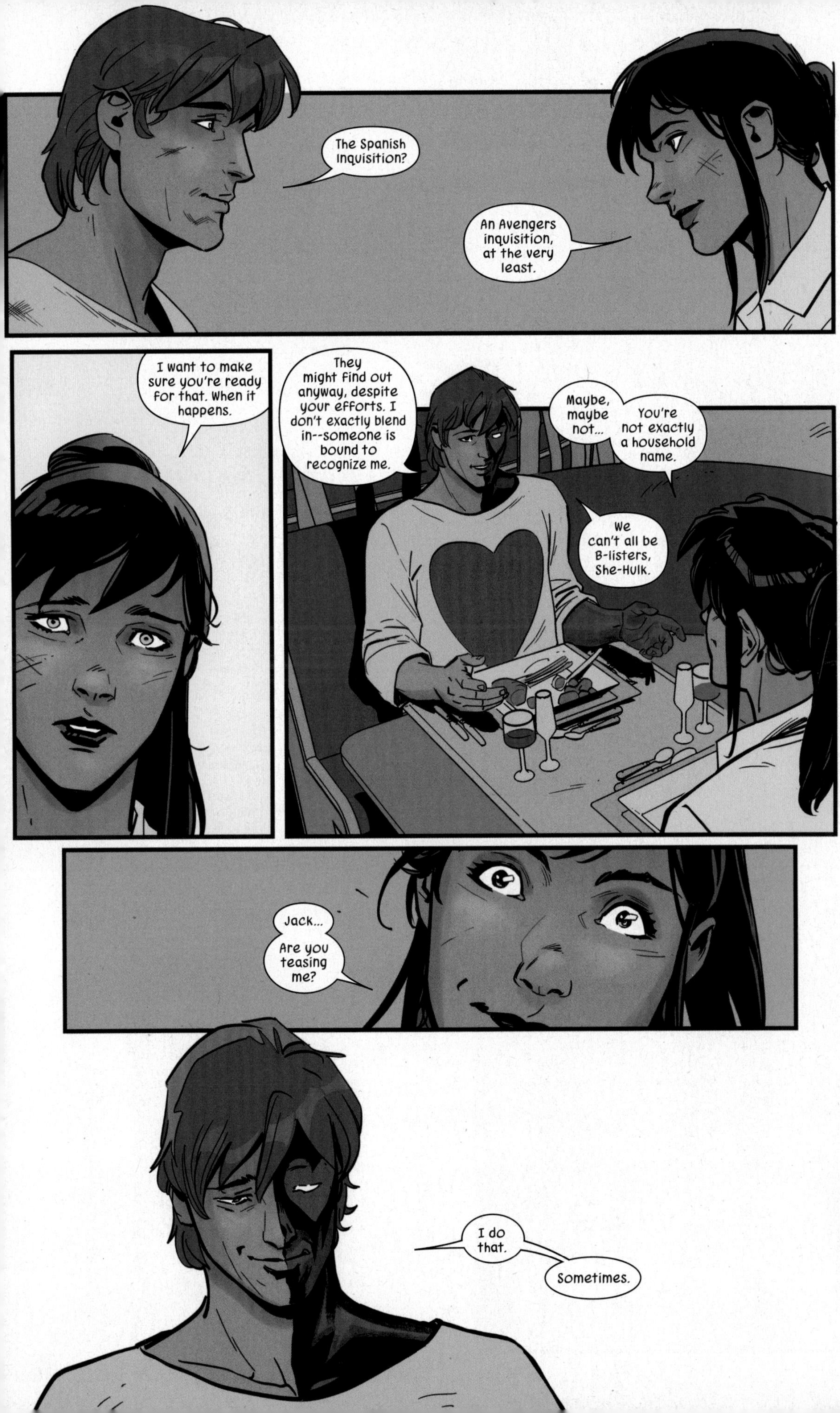
The Spanish Inquisition?
An Avengers inquisition, at the very least.
I want to make sure you're ready for that. When it happens.
They might find out anyway, despite your efforts. I don't exactly blend in--someone is bound to recognize me.
Maybe, maybe not...
You're not exactly a household name.
We can't all be B-listers, She-Hulk.
Jack...
Are you teasing me?
I do that.
Sometimes.

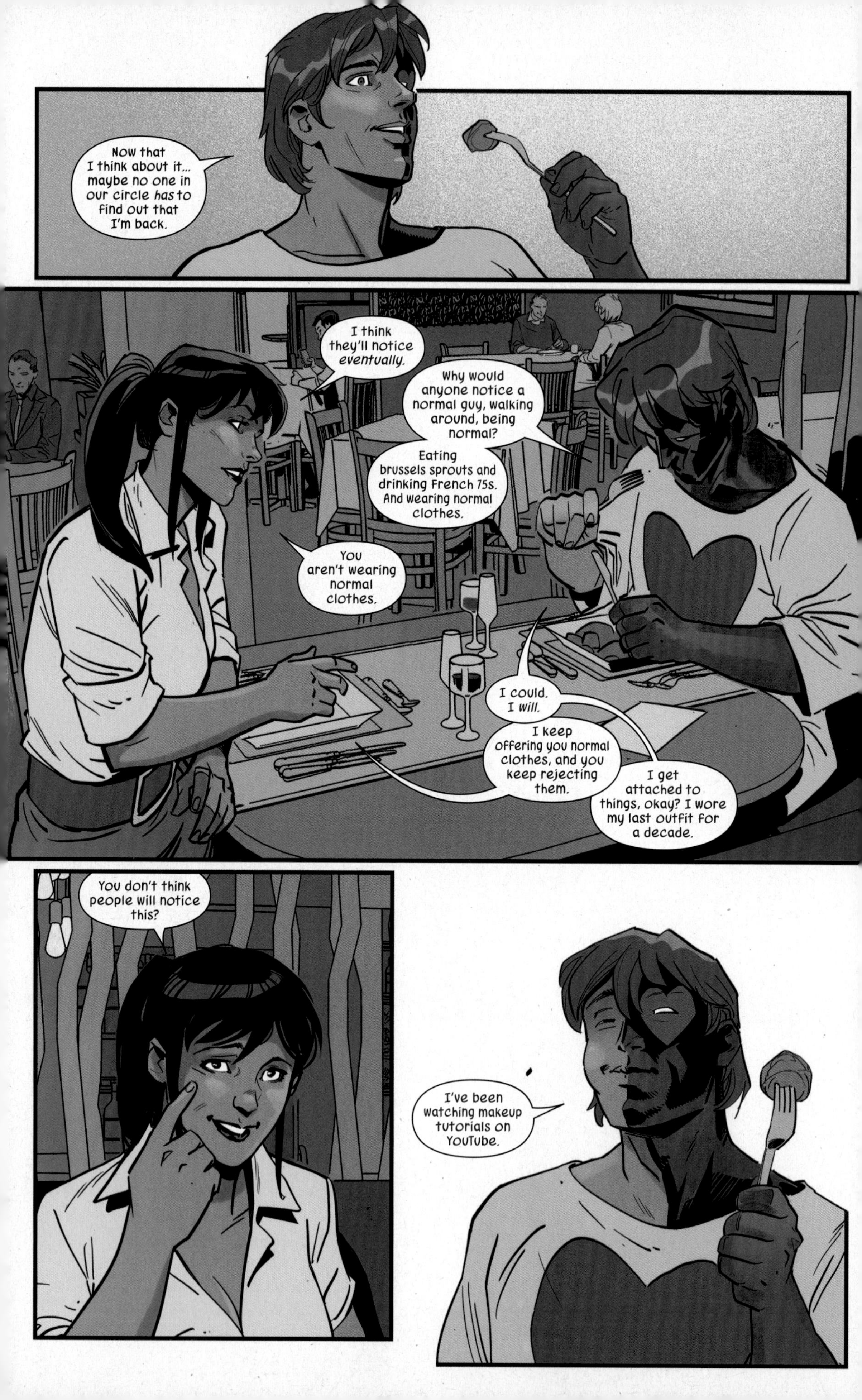

Now that I think about it... maybe no one in our circle *has* to find out that I'm back.
I think they'll notice *eventually.*
Why would anyone notice a normal guy, walking around, being normal?
Eating brussels sprouts and drinking French 75s. And wearing normal clothes.
You aren't wearing normal clothes.
I could. I *will.*
I keep offering you normal clothes, and you keep rejecting them.
I get attached to things, okay? I wore my last outfit for a decade.
You don't think people will notice this?
I've been watching makeup tutorials on YouTube.

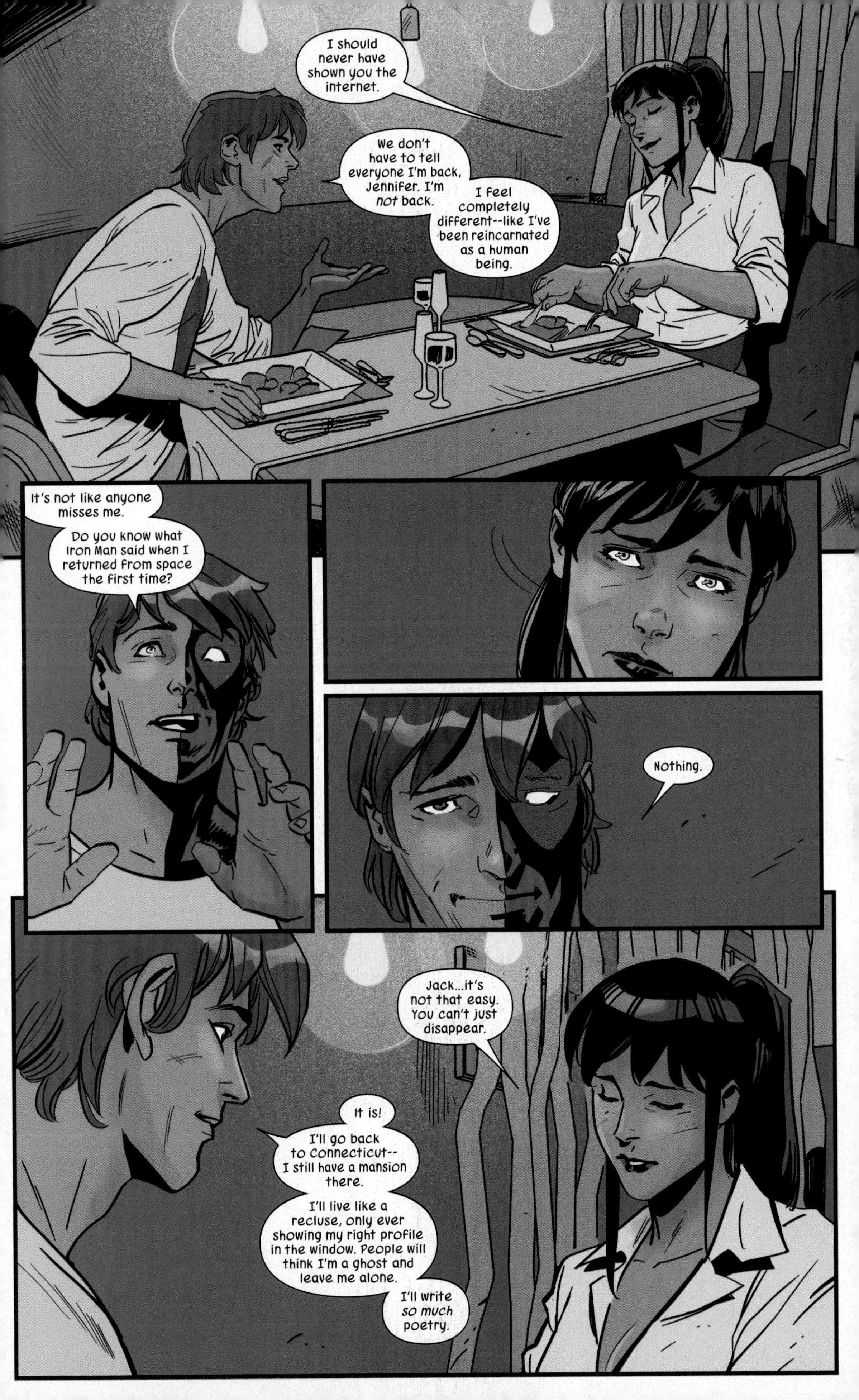
I should never have shown you the internet.
We don't have to tell everyone I'm back, Jennifer. I'm *not* back.
I feel completely different--like I've been reincarnated as a human being.
It's not like anyone misses me.
Do you know what Iron Man said when I returned from space the first time?
Nothing.
Jack...it's not that easy. You can't just disappear.
It is!
I'll go back to Connecticut-- I still have a mansion there.
I'll live like a recluse, only ever showing my right profile in the window. People will think I'm a ghost and leave me alone.
I'll write *so much* poetry.

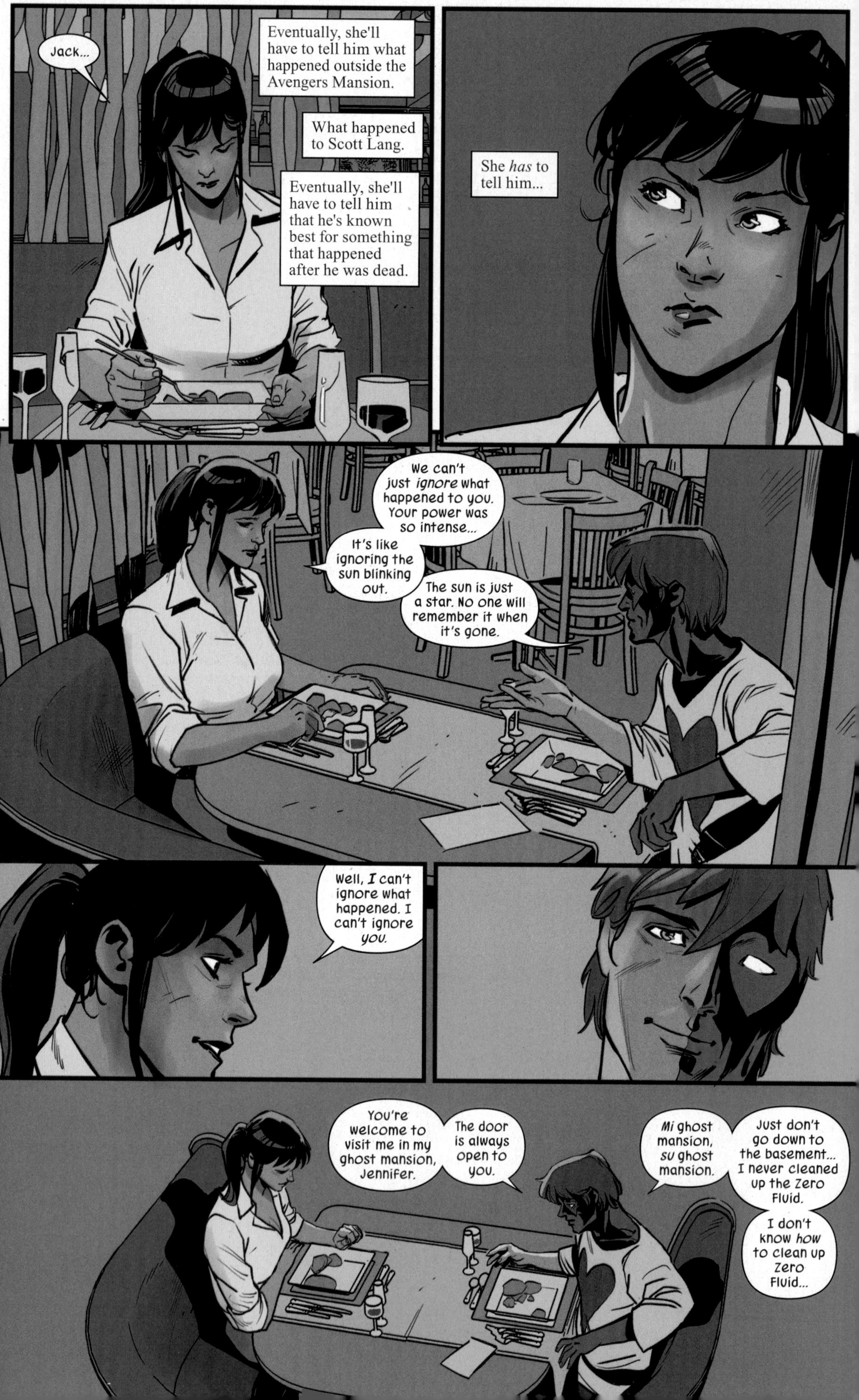
Jack...
Eventually, she'll have to tell him what happened outside the Avengers Mansion.
What happened to Scott Lang.
Eventually, she'll have to tell him that he's known best for something that happened after he was dead.
She *has* to tell him...
We can't just *ignore* what happened to you. Your power was so intense...
It's like ignoring the sun blinking out.
The sun is just a star. No one will remember it when it's gone.
Well, *I* can't ignore what happened. I can't ignore *you*.
You're welcome to visit me in my ghost mansion, Jennifer.
The door is always open to you.
Mi ghost mansion, *su* ghost mansion.
Just don't go down to the basement... I never cleaned up the Zero Fluid.
I don't know *how* to clean up Zero Fluid...

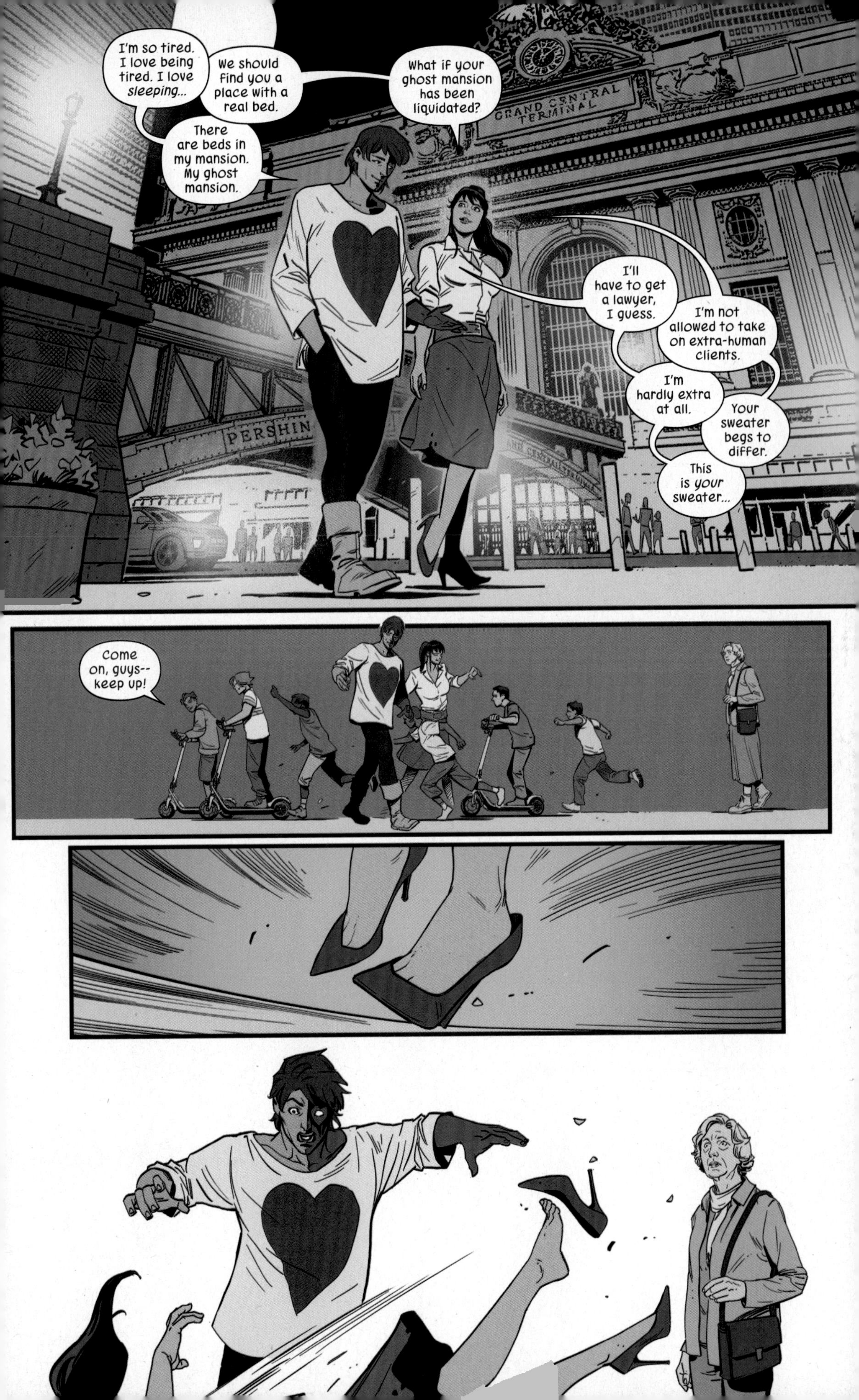
I'm so tired. I love being tired. I love *sleeping*...
We should find you a place with a real bed.
There are beds in my mansion. My ghost mansion.
What if your ghost mansion has been liquidated?
GRAND CENTRAL TERMINAL
I'll have to get a lawyer, I guess.
I'm not allowed to take on extra-human clients.
I'm hardly extra at all.
Your sweater begs to differ.
This is *your* sweater...
PERSHIN
Come on, guys-- keep up!

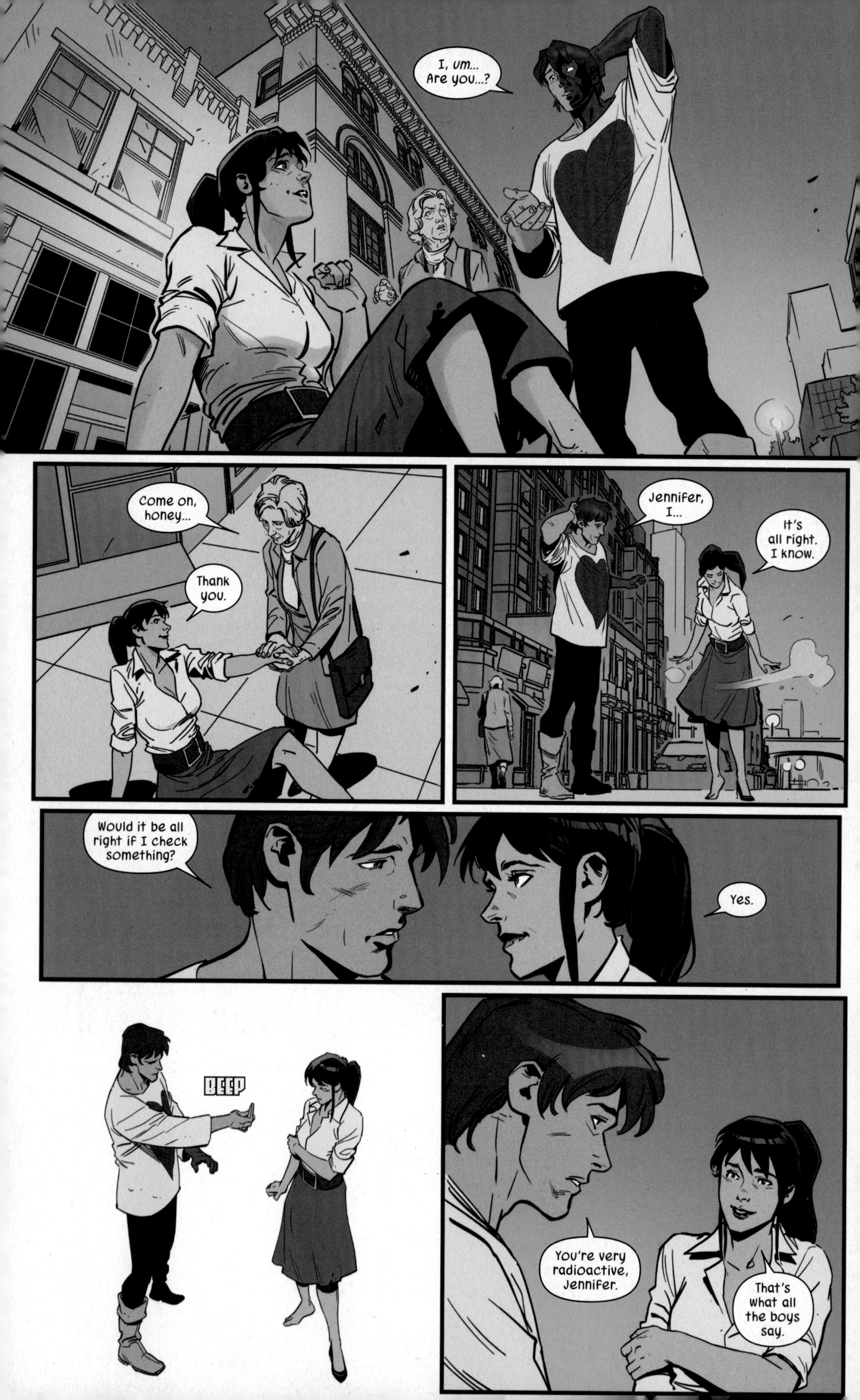
I, um...
Are you...?
Come on, honey...
Thank you.
Jennifer, I...
It's all right. I know.
Would it be all right if I check something?
Yes.
BEEP
You're very radioactive, Jennifer.
That's what all the boys say.

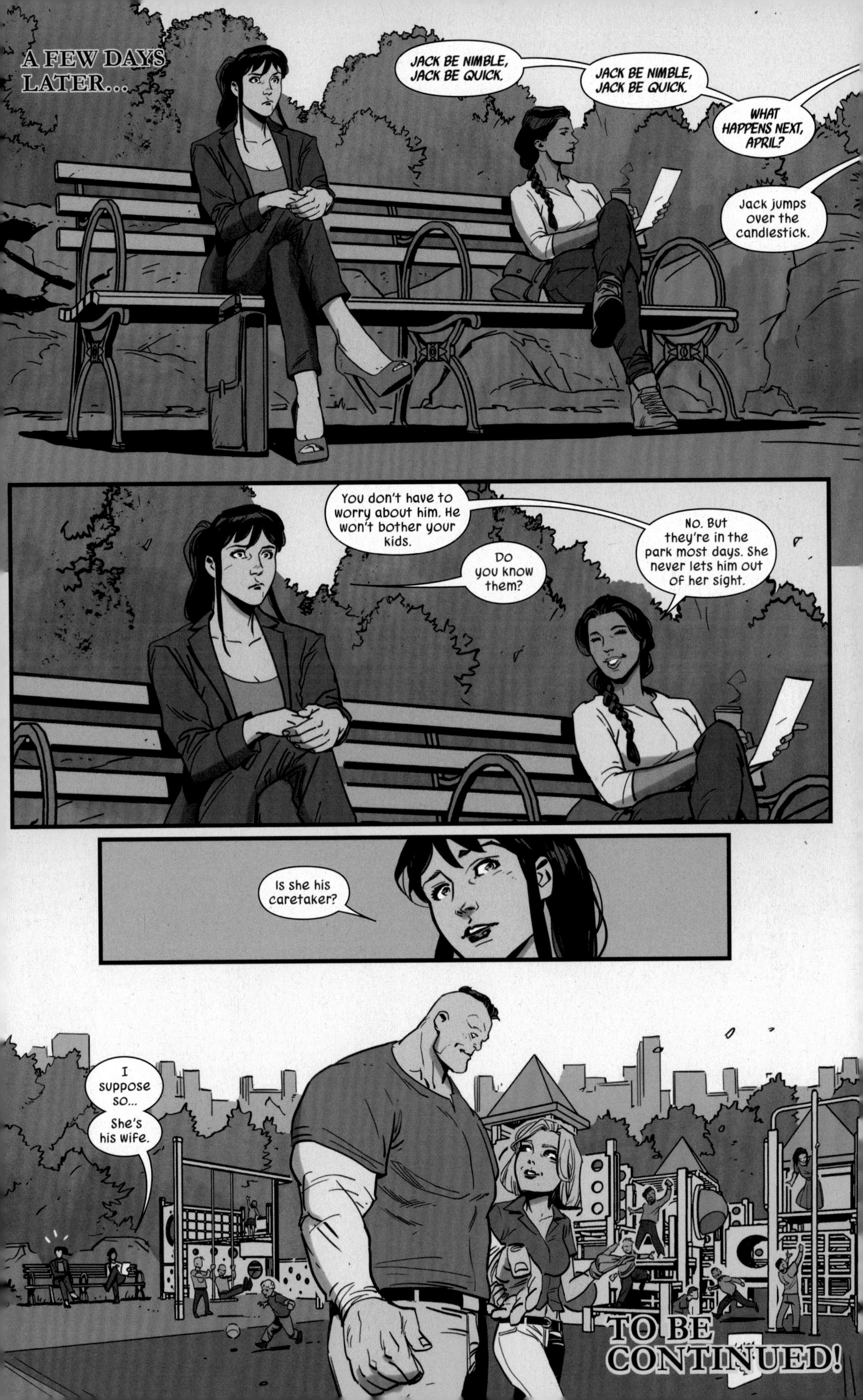
A FEW DAYS LATER...
JACK BE NIMBLE, JACK BE QUICK.
JACK BE NIMBLE, JACK BE QUICK.
WHAT HAPPENS NEXT, APRIL?
Jack jumps over the candlestick.
You don't have to worry about him. He won't bother your kids.
Do you know them?
No. But they're in the park most days. She never lets him out of her sight.
Is she his caretaker?
I suppose so...
She's his wife.
TO BE CONTINUED!

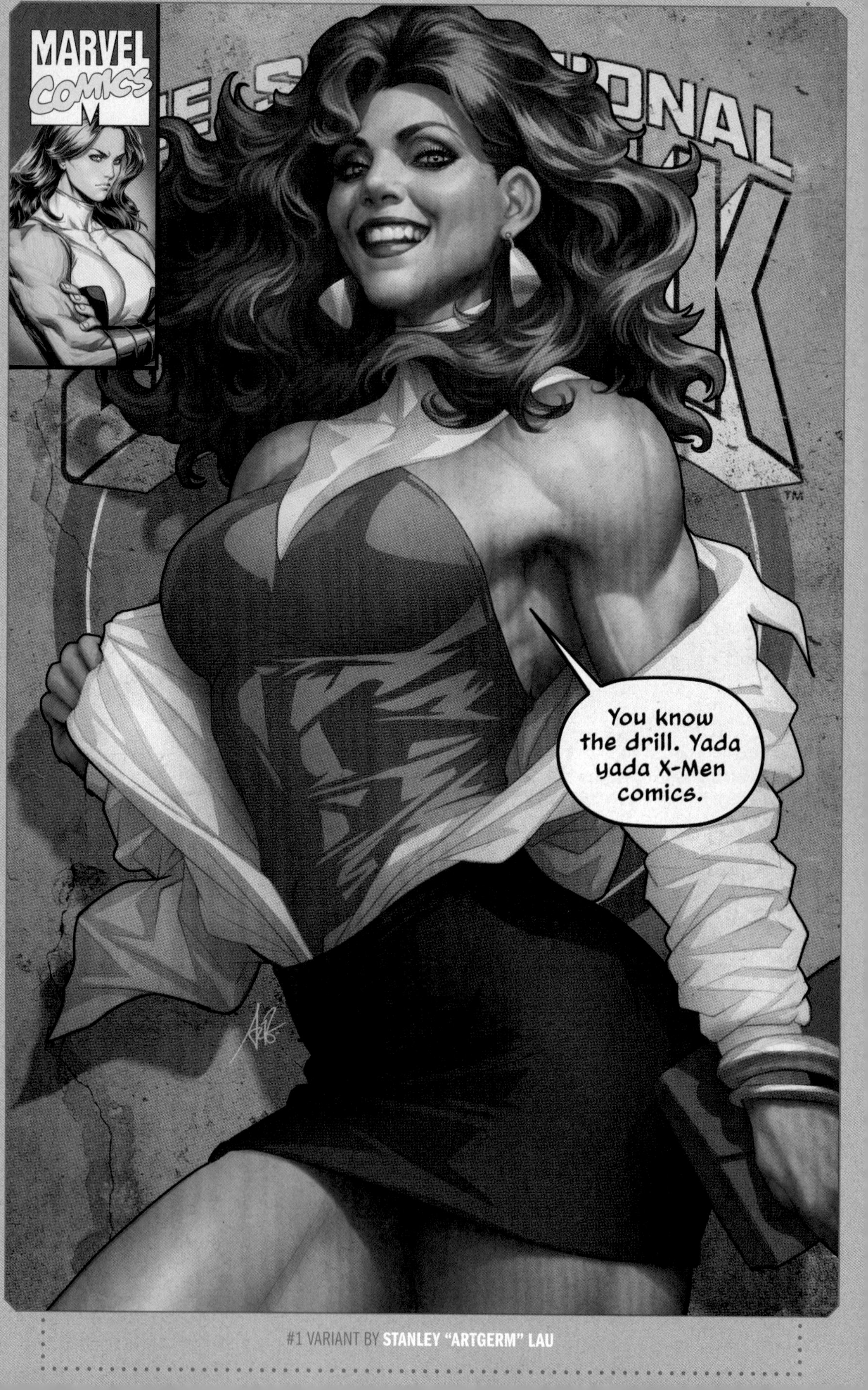
MARVEL COMICS
You know the drill. Yada yada X-Men comics.

#1 VARIANT BY **STANLEY "ARTGERM" LAU**

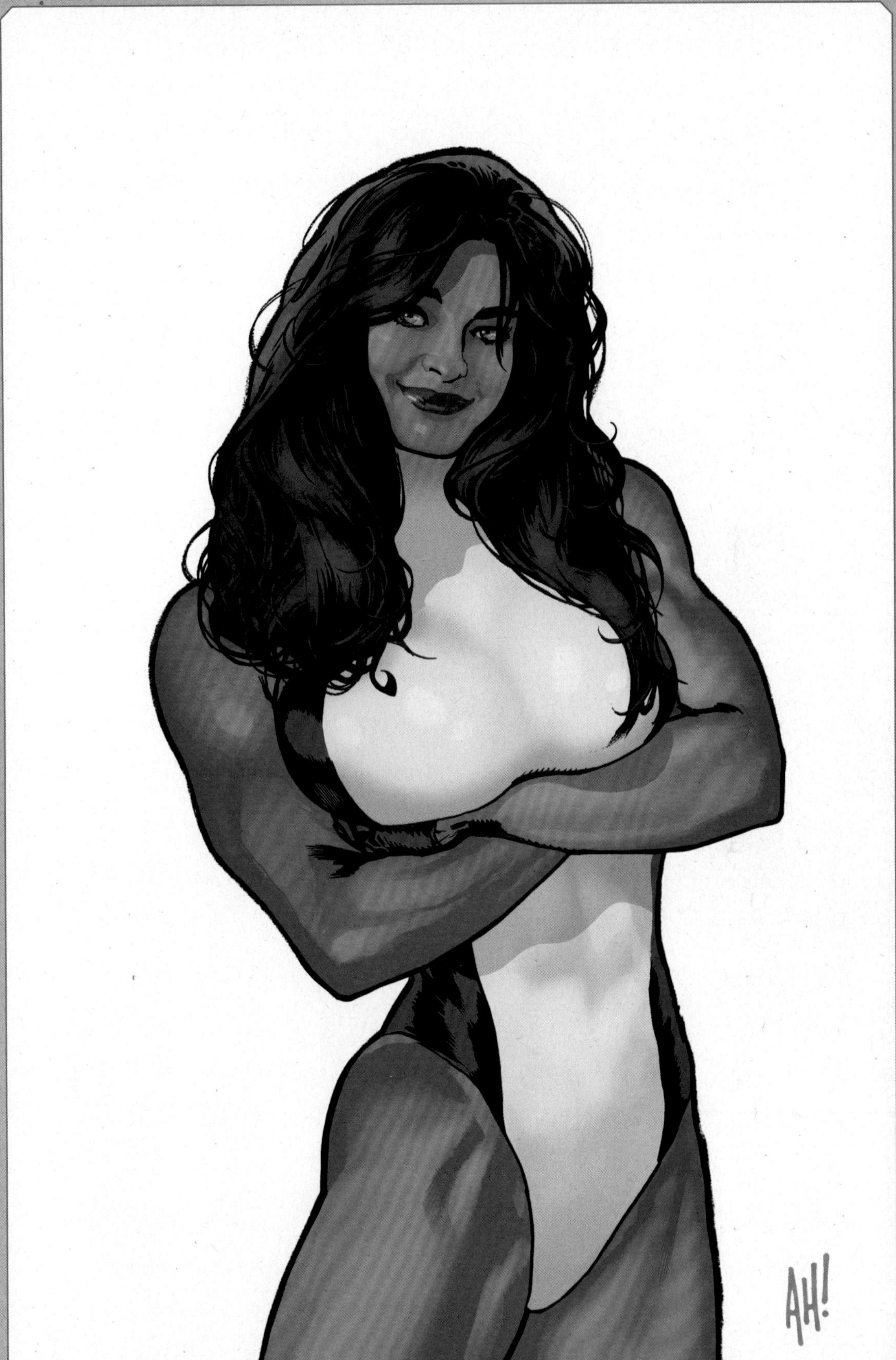
AH!

#1 VARIANT BY **ADAM HUGHES**

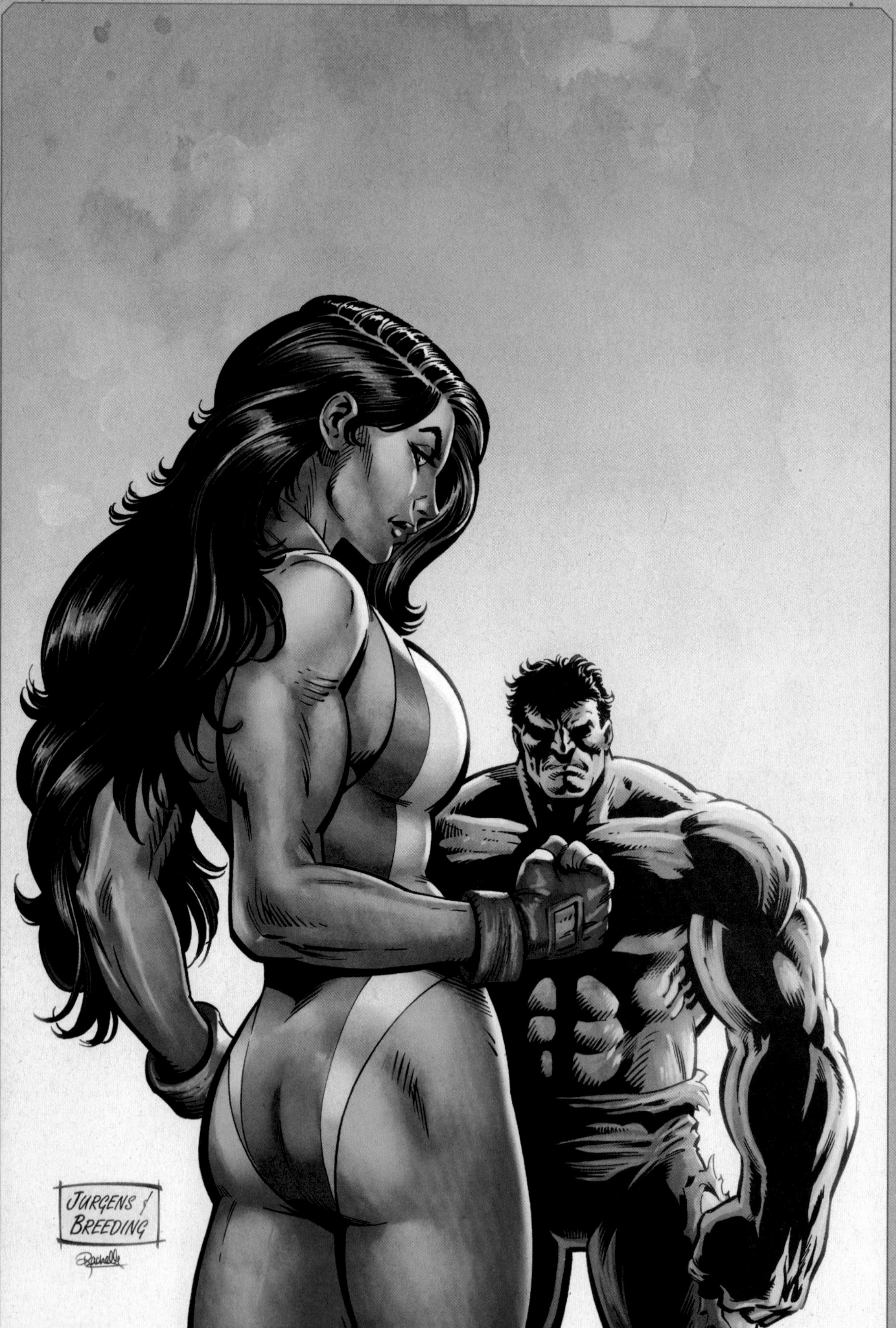
JURGENS & BREEDING
Rachelle

#1 VARIANT BY **DAN JURGENS**, **BRETT BREEDING** & **RACHELLE ROSENBERG**

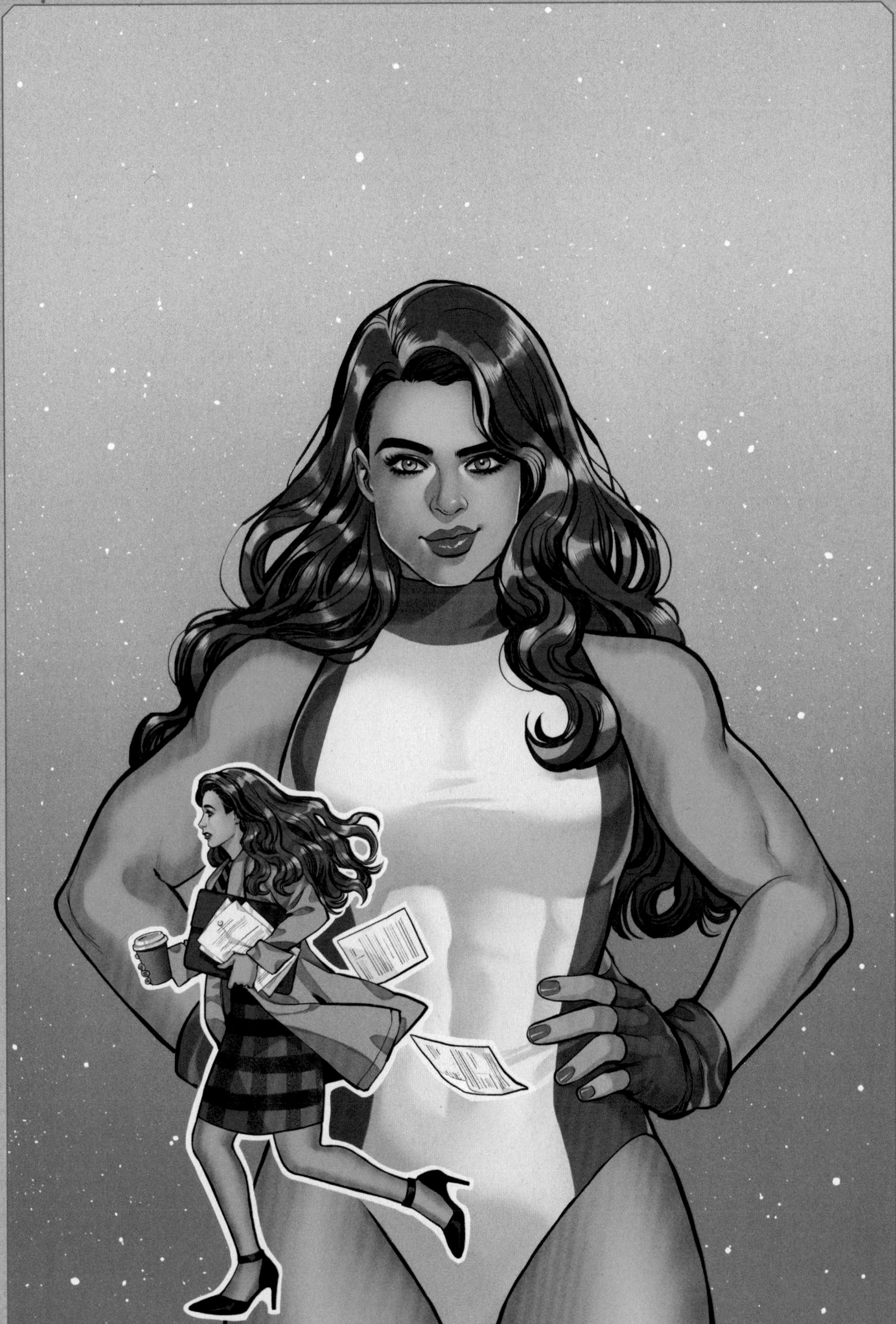

#2 VARIANT BY **ROMY JONES**

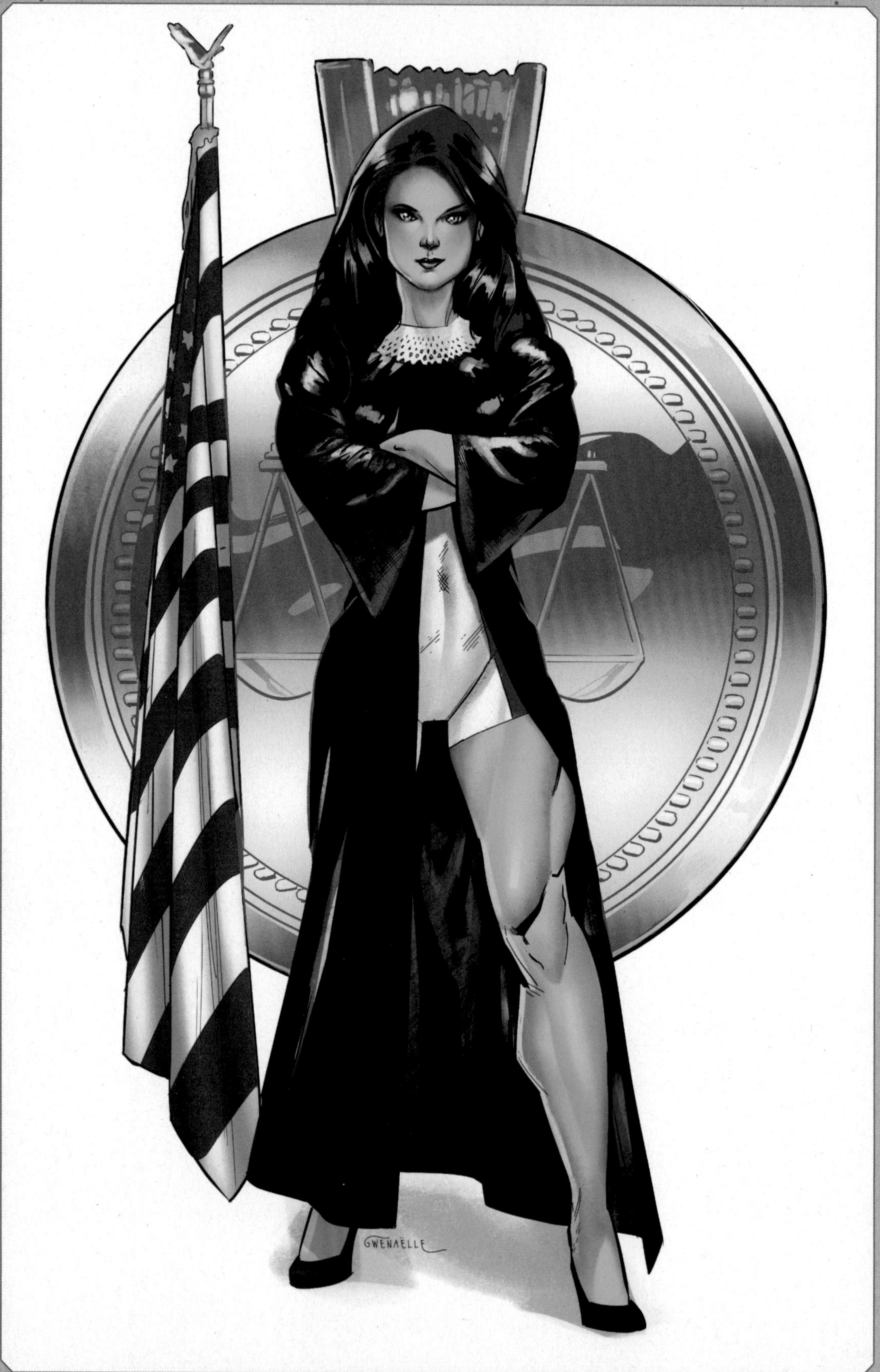
GWENAËLLE

#3 WOMEN'S HISTORY MONTH VARIANT BY **JAN BAZALDUA** & **GWENAËLLE DALIGAULT**

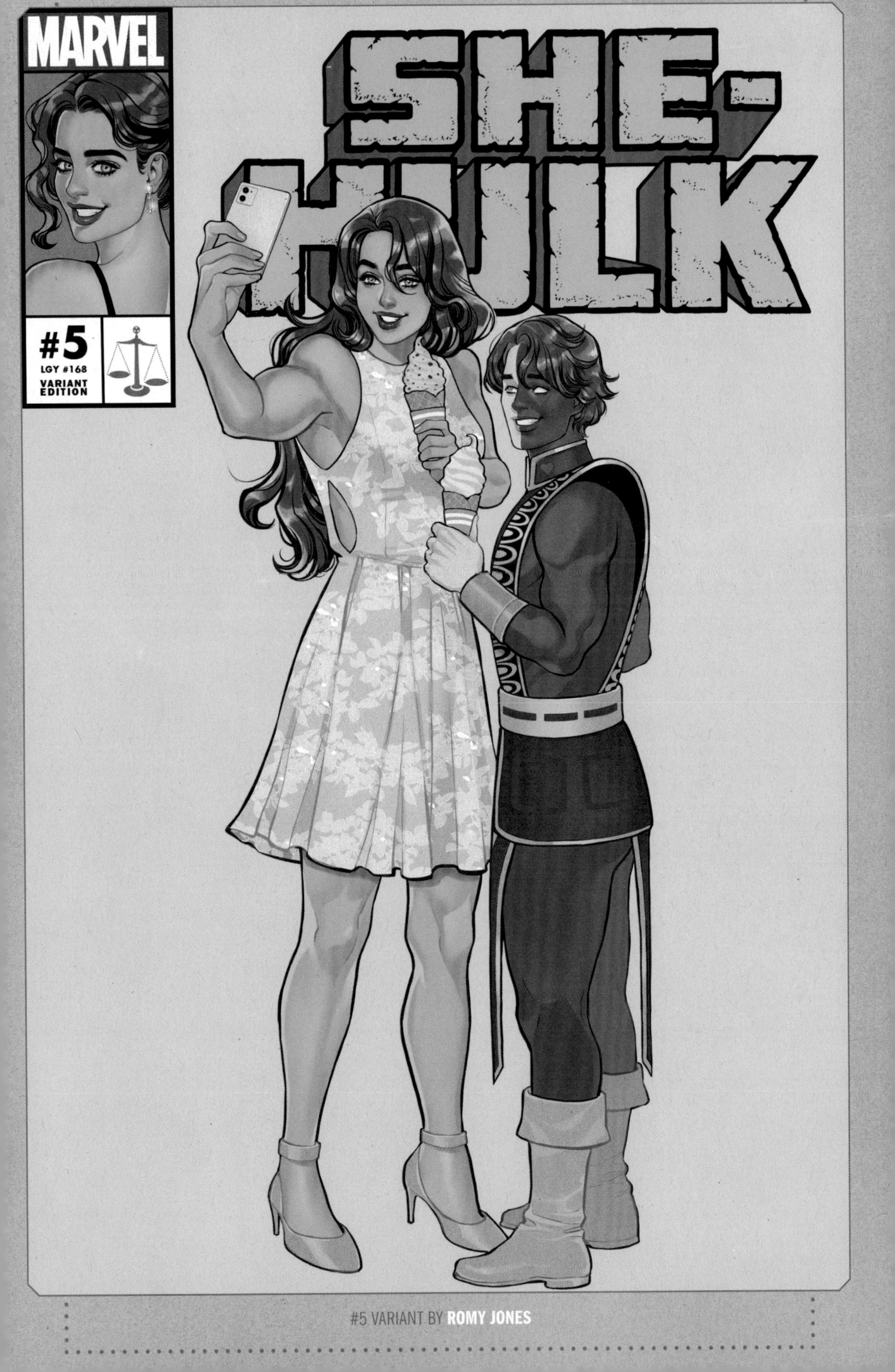
MARVEL
SHE-HULK
#5
LGY #168
VARIANT EDITION

#5 VARIANT BY **ROMY JONES**

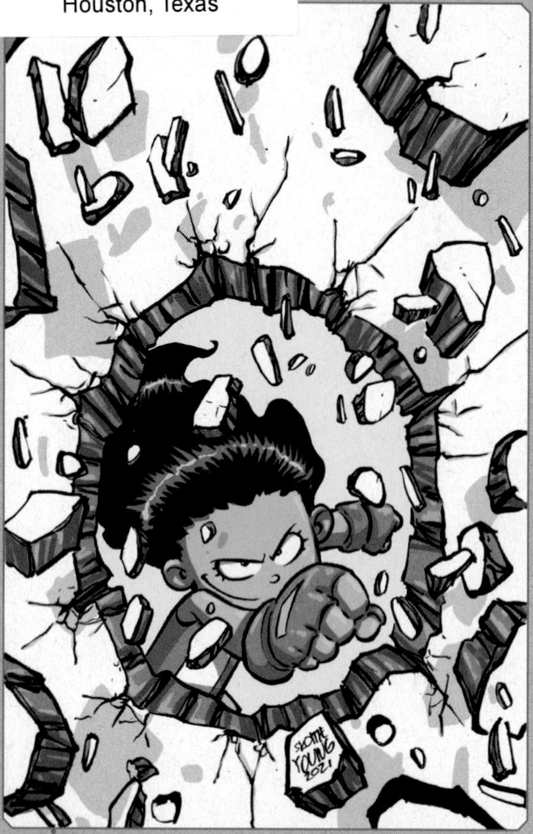
SKOTTIE YOUNG 2021

#1 VARIANT BY **SKOTTIE YOUNG**

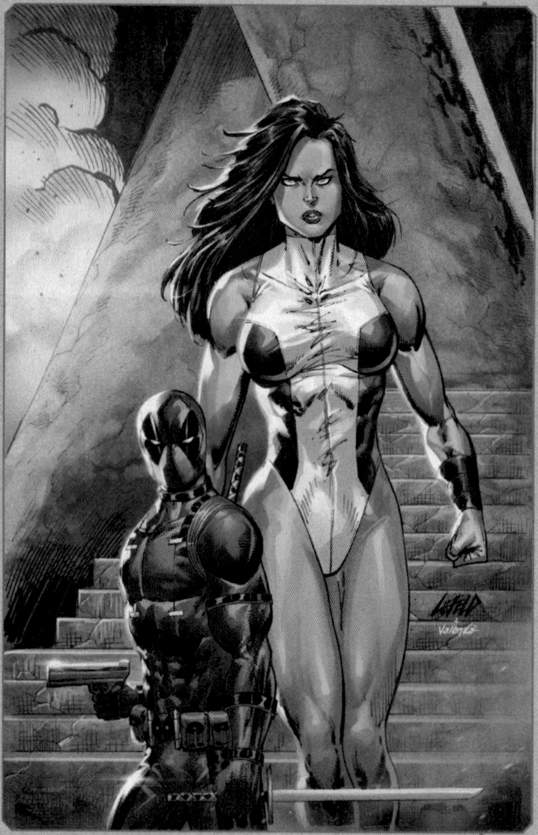

#1 DEADPOOL 30TH ANNIVERSARY VARIANT BY **ROB LIEFELD**

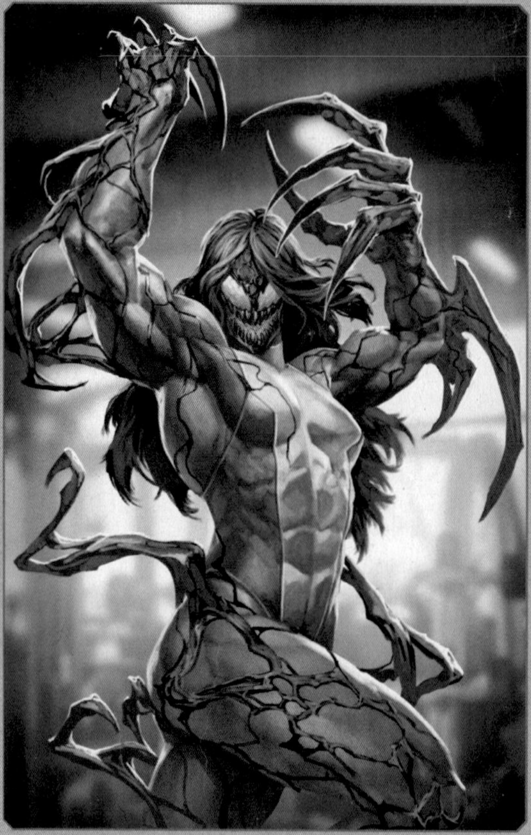

#3 CARNAGE FOREVER VARIANT BY **SKAN**

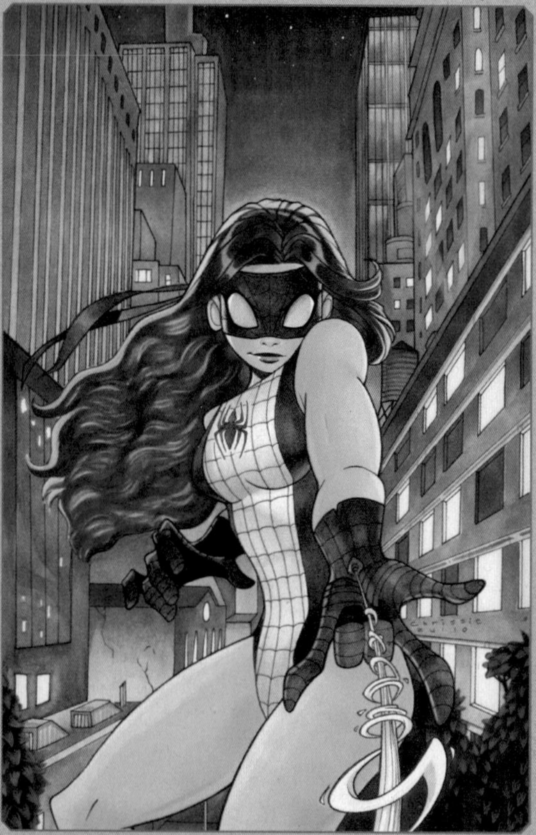

#4 SPIDER-MAN VARIANT BY **CHRISSIE ZULLO**

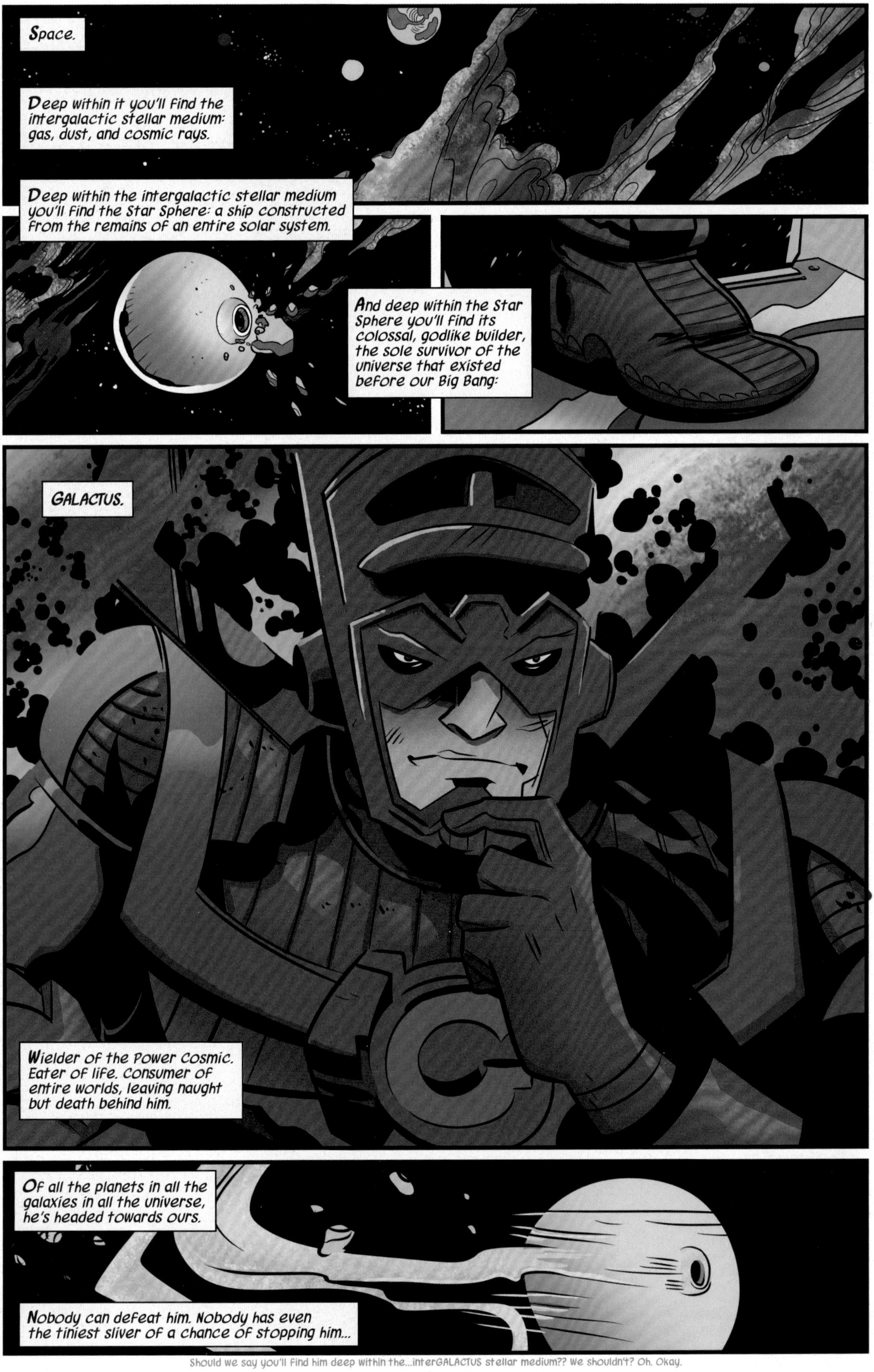
Space.
Deep within it you'll find the intergalactic stellar medium: gas, dust, and cosmic rays.
Deep within the intergalactic stellar medium you'll find the Star Sphere: a ship constructed from the remains of an entire solar system.
And deep within the Star Sphere you'll find its colossal, godlike builder, the sole survivor of the universe that existed before our Big Bang:
GALACTUS.
Wielder of the Power Cosmic. Eater of life. Consumer of entire worlds, leaving naught but death behind him.
Of all the planets in all the galaxies in all the universe, he's headed towards ours.
Nobody can defeat him. Nobody has even the tiniest sliver of a chance of stopping him...

Should we say you'll find him deep within the...interGALACTUS stellar medium?? We shouldn't? Oh. Okay.

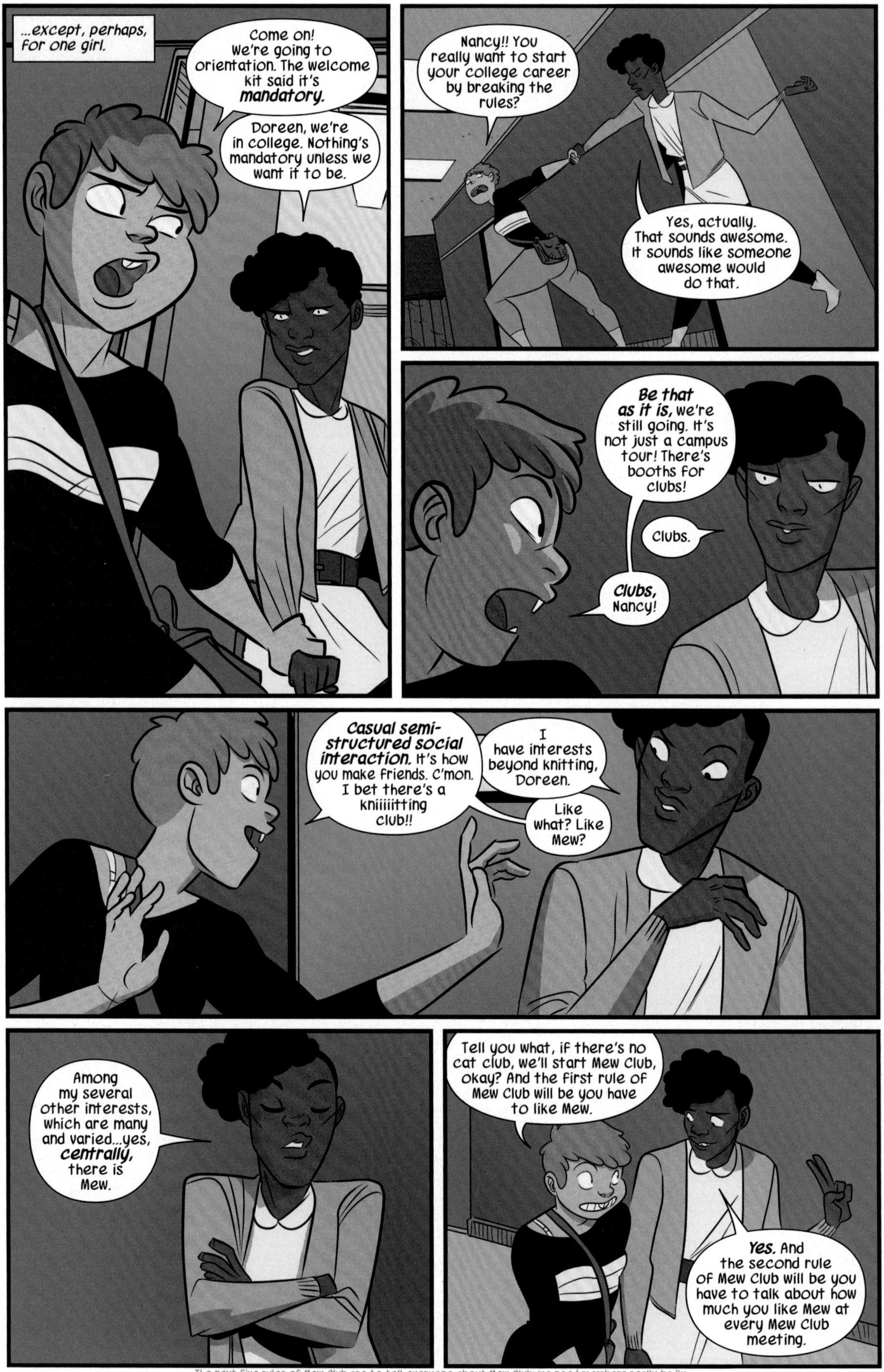
...except, perhaps, for one girl.
Come on! We're going to orientation. The welcome kit said it's *mandatory.*
Doreen, we're in college. Nothing's mandatory unless we want it to be.
Nancy!! You really want to start your college career by breaking the rules?
Yes, actually. That sounds awesome. It sounds like someone awesome would do that.
Be that as it is, we're still going. It's not just a campus tour! There's booths for clubs!
Clubs.
Clubs, Nancy!
Casual semi-structured social interaction. It's how you make friends. C'mon. I bet there's a kniiiiitting club!!
I have interests beyond knitting, Doreen.
Like what? Like Mew?
Among my several other interests, which are many and varied...yes, *centrally,* there is Mew.
Tell you what, if there's no cat club, we'll start Mew Club, okay? And the first rule of Mew Club will be you have to like Mew.
Yes. And the second rule of Mew Club will be you have to talk about how much you like Mew at every Mew Club meeting.

The next five rules of Mew Club are to tell everyone about Mew Club; we need members really badly

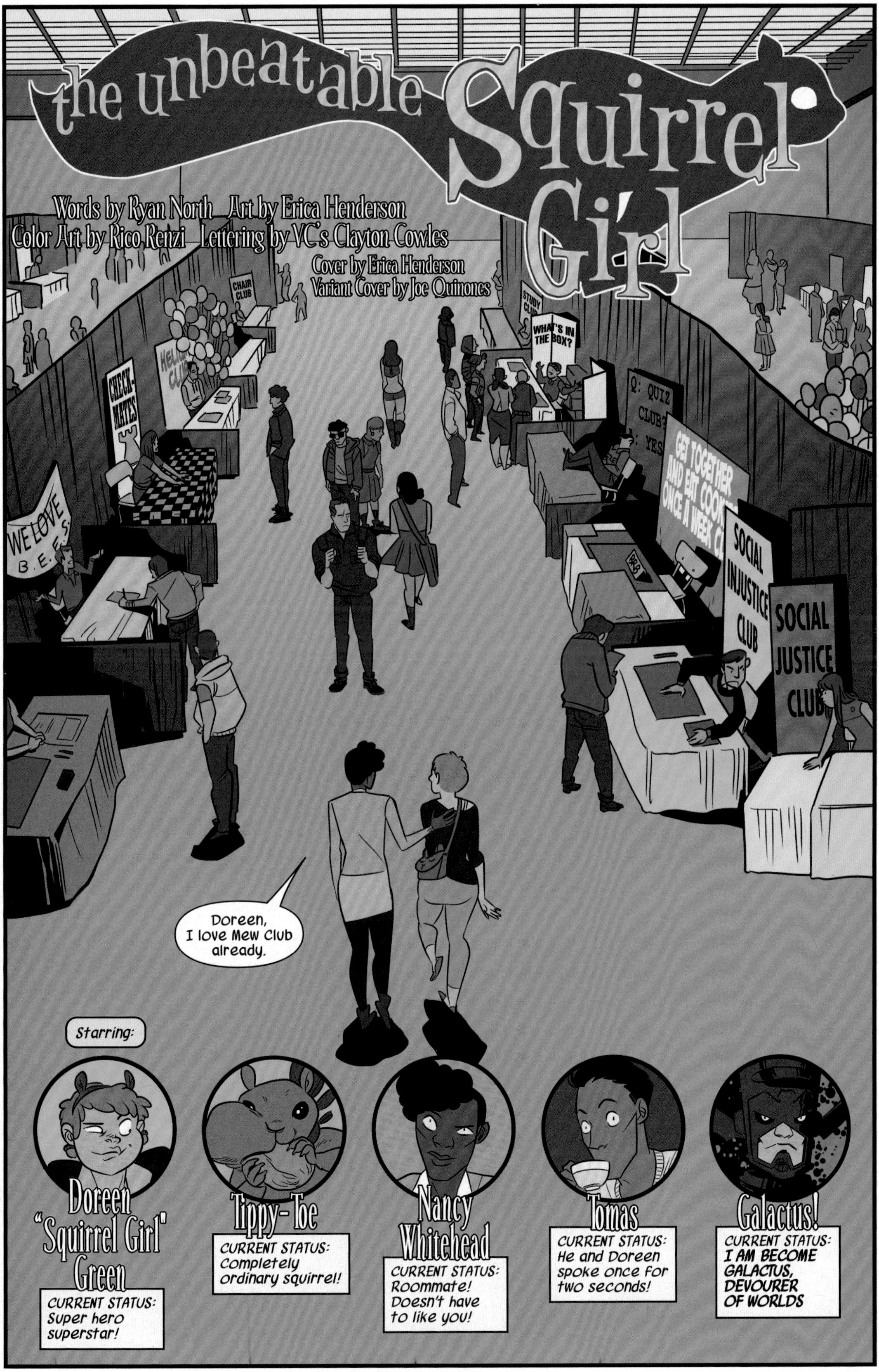
the unbeatable Squirrel Girl
Words by Ryan North Art by Erica Henderson
Color Art by Rico Renzi Lettering by VC's Clayton Cowles
Cover by Erica Henderson
Variant Cover by Joe Quinones
CHAIR CLUB
STUDY CLUB
WHAT'S IN THE BOX?
CHECK-MATES
Q: QUIZ CLUB? A: YES
GET TOGETHER AND EAT COOKIES ONCE A WEEK CL
WE LOVE B.E.E.S.
BRB
SOCIAL INJUSTICE CLUB
SOCIAL JUSTICE CLUB
Doreen, I love Mew Club already.
Starring:
Doreen "Squirrel Girl" Green
CURRENT STATUS: Super hero superstar!
Tippy-Toe
CURRENT STATUS: Completely ordinary squirrel!
Nancy Whitehead
CURRENT STATUS: Roommate! Doesn't have to like you!
Tomas
CURRENT STATUS: He and Doreen spoke once for two seconds!
Galactus!
CURRENT STATUS: I AM BECOME GALACTUS, DEVOURER OF WORLDS

Not pictured: Way Too Lazy To Set Up A Booth Club

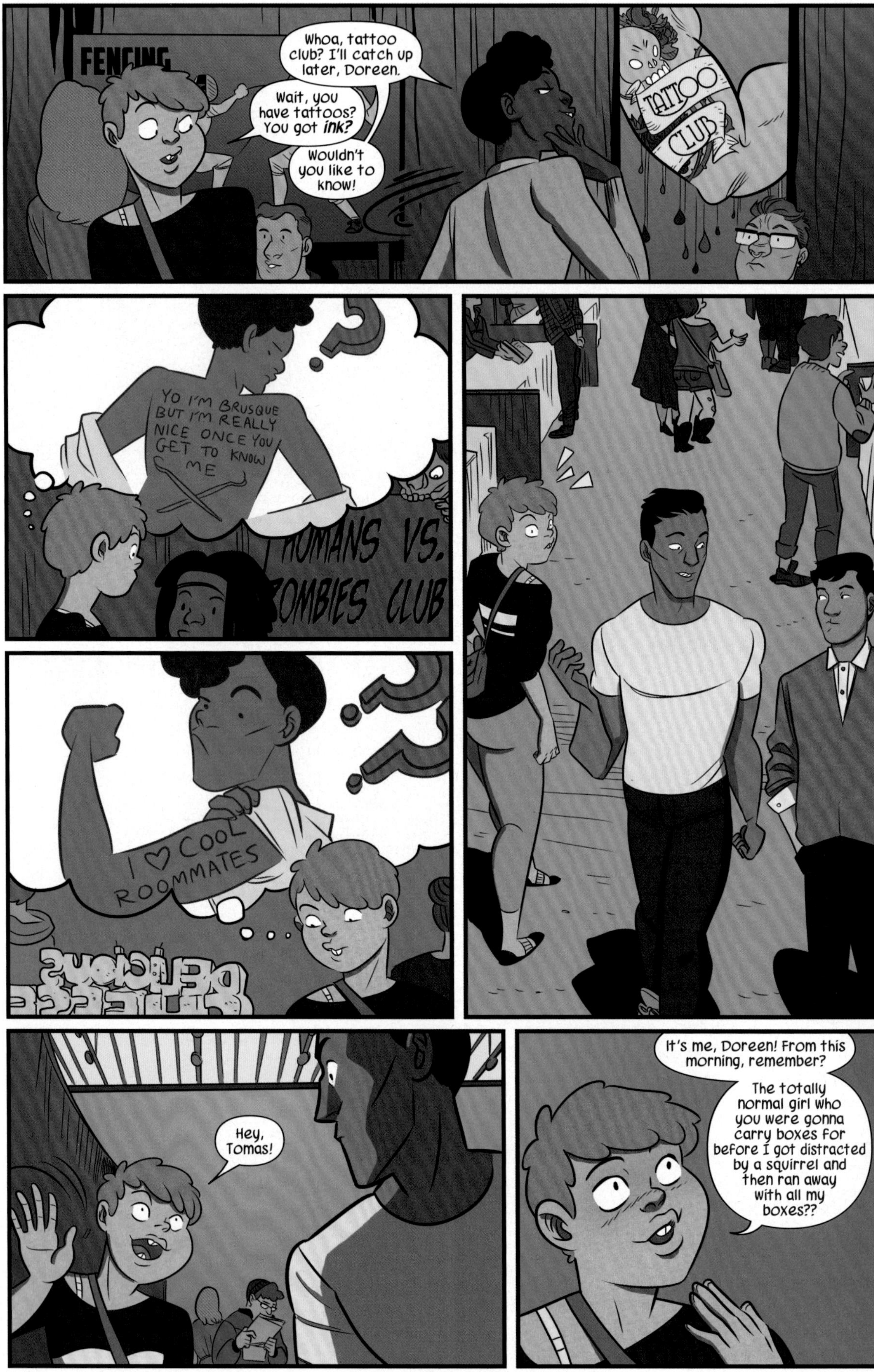
FENCING
Whoa, tattoo club? I'll catch up later, Doreen.
Wait, you have tattoos? You got *ink?*
Wouldn't you like to know!
TATTOO CLUB
YO I'M BRUSQUE BUT I'M REALLY NICE ONCE YOU GET TO KNOW ME
HUMANS VS. ZOMBIES CLUB
I ♡ COOL ROOMMATES
Hey, Tomas!
It's me, Doreen! From this morning, remember?
The totally normal girl who you were gonna carry boxes for before I got distracted by a squirrel and then ran away with all my boxes??

Hey, did you know you can give yourself tattoos at home? It's true! ***But don't tell any authority figures I told you,*** I don't want to get in trouble

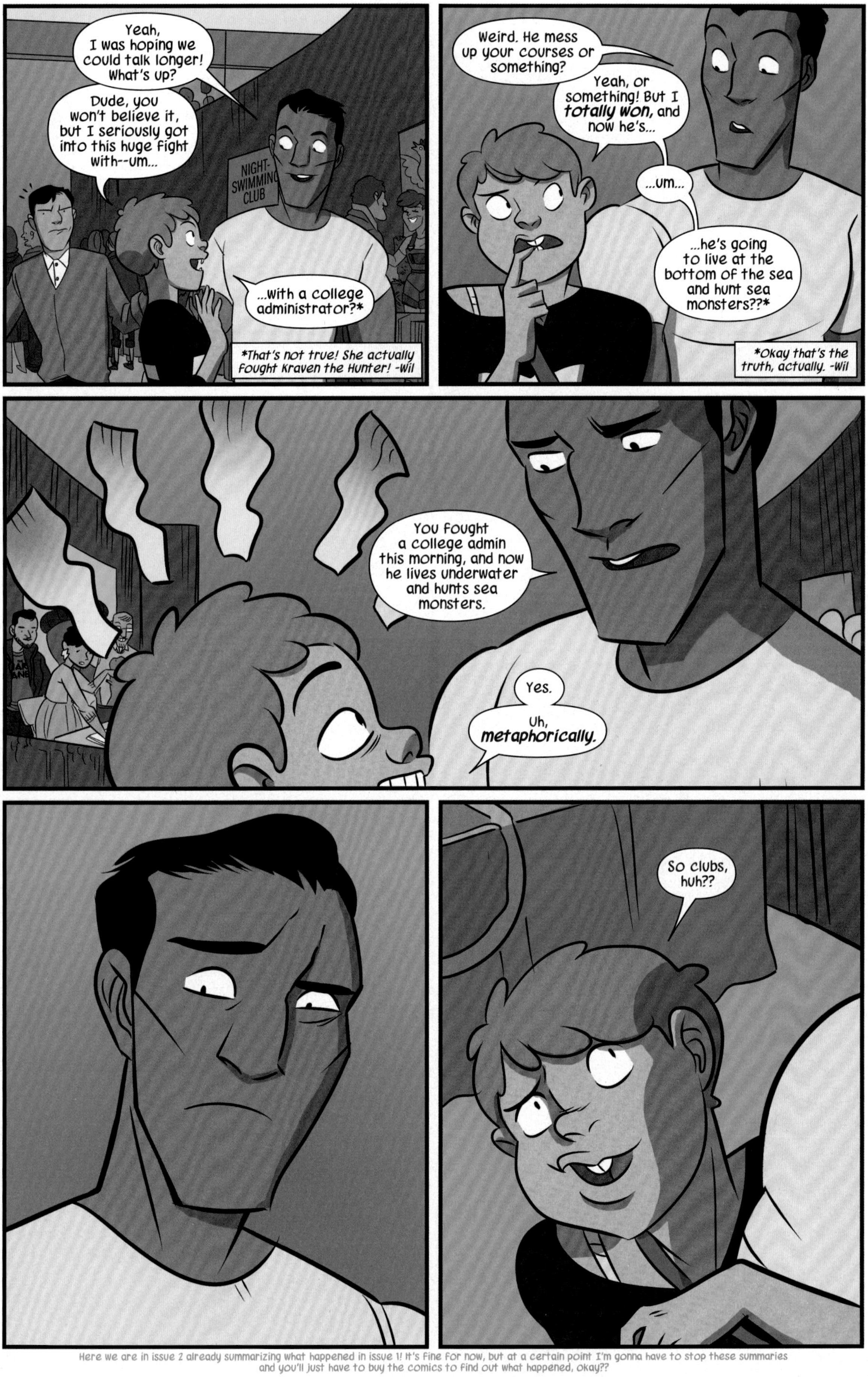
Yeah, I was hoping we could talk longer! What's up?
Dude, you won't believe it, but I seriously got into this huge fight with--um...
NIGHT-SWIMMING CLUB
...with a college administrator?*
*That's not true! She actually fought Kraven the Hunter! -Wil
Weird. He mess up your courses or something?
Yeah, or something! But I totally won, and now he's...
...um...
...he's going to live at the bottom of the sea and hunt sea monsters??*
*Okay that's the truth, actually. -Wil
You fought a college admin this morning, and now he lives underwater and hunts sea monsters.
Yes.
Uh, metaphorically.
So clubs, huh??

Here we are in issue 2 already summarizing what happened in issue 1! It's fine for now, but at a certain point I'm gonna have to stop these summaries and you'll just have to buy the comics to find out what happened, okay??

Yeah, I thought I'd check it out. There's a fencing club I was looking at, but I dunno. I've never thought of fencing before; it just looks fun.

Well, I mean, they'd teach you, right?

COMEDY CLUB

Doreen! You've barely been here a day and *already* you're making friends with people who haven't been assigned to live with you. You're awesome!

I guess! I mainly just want to be ready in case I find myself in a swordfight where I have to swing from chandeliers and roguishly smile as swords clash, saying things like *"Let's get right to the point!"*

Hah!

SHORT BLUDGEONING STAFF CLUB aka CLUB CLUB

Although this Tomas guy doesn't *really* know who I am. What if I tell him I'm Squirrel Girl and he *flips out* or something?

So I'm there in front of their table, looking up *"fencing"* on my phone because I'm suddenly not sure if what I have in mind is even called that, you know?

Like he's all "Oh no, the fact that you're so awesome and dress up in an awesome outfit and fight crime awesomely is terrible to me!"

Uh-huh.

Anyway, it turns out there's three kinds of fencing: foil, sabre, and epee, and what I had in mind is none of those. Mine imaginary swashbuckler turns out the actual *really* mad when you what they do.

Though, if he *did* say that, that at least tells me he's a jerk and saves me the time of getting to know him any more.

Dang, though. He sure is handsome.

Uh-huh.

And they'll challenge you at's

Look at me, chatting up a megahunk like it isn't even a big deal!! Not bad, self, *not bad*.

Uh-huh.

Doreen? Did my fencing club story lose you?

Uh...

...huh?

Hello. I, uh, need Doreen to join me in the ladies' room for a second.

Whoa!!

I believe the canonical attractiveness hierarchy runs--when going from most to least hunky--from hyperhunk, to megahunk, to hunk, to minihunk, and, finally, to nanohunk.

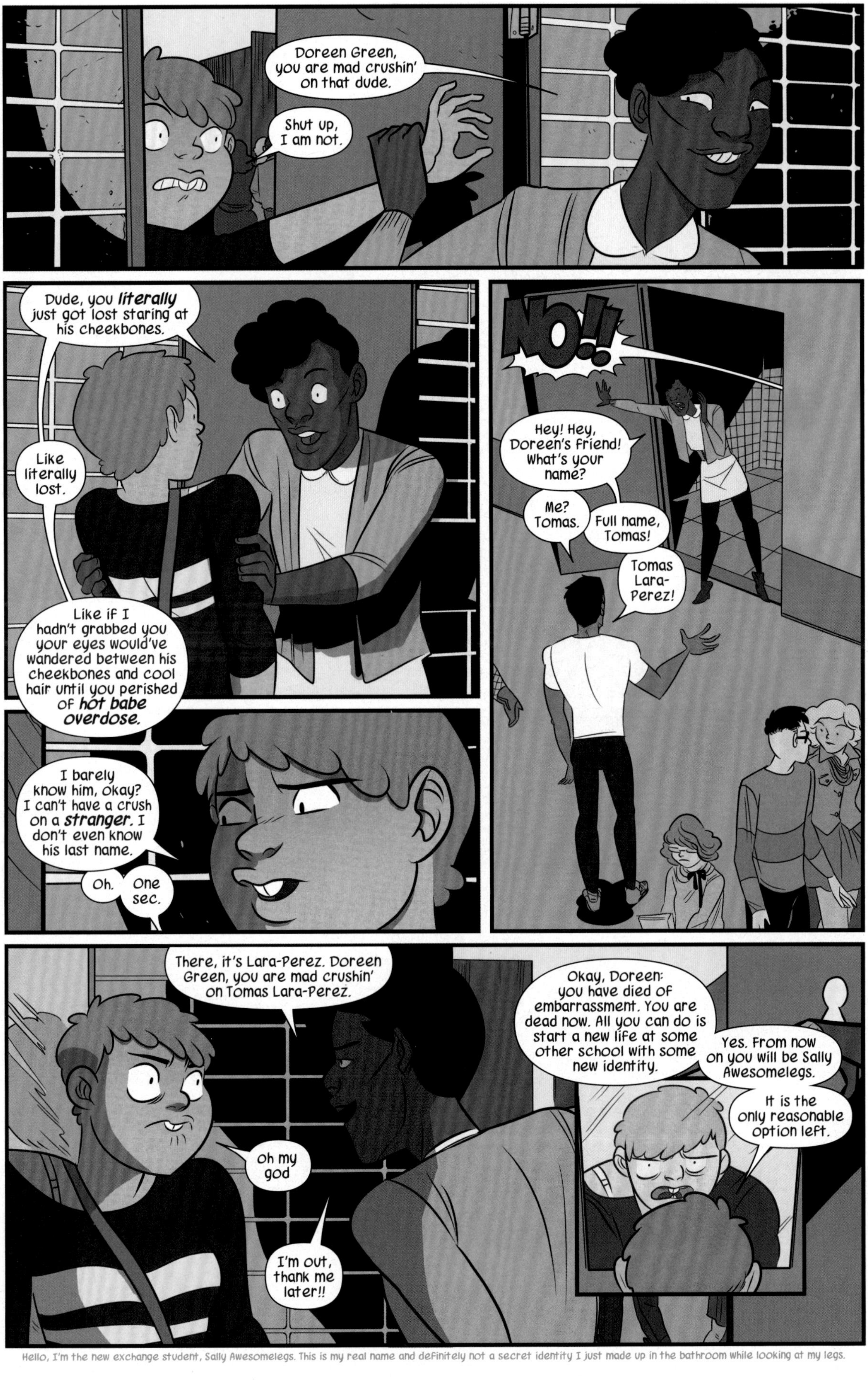
Doreen Green, you are mad crushin' on that dude.
Shut up, I am not.
Dude, you *literally* just got lost staring at his cheekbones.
Like literally lost.
Like if I hadn't grabbed you your eyes would've wandered between his cheekbones and cool hair until you perished of *hot babe overdose.*
I barely know him, okay? I can't have a crush on a *stranger.* I don't even know his last name.
Oh.
One sec.
NO!!
Hey! Hey, Doreen's friend! What's your name?
Me? Tomas.
Full name, Tomas!
Tomas Lara-Perez!
There, it's Lara-Perez. Doreen Green, you are mad crushin' on Tomas Lara-Perez.
Oh my god
I'm out, thank me later!!
Okay, Doreen: you have died of embarrassment. You are dead now. All you can do is start a new life at some other school with some new identity.
Yes. From now on you will be Sally Awesomelegs.
It is the only reasonable option left.

Hello, I'm the new exchange student, Sally Awesomelegs. This is my real name and definitely not a secret identity I just made up in the bathroom while looking at my legs.

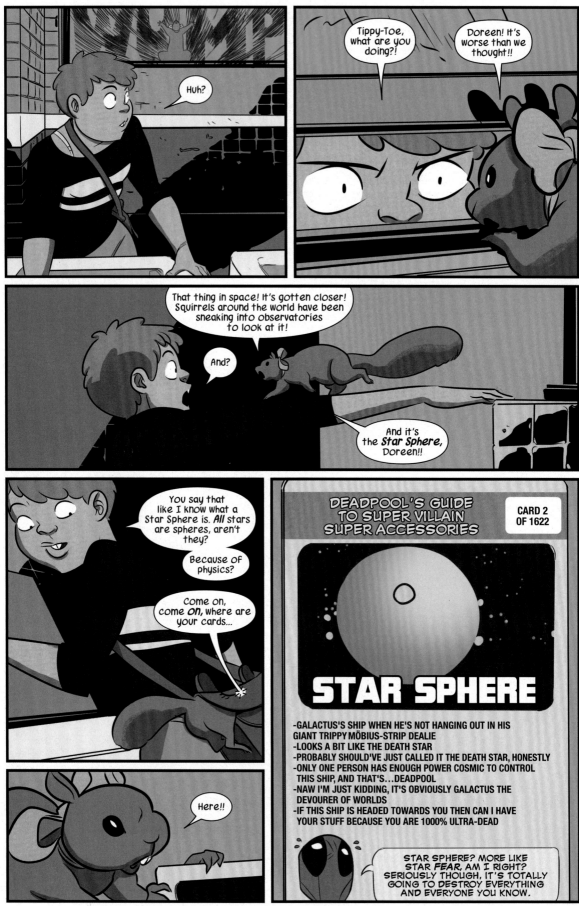

Huh?

Tippy-Toe, what are you doing?!

Doreen! It's worse than we thought!!

That thing in space! It's gotten closer! Squirrels around the world have been sneaking into observatories to look at it!

And?

And it's the *Star Sphere*, Doreen!!

You say that like I know what a Star Sphere is. *All* stars are spheres, aren't they?

Because of physics?

Come on, come *ON*, where are your cards...

Here!!

DEADPOOL'S GUIDE TO SUPER VILLAIN SUPER ACCESSORIES

CARD 2 OF 1622

STAR SPHERE

- GALACTUS'S SHIP WHEN HE'S NOT HANGING OUT IN HIS GIANT TRIPPY MÖBIUS-STRIP DEALIE
- LOOKS A BIT LIKE THE DEATH STAR
- PROBABLY SHOULD'VE JUST CALLED IT THE DEATH STAR, HONESTLY
- ONLY ONE PERSON HAS ENOUGH POWER COSMIC TO CONTROL THIS SHIP, AND THAT'S...DEADPOOL
- NAW I'M JUST KIDDING, IT'S OBVIOUSLY GALACTUS THE DEVOURER OF WORLDS
- IF THIS SHIP IS HEADED TOWARDS YOU THEN CAN I HAVE YOUR STUFF BECAUSE YOU ARE 1000% ULTRA-DEAD

STAR SPHERE? MORE LIKE STAR *FEAR*, AM I RIGHT? SERIOUSLY THOUGH, IT'S TOTALLY GOING TO DESTROY EVERYTHING AND EVERYONE YOU KNOW.

Yes, Tippy-Toe did absolutely start this page imagining that window would dramatically smash around her as she leapt through it.

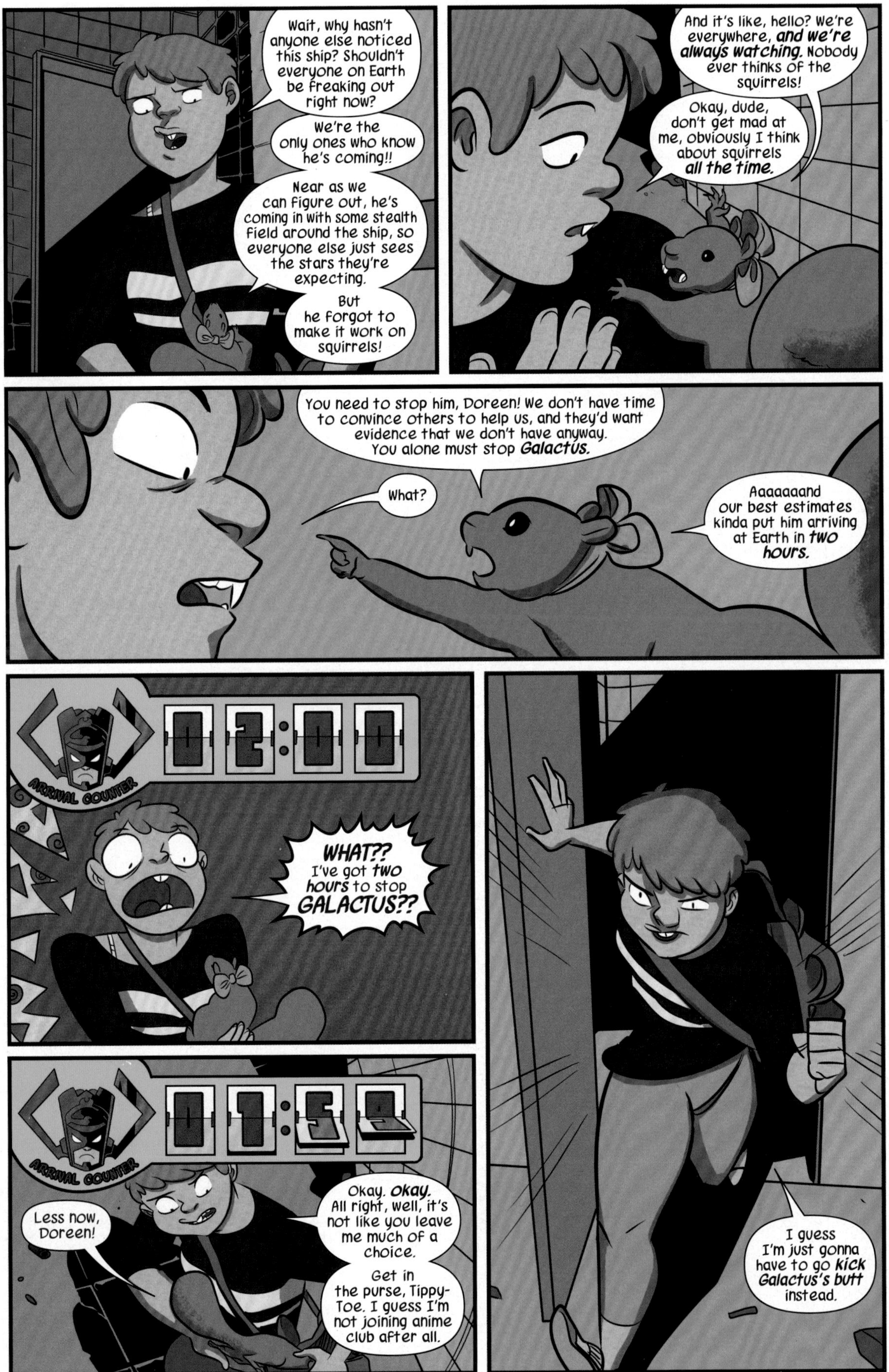
Wait, why hasn't anyone else noticed this ship? Shouldn't everyone on Earth be freaking out right now?
We're the only ones who know he's coming!!
Near as we can figure out, he's coming in with some stealth field around the ship, so everyone else just sees the stars they're expecting.
But he forgot to make it work on squirrels!
And it's like, hello? We're everywhere, and we're always watching. Nobody ever thinks of the squirrels!
Okay, dude, don't get mad at me, obviously I think about squirrels all the time.
You need to stop him, Doreen! We don't have time to convince others to help us, and they'd want evidence that we don't have anyway. You alone must stop Galactus.
What?
Aaaaaaand our best estimates kinda put him arriving at Earth in two hours.
ARRIVAL COUNTER
02:00
WHAT?? I've got two hours to stop GALACTUS??
ARRIVAL COUNTER
01:59
Less now, Doreen!
Okay. Okay. All right, well, it's not like you leave me much of a choice.
Get in the purse, Tippy-Toe. I guess I'm not joining anime club after all.
I guess I'm just gonna have to go kick Galactus's butt instead.

Honestly I wish there was time to do both, but there's not, and a girl has to make choices sometimes. Someone else join anime club for me, I'll catch up later.

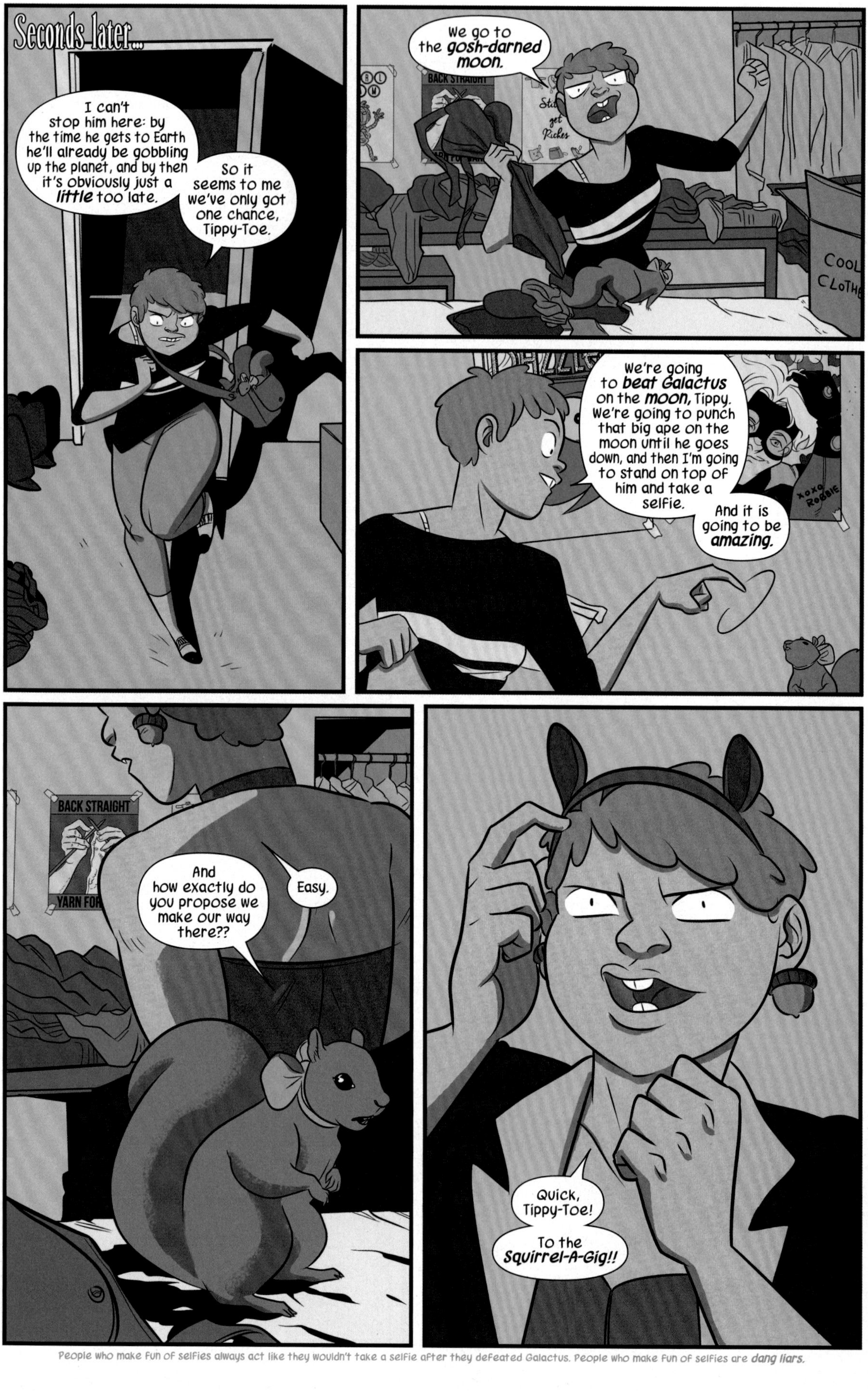
Seconds later...
I can't stop him here: by the time he gets to Earth he'll already be gobbling up the planet, and by then it's obviously just a *little* too late.
So it seems to me we've only got one chance, Tippy-Toe.
We go to the *gosh-darned moon.*
BACK STRAIGHT
COOL
We're going to *beat Galactus* on the *moon,* Tippy. We're going to punch that big ape on the moon until he goes down, and then I'm going to stand on top of him and take a selfie.
And it is going to be *amazing.*
xoxo ROBBIE
BACK STRAIGHT
And how exactly do you propose we make our way there??
Easy.
Quick, Tippy-Toe!
To the *Squirrel-A-Gig!!*

People who make fun of selfies always act like they wouldn't take a selfie after they defeated Galactus. People who make fun of selfies are *dang liars.*

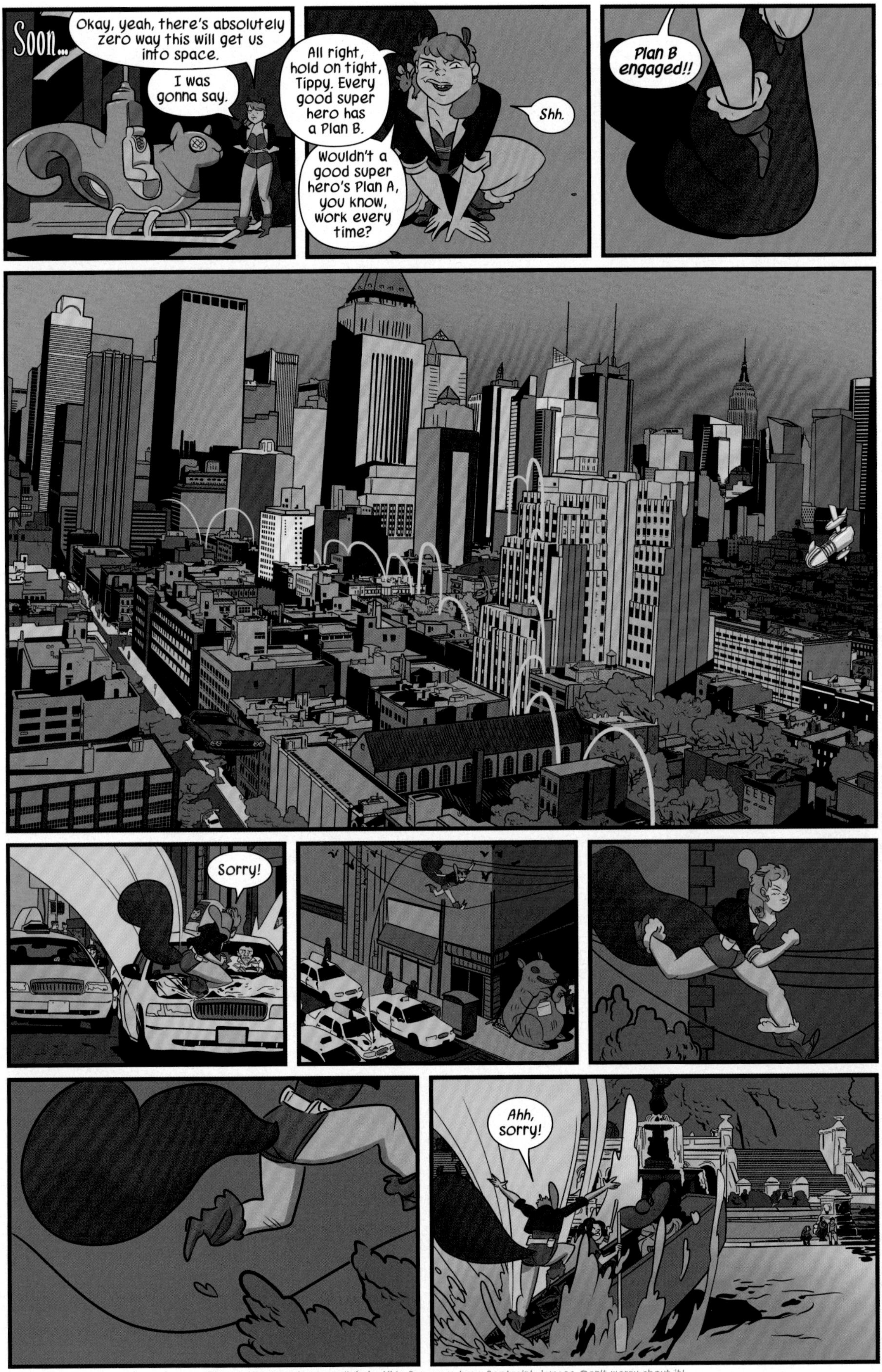
Soon...
Okay, yeah, there's absolutely zero way this will get us into space.
I was gonna say.
All right, hold on tight, Tippy. Every good super hero has a Plan B.
Wouldn't a good super hero's Plan A, you know, work every time?
Shh.
Plan B engaged!!
Sorry!
Ahh, sorry!

NYC cab insurance has a small deductible for super hero footprint damage. Don't worry about it!

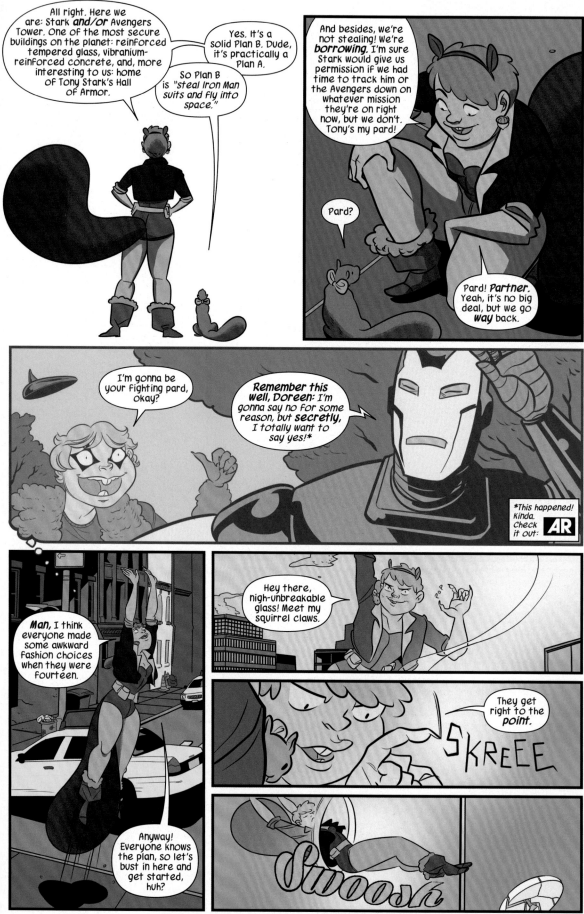

All right. Here we are: Stark **and/or** Avengers Tower. One of the most secure buildings on the planet: reinforced tempered glass, vibranium-reinforced concrete, and, more interesting to us: home of Tony Stark's Hall of Armor.

Yes. It's a solid Plan B. Dude, it's practically a Plan A.

So Plan B is "steal Iron Man suits and fly into space."

And besides, we're not stealing! We're **borrowing**. I'm sure Stark would give us permission if we had time to track him or the Avengers down on whatever mission they're on right now, but we don't. Tony's my pard!

Pard?

Pard! **Partner.** Yeah, it's no big deal, but we go **way** back.

I'm gonna be your fighting pard, okay?

Remember this well, Doreen: I'm gonna say no for some reason, but **secretly**, I totally want to say yes!*

*This happened! Kinda. Check it out: AR

Man, I think everyone made some awkward fashion choices when they were fourteen.

Hey there, nigh-unbreakable glass! Meet my squirrel claws.

POP

They get right to the **point.**

SKREEE

Anyway! Everyone knows the plan, so let's bust in here and get started, huh?

Swoosh

Shoulda paid extra to get rid of that *"nigh"* in front of *"unbreakable glass,"* Tony!

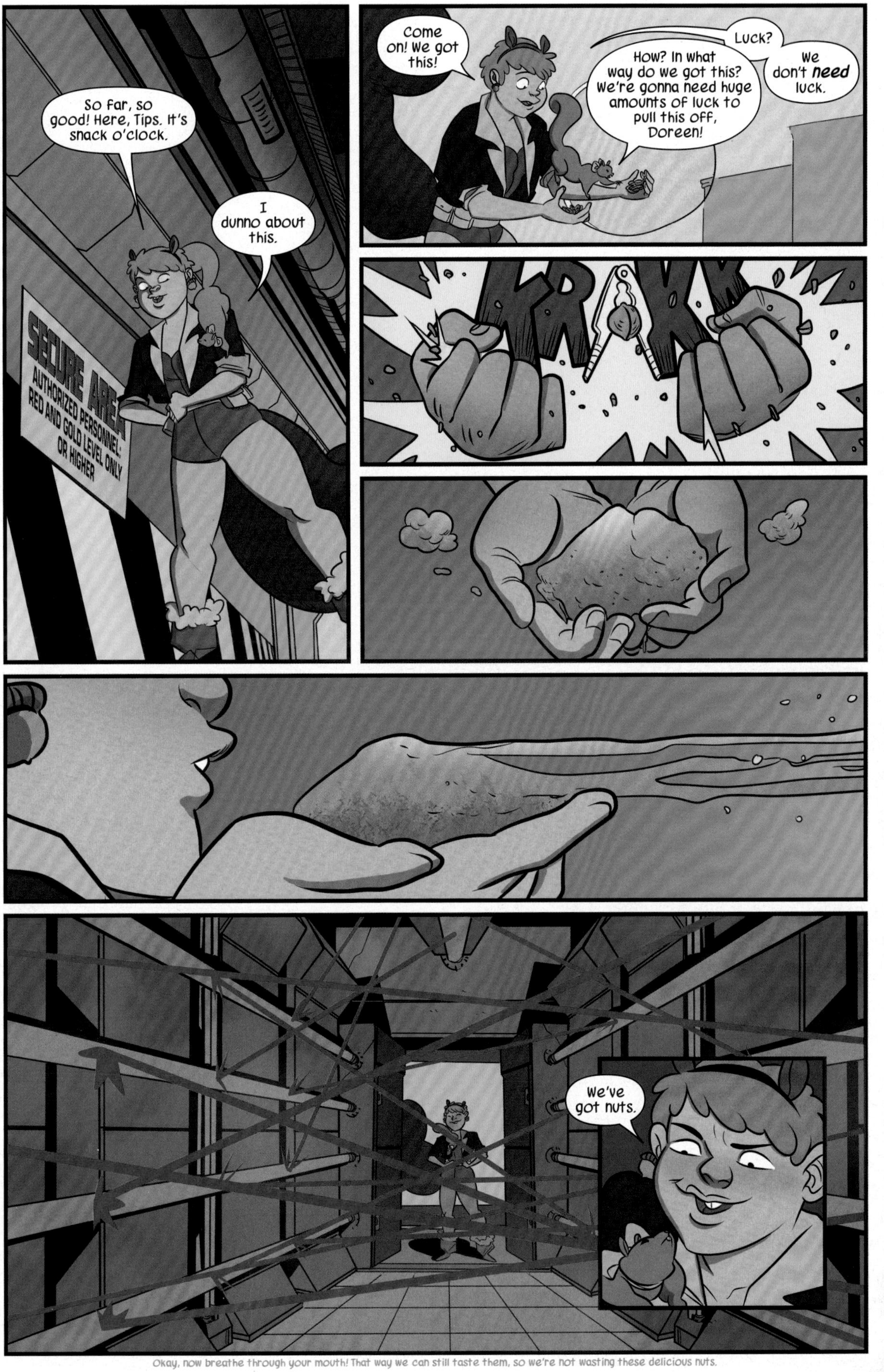
So far, so good! Here, Tips. It's snack o'clock.
I dunno about this.
SECURE AREA
AUTHORIZED PERSONNEL: RED AND GOLD LEVEL ONLY OR HIGHER
Come on! We got this!
How? In what way do we got this? We're gonna need huge amounts of luck to pull this off, Doreen!
Luck?
We don't **need** luck.
We've got nuts.

Okay, now breathe through your mouth! That way we can still taste them, so we're not wasting these delicious nuts.

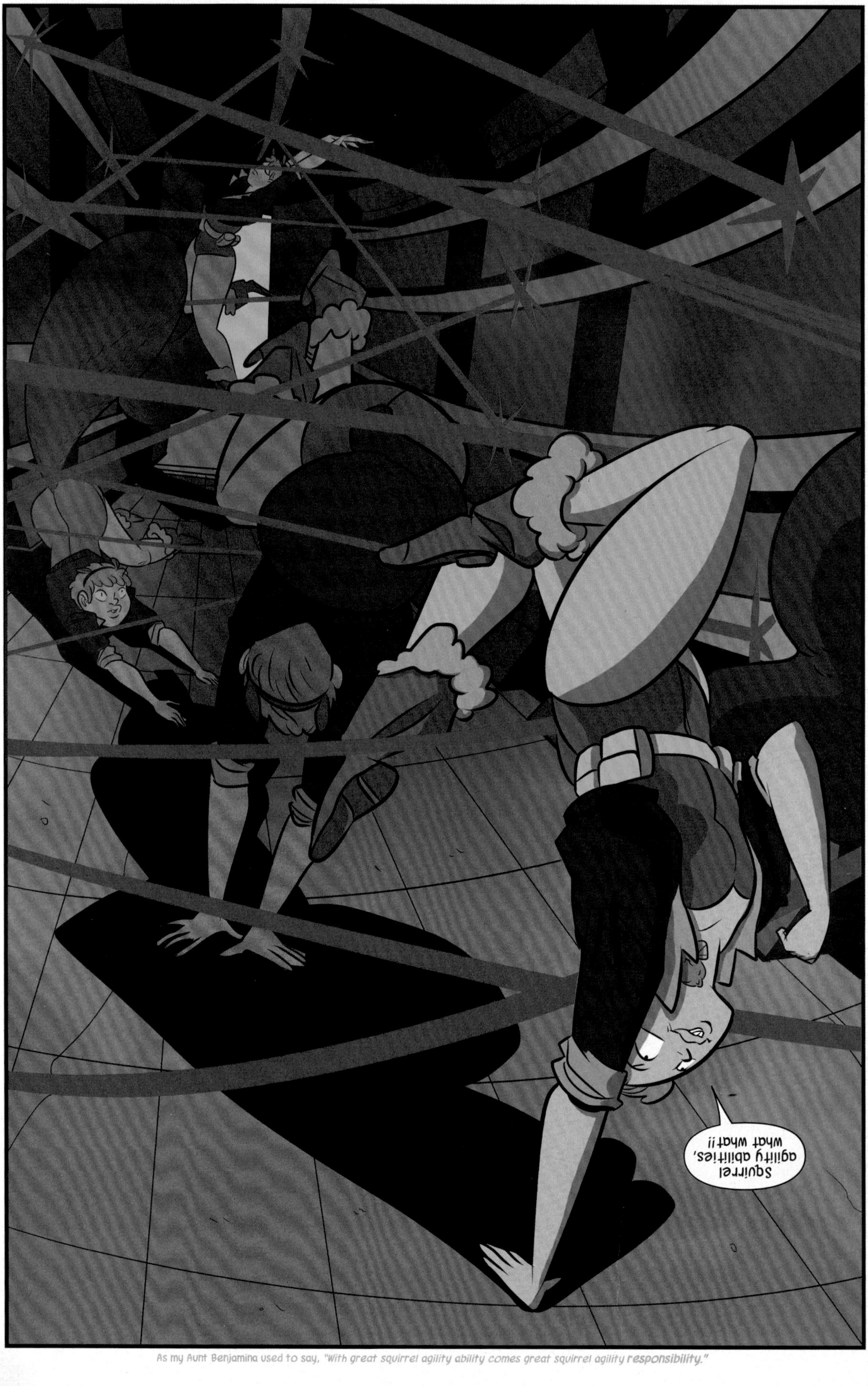
squirrel
agility abilities,
what what!!

As my Aunt Benjamina used to say, *"With great squirrel agility ability comes great squirrel agility* ***responsibility.****"*

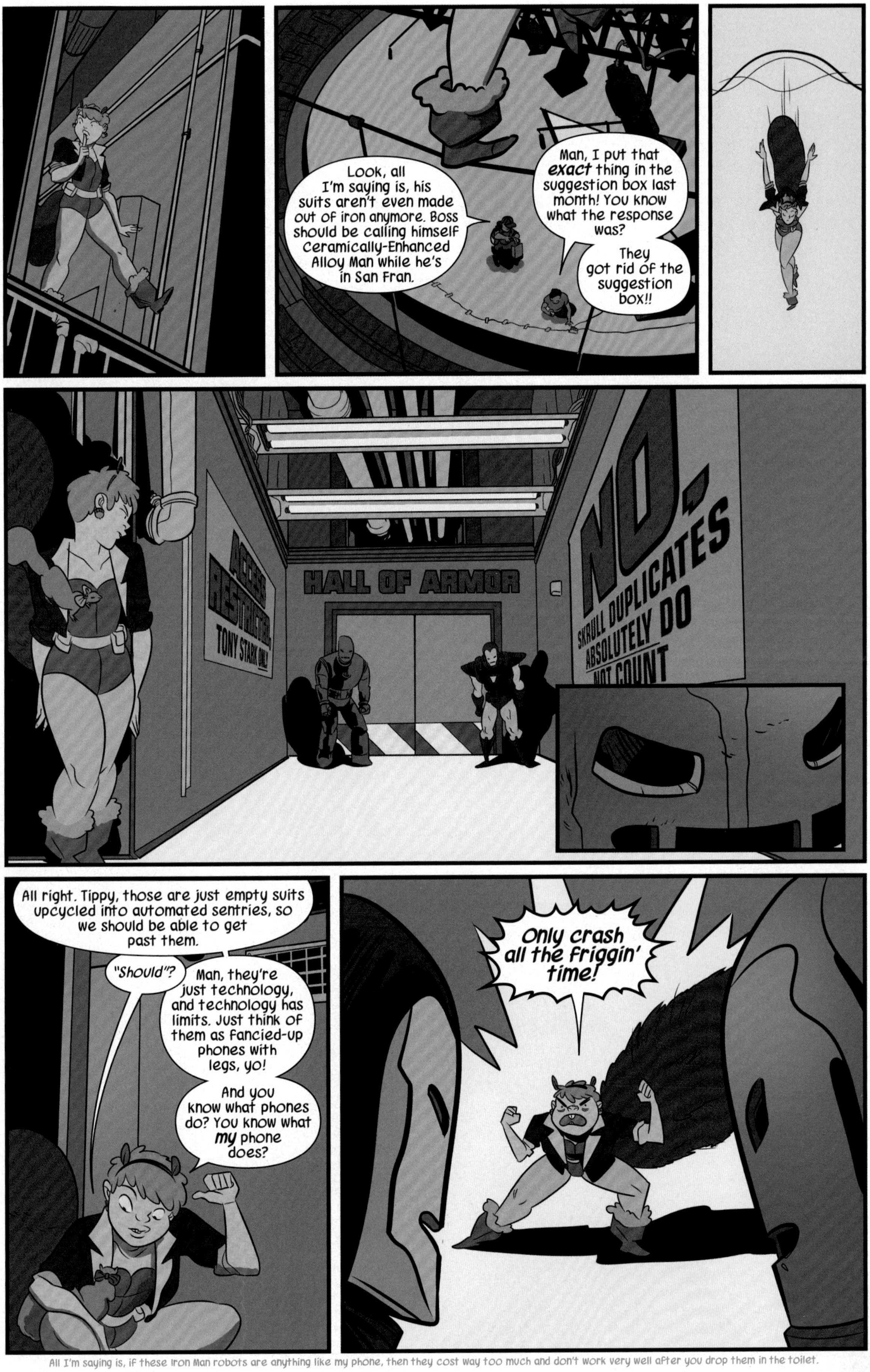
Look, all I'm saying is, his suits aren't even made out of iron anymore. Boss should be calling himself Ceramically-Enhanced Alloy Man while he's in San Fran.
Man, I put that *exact* thing in the suggestion box last month! You know what the response was?
They got rid of the suggestion box!!
HALL OF ARMOR
ACCESS RESTRICTED. TONY STARK ONLY
NO. SKRULL DUPLICATES ABSOLUTELY DO NOT COUNT
All right. Tippy, those are just empty suits upcycled into automated sentries, so we should be able to get past them.
"Should"?
Man, they're just technology, and technology has limits. Just think of them as fancied-up phones with legs, yo!
And you know what phones do? You know what *my* phone does?
Only crash all the friggin' time!

All I'm saying is, if these Iron Man robots are anything like my phone, then they cost way too much and don't work very well after you drop them in the toilet.

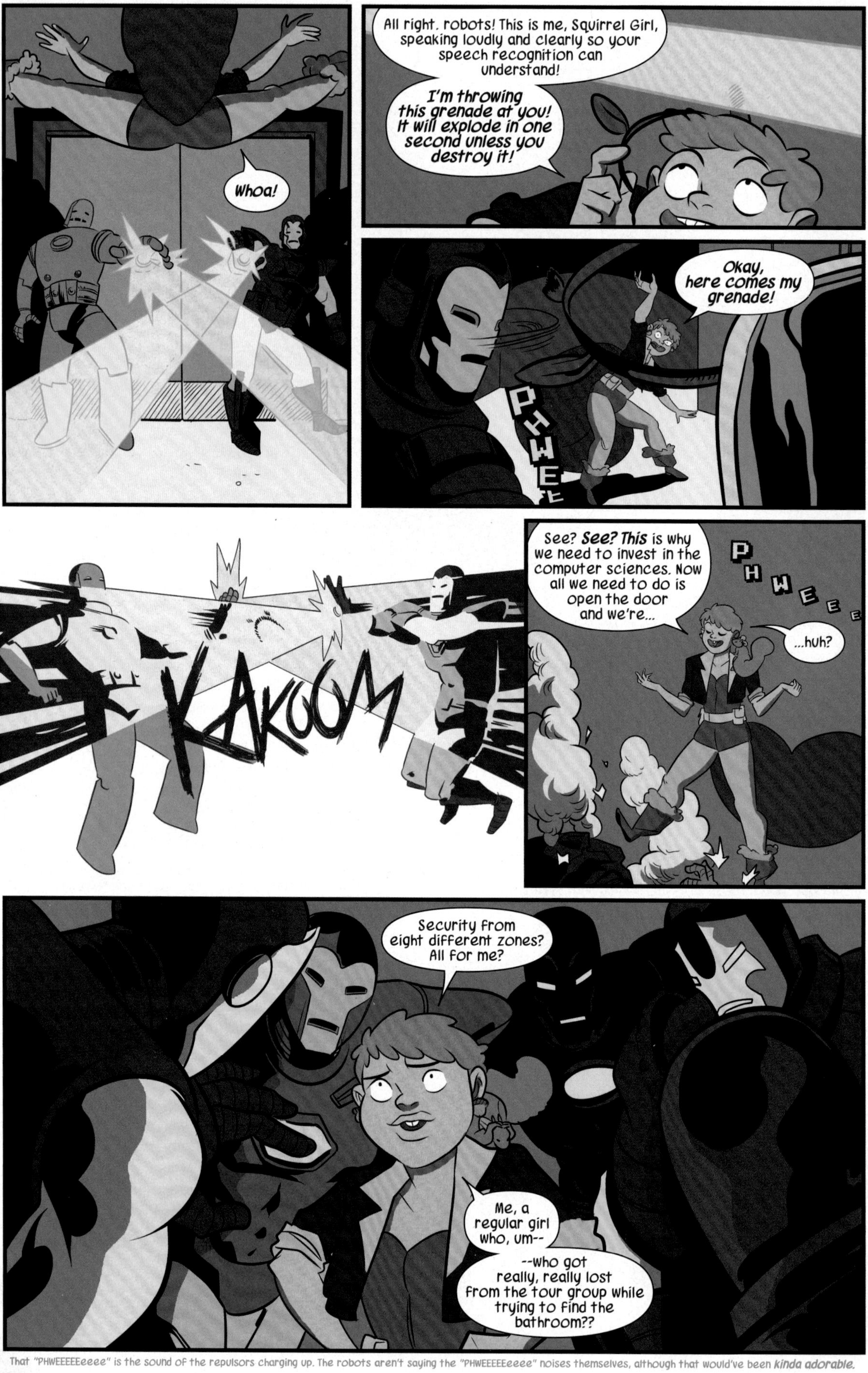
Whoa!
All right, robots! This is me, Squirrel Girl, speaking loudly and clearly so your speech recognition can understand!
I'm throwing this grenade at you! It will explode in one second unless you destroy it!
Okay, here comes my grenade!
PHWEE
KAKOOM
See? *See? This* is why we need to invest in the computer sciences. Now all we need to do is open the door and we're...
PHWEEE
...huh?
Security from eight different zones? All for me?
Me, a regular girl who, um--
--who got really, really lost from the tour group while trying to find the bathroom??

That "PHWEEEEEeeee" is the sound of the repulsors charging up. The robots aren't saying the "PHWEEEEEeeee" noises themselves, although that would've been ***kinda adorable.***

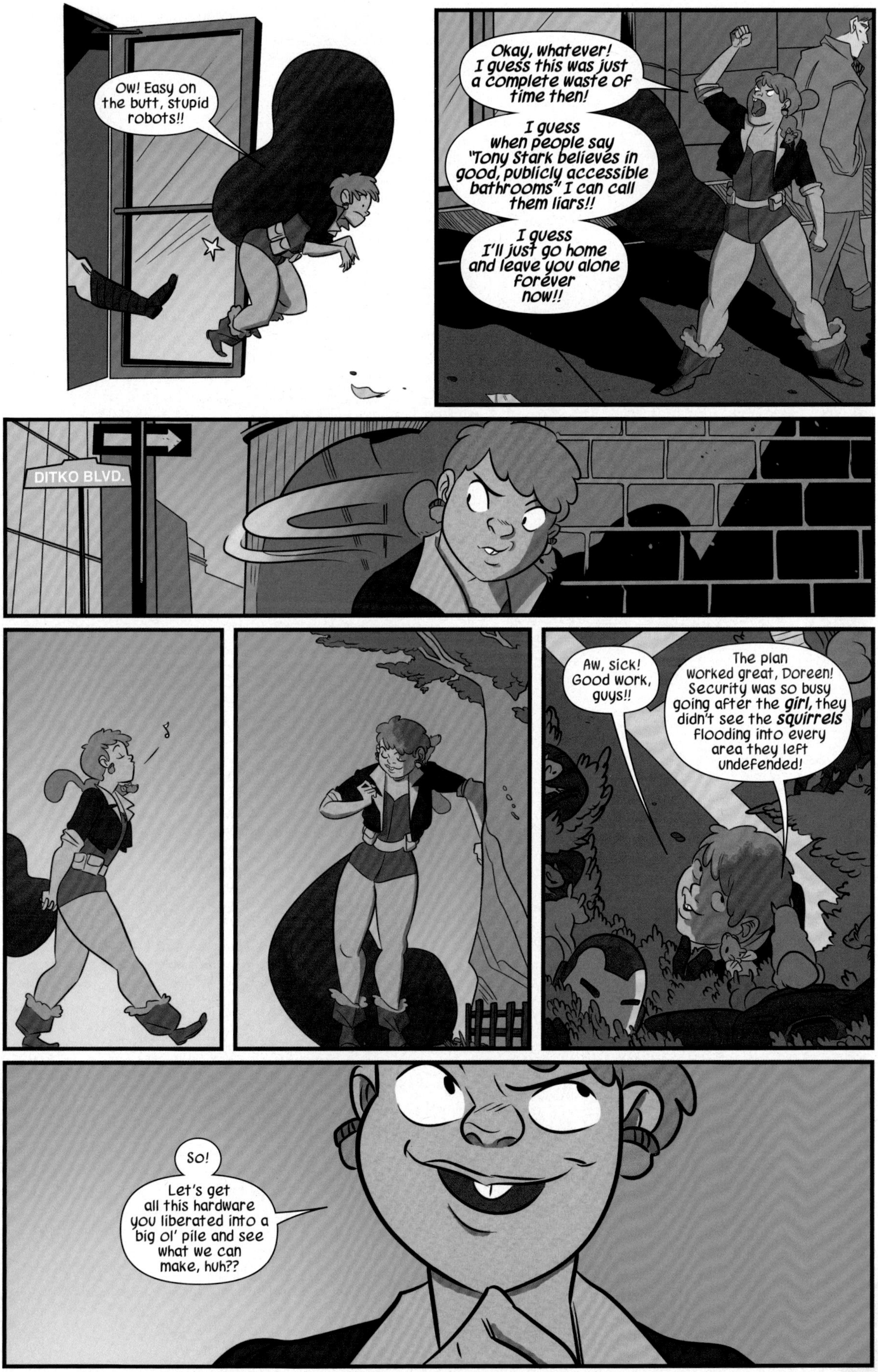
Ow! Easy on the butt, stupid robots!!
Okay, whatever! I guess this was just a complete waste of time then!
I guess when people say "Tony Stark believes in good, publicly accessible bathrooms" I can call them liars!!
I guess I'll just go home and leave you alone forever now!!
DITKO BLVD.
Aw, sick! Good work, guys!!
The plan worked great, Doreen! Security was so busy going after the *girl*, they didn't see the *squirrels* flooding into every area they left undefended!
So!
Let's get all this hardware you liberated into a big ol' pile and see what we can make, huh??

I didn't let you, the reader, know her plan before now because it's a better narrative surprise this way! ***Also:*** how do I know I can trust you, huh??
You could be *literally anyone.*

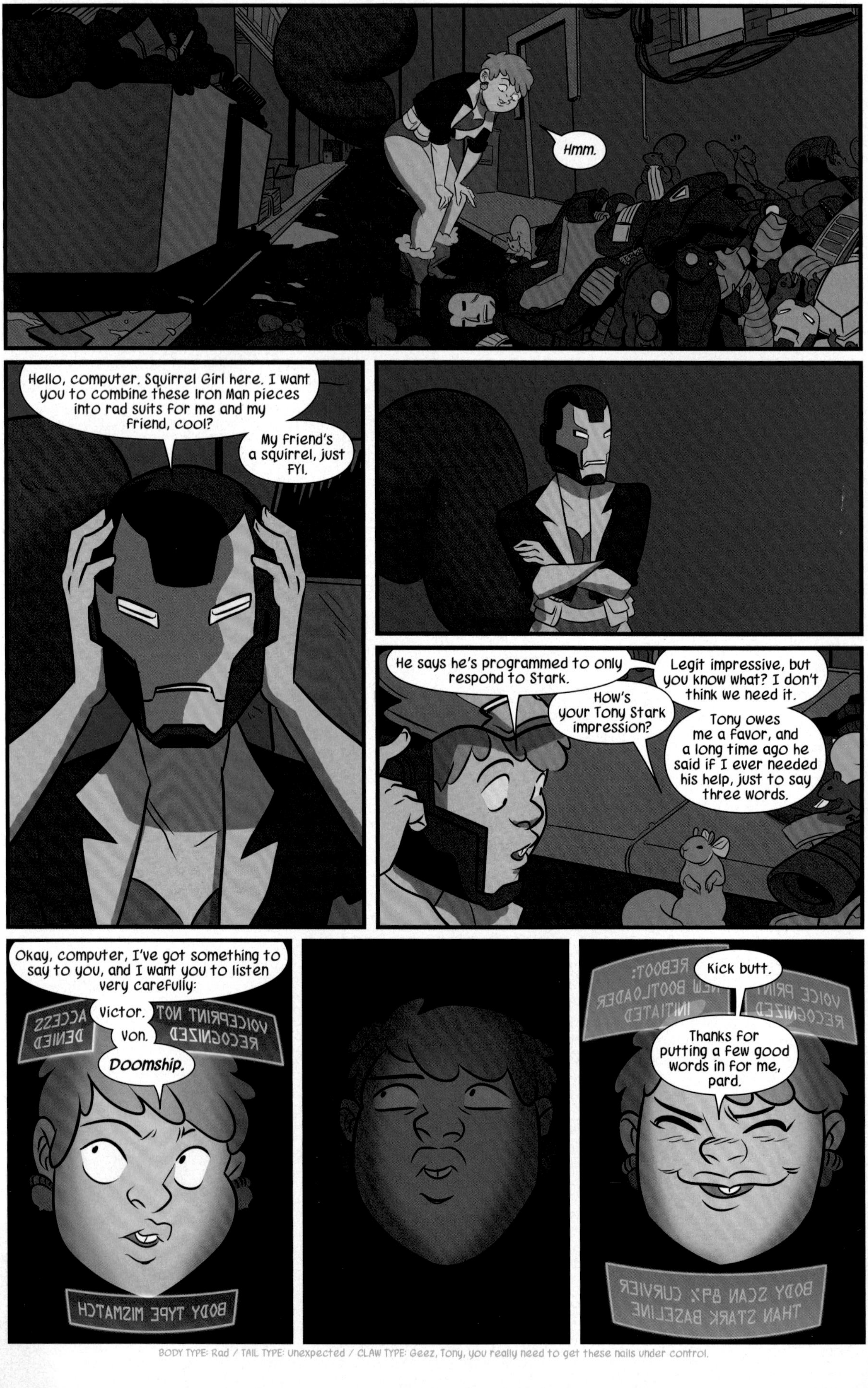
Hmm.
Hello, computer. Squirrel Girl here. I want you to combine these Iron Man pieces into rad suits for me and my friend, cool?
My friend's a squirrel, just FYI.
He says he's programmed to only respond to Stark.
How's your Tony Stark impression?
Legit impressive, but you know what? I don't think we need it.
Tony owes me a favor, and a long time ago he said if I ever needed his help, just to say three words.
Okay, computer, I've got something to say to you, and I want you to listen very carefully:
ACCESS DENIED
VOICEPRINT NOT RECOGNIZED
Victor.
Von.
Doomship.
BODY TYPE MISMATCH
REBOOT: NEW BOOTLOADER INITIATED
VOICE PRINT RECOGNIZED
Kick butt.
Thanks for putting a few good words in for me, pard.
BODY SCAN 89% CURVIER THAN STARK BASELINE

BODY TYPE: Rad / TAIL TYPE: Unexpected / CLAW TYPE: Geez, Tony, you really need to get these nails under control.

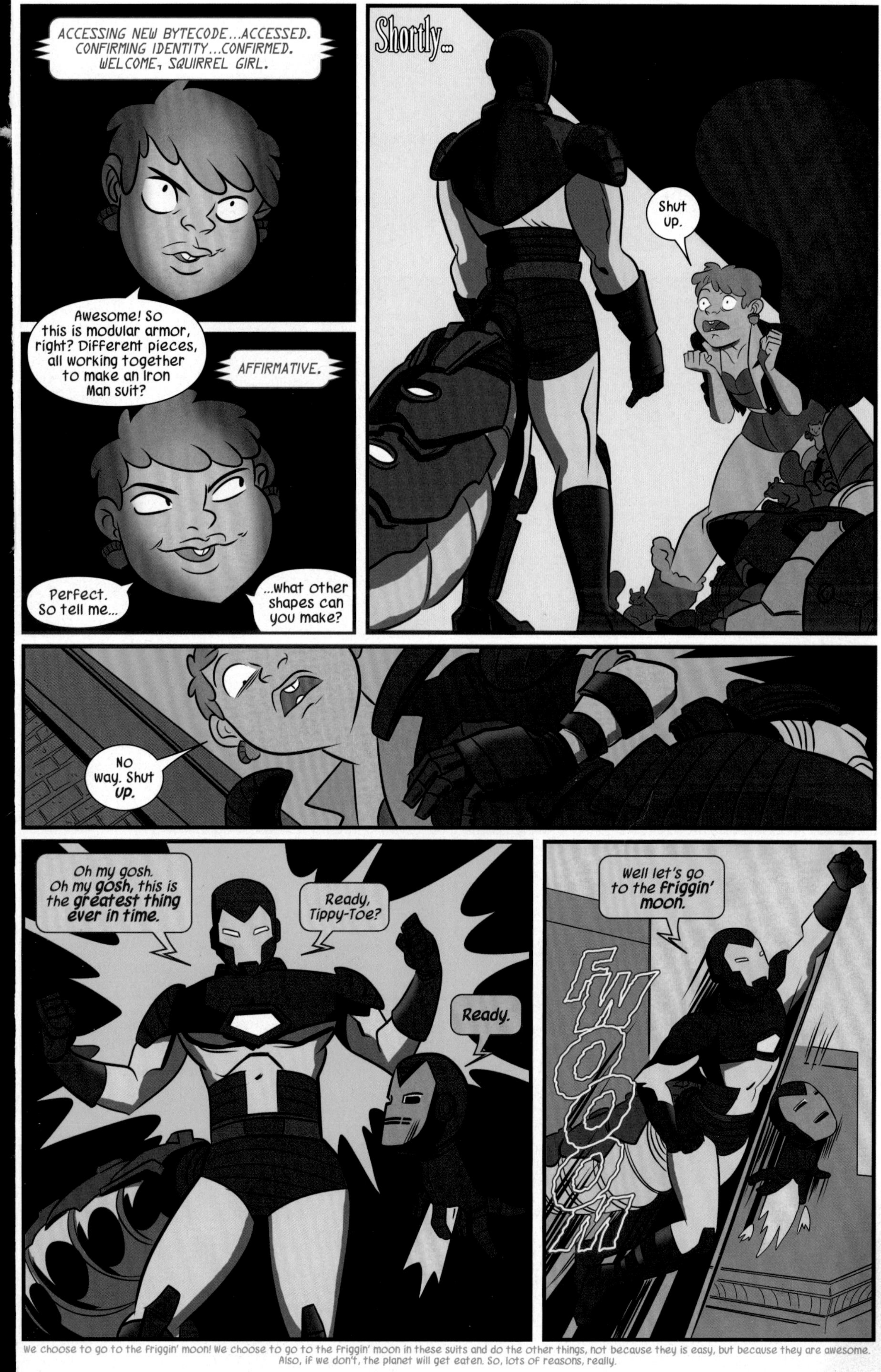
ACCESSING NEW BYTECODE...ACCESSED. CONFIRMING IDENTITY...CONFIRMED. WELCOME, SQUIRREL GIRL.
Awesome! So this is modular armor, right? Different pieces, all working together to make an Iron Man suit?
AFFIRMATIVE.
Perfect. So tell me...
...what other shapes can you make?
Shortly...
Shut up.
No way. Shut up.
Oh my gosh. Oh my gosh, this is the greatest thing ever in time.
Ready, Tippy-Toe?
Ready.
Well let's go to the friggin' moon.
FWOOOOM

We choose to go to the friggin' moon! We choose to go to the friggin' moon in these suits and do the other things, not because they is easy, but because they are awesome. Also, if we don't, the planet will get eaten. So, lots of reasons, really.

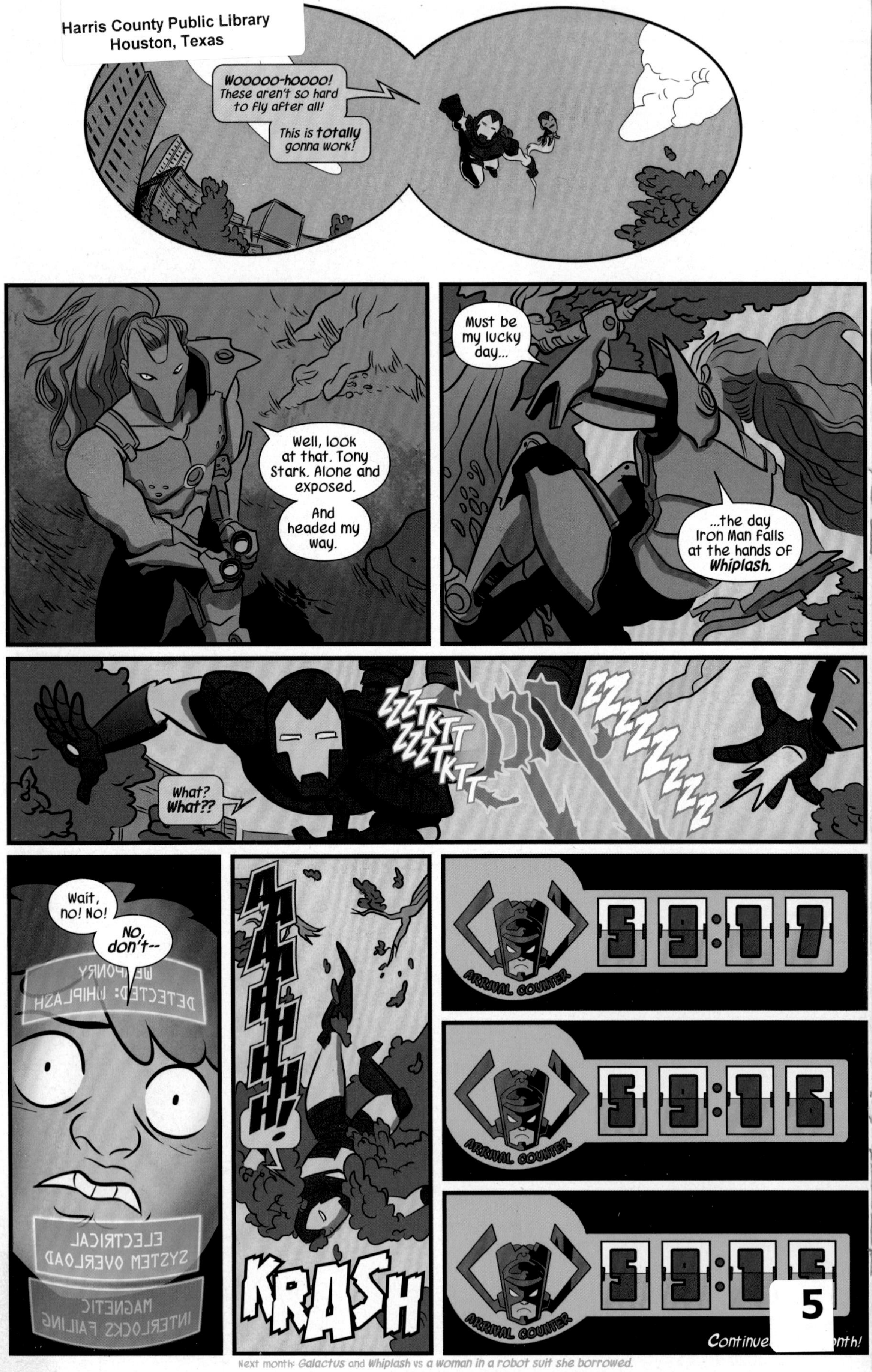
Wooooo-hoooo! These aren't so hard to fly after all!
This is totally gonna work!
Well, look at that. Tony Stark. Alone and exposed.
And headed my way.
Must be my lucky day...
...the day Iron Man falls at the hands of Whiplash.
ZZZTKTT
ZZZTKTT
What? What??
ZZZZZZZZZ
Wait, no! No!
No, don't--
WEAPONRY DETECTED: WHIPLASH
ELECTRICAL SYSTEM OVERLOAD
MAGNETIC INTERLOCKS FAILING
AAAAHHHH!
KRASH
ARRIVAL COUNTER
59:17
ARRIVAL COUNTER
59:16
ARRIVAL COUNTER
Continue
onth!

Next month: *Galactus* and *Whiplash* vs *a woman in a robot suit she borrowed.*